LUTHER'S WORKS

LUTHER'S WORKS

COMPANION VOLUME

LUTHER THE EXPOSITOR

*Introduction to the Reformer's
Exegetical Writings*

By

JAROSLAV PELIKAN

CONCORDIA PUBLISHING HOUSE · SAINT LOUIS

MANUFACTURED IN THE UNITED STATES OF AMERICA

5 6 7 8 9 10 11 12 13 TS 89 88 87 86 85 84 83 82

Contents

Publisher's Preface

SINCE the first thirty volumes of the American edition of *Luther's Works* are devoted to exegetical writings from the pen of the Reformer, the publisher has considered it helpful to issue a work dealing specifically with Luther's skill and significance as an expositor of Holy Writ. Although each of the volumes has a brief introduction giving pertinent information as to the historical setting of its contents, a thorough understanding of the Reformer's role and achievements in the important field of exegesis requires an acquaintance with the principles that guided the great doctor of theology when he expounded the words of the Bible.

In *Luther the Expositor* Jaroslav Pelikan provides the reader and student with some of the tools that are needed for a proper appreciation of Luther's exegetical writings. This companion volume shows conclusively that "in his exegesis — as in his doctrine, piety, and ethic — the Reformer" was "a son of the church" and "a witness to the Word of God revealed in Jesus Christ and documented in the Sacred Scriptures."

CONCORDIA PUBLISHING HOUSE

Introduction

THIS volume is an introduction to Luther's exegetical works and a study of Luther as an expositor of the Scriptures. The exegetical works of Luther, which constitute the first thirty volumes of this American edition, cover much of the Old and the New Testament. The dates of their composition span the entire third-century of Luther's theological career. Some of these exegetical works were delivered in the form of sermons; others were lectures from Luther's classroom; still others were the product of Luther's literary labors. The individual introductions to the various volumes of the exegetical works seek to describe the circumstances in which they were composed, to untangle the ofttimes complex problems of dating the works, to determine the role of Luther's editors in the compilation of the commentaries, and to settle similar issues of a literary and historical nature. Thus the separate historical introductions to the exegetical works deliberately confine themselves to the immediate historical setting of the works.

Yet these historical introductions do not exhaust the information to which the reader is entitled if he is to read the exegetical works of Luther intelligently. For while the proper introduction to Luther's *Bondage of the Will* is a rehearsal of the controversy between him and Erasmus, the only adequate way to introduce the reader to a commentary on Genesis or St. John is to recite the principles that guided Luther in the composition of such Biblical commentaries. Without a knowledge of these principles the reader is at a loss to recognize what is at stake in Luther's exegetical works; both the contrasts and the continuities in those works will elude him. It would, of course, be repetitious to attach a discussion of Luther's exegetical principles to each of the exegetical works. Instead, we have reserved that discussion for this companion volume.

This volume is intended, therefore, to provide the reader and student of Luther's works with some of the tools he needs for an appreciation of Luther's exegesis. These tools should enable him to identify Luther's procedures in these commentaries on the Scriptures. When Luther discovered the doctrine of the Trinity in a psalm or in Isaiah; when he took a passage in the Sermon on the Mount as an occasion to strike out at the Anabaptists; when he devoted meticulous attention to the grammar or the metaphorical language of a text in St. Paul; when he interpreted the struggles of the patriarchs as though they had been Martin Luther fighting the papacy — when Luther proceeded in these and similar ways, he was not simply playing by ear in his exegesis, even though it sometimes seems that way. He was enunciating and illustrating fundamental principles of Biblical interpretation. It is clear that relatively few interpreters of the Bible today would be willing to follow him in all these principles, much less in his practice of them. But it is even clearer that no interpreter of Luther today is in a position to make up his mind whether he can follow Luther's exegetical principles or not unless he can see them at work.

It is not an editor's prerogative to prejudge the issue of how much in Luther's exegesis is acceptable to the church of the twentieth century, but it is an editor's obligation to introduce the reader of Luther to this issue and to make possible an informed judgment upon it. Such a judgment about Luther's exegesis necessarily involves a consideration of both the principles and the practice of Luther's exegetical

work. Part One of this volume discusses the principles. It
opens by setting the study of Luther's exegetical works into
the context of the history of exegesis, which is currently
enjoying a great revival of interest. Chapter one thus seeks
to show that the examination of the history of exegesis is
an important and neglected resource for the study of the
history of Christian thought. Chapter two applies this judgment to the exegetical works of Luther, pointing out how
the renewed attention to the works contained in these volumes promises to revise and to amplify the understanding of
his theology. The next four chapters review some of the
basic formal principles at work in the exegetical volumes of
Luther's Works: the authority of the Word of God in the
Bible, the role of the dogmatic tradition, the Bible as the
history of the people of God, and the importance of controversy for the determination of what the Scriptures meant.
In the interaction between these principles lies much of the
dynamic of Luther's method as a Biblical expositor; for
a study of the exegetical works presented in this set will
show that all these principles were at work throughout Luther's exegesis, even though in one or another commentary
some of these principles appear to have predominated.

Part One is based, therefore, directly on the exegetical
works; it attempts to isolate the principles and presuppositions underlying those works. Yet Luther acted as an expositor also when he was not preaching or teaching on the
basis of a Biblical text. This introduction to his exegetical
works may not content itself with the principles of his teaching and preaching. It must also examine how his exegesis
worked itself out in his theology as a whole. For, as chapter
six points out, there was a subtle connection between polemics and exegesis in Luther, as there has been in other theologians. Almost every commentary in the following volumes
contains a vast amount of polemics, as chapter five illustrates

from Luther's *Lectures on Genesis*. On the other hand, Luther's polemics deals with exegetical issues. The exegetical import of his polemics belongs in a volume on Luther the expositor.

In Part Two the exegesis of texts on the Lord's Supper is employed as a case study of his work as an expositor. This was one of the few issues on which Luther contended with both his Roman Catholic and his Protestant opponents. That conflict compelled Luther to think through his exegesis of the Bible as no other controversy in his career managed to do. The exegesis of eucharistic texts is the prime instance of Luther the expositor in action. It is at the same time the prime instance of the hiatus between Reformation exegesis and present-day trends in Biblical interpretation. Even the current debates over the meaning of justification in the New Testament as contrasted with its meaning in the exegesis of the reformers are not as far-reaching in their import as are the discussions on the exegetical foundation for the doctrine of the Lord's Supper. Confessional theology, whether on the Roman Catholic or the Reformed or the Lutheran side, dare not ignore the implications of what New Testament exegetes of all confessions have to say about the primitive meaning of the passages on the Lord's Supper. Nor dare the exegetes proceed as though they were free of confessional bias or as though the exegesis in the confessional traditions were irrelevant to the exegetical assignment of the twentieth century.

Such considerations as these have suggested the choice of the doctrine of the Lord's Supper as a case study for the consideration of Luther the expositor. The titles of the chapters in Part Two indicate several texts that have figured prominently in the history of exegesis. Each of these texts occupied Luther as an expositor and as a controversialist. Taken together, they provide a neat summary of how Luther the expositor applied the principles of his exegesis to the actual practice of expounding the New Testament. The conclusion of the volume is a brief consideration of the present relevance of Luther's exegetical works.

During the five years since this volume was begun, various of its chapters have been delivered as lectures. Chapter five was a paper before the First International Congress on Luther Research at Aarhus, Denmark, in 1956. Other chapters were presented at Concordia, Luther, Northwestern, and Wartburg theological seminaries (at this last as the Reu Memorial Lectures), and at the Harvard Divinity School. Still others were given before conventions or pastoral conferences of the Atlantic, Central, English, Michigan, Minnesota, Northern Illinois, Southeastern, and Western districts of The Lutheran Church — Missouri Synod.

LUTHER THE EXPOSITOR

Introduction to the Reformer's
Exegetical Writings

by

JAROSLAV PELIKAN

PART ONE

The Principles of Luther's Exegesis

CHAPTER ONE

Exegesis and the History of Theology

THE history of theology is the record of how the church has interpreted the Scriptures. In fact, as Gerhard Ebeling has suggested, not only the history of Christian theology but the entire history of the Christian Church could be read as the account of its efforts to find and to articulate the meaning of the Scriptures among the manifold changes of its historical development.[1] Thus, for example, the history of monasticism is a lengthy commentary on the statement of Peter in Matt. 19:27: "We have left everything and followed You."[2] The history of papal claims to supremacy over the church, on the other hand, is a lengthy commentary on the statement to Peter in Matt. 16:18: "You are Peter, and on this rock I will build My church."[3] In this way it would be possible to interpret many aspects of the church's history in the light of the Biblical imperative to which they have sought to give expression. The history of theology is, of course, the most obvious aspect of Christian history in which the interpretation of the Scriptures has figured very prominently — especially if the history of theology includes, as it should, the history of Christian preaching.

[1] Gerhard Ebeling, *Kirchengeschichte als Geschichte der Auslegung der Heiligen Schrift* (Tübingen, 1947).

[2] Cf. St. Maximus the Confessor, *The Ascetic Life*, tr. by Polycarp Sherwood, *Ancient Christian Writers*, henceforth abbreviated as ACW, 21, 105.

[3] Jaroslav Pelikan, *The Riddle of Roman Catholicism* (Nashville, 1959), pp. 77—93, with bibliography on the history of the interpretation of this passage.

As an interpretation of what has actually happened in the development of the church and of its thought this generalization is true, and it is not true. It is true that the history of theology has been dominated by themes and issues set down in the Scriptures, and that the theologians of the church have repeatedly found it necessary to reappropriate these Scriptural themes and issues. At the same time this generalization as it stands seems to assign to other phases and factors of theological and ecclesiastical history only an ancillary function in relation to the exegesis of the Scriptures.[4] One may or may not wish that it were accurate to describe the history of Christian thought and institutions as the record of its exegesis. But it remains true that any such interpretation would fail to account for the variety of motifs and movements in the history of the Christian community.

This much, however, seems sure: the interpretation of the Scriptures *has* played a role of greater import and influence in the history of theology than it does in the histories of theology composed by many modern historians and theologians. Entire histories have been written — histories of a whole section of the church, of an era in church history, or of a major theological problem — which do not seriously consider the possibility that at least one of the decisive elements in the thought and action of a Christian man or group may have been the way they interpreted the Bible.[5] And

[4] As H. Richard Niebuhr comments, "Opinions as to church polity, varying from denomination to denomination, have been based in theory on New Testament reports of primitive church organization. The episcopal, the presbyterian, and the congregational forms have each been set forth as representing the original and ideal constitution of the Christian church. Yet the relationship of these forms to the political experience and desire of various groups is considerably more pertinent than is their relationship to the New Testament." *The Social Sources of Denominationalism* (New York, 1929), pp. 14–15.

[5] See the astute discussion by Werner Elert, *Der Ausgang der altkirchlichen Christologie* (Berlin, 1957), pp. 313–333, on *Die Kirche und ihre Dogmengeschichte*.

this in the face of the fact that these men and groups frequently made the claim that they were speaking and acting as expounders of the Sacred Scriptures. Historians have sought to assess the influence of everything from the theologian's vanity to the theologian's viscera upon the formulation of theological doctrines, meanwhile regarding as naive and uninformed the suggestion that the Bible may be a source of these doctrines. Influenced by recent trends in systematic theology and influencing them in turn, church history and the history of theology have begun to reappraise the significance of exegesis for the development of Christian thought. This reappraisal is one of the principal shifts in the study of the history of theology during recent decades.

One area of theological study which will benefit greatly from this reappraisal is the history of dogma, the narrative of how the official creeds and confessions of the church have come into being. The study of the history of Christian thought as a separate theological field began in the period of the Enlightenment as the history of dogma.[6] Its aim was to show the historical setting and, therefore, the relativity of dogmas which Protestant orthodoxy regarded as absolute and binding. Eventually the historians of dogma came to defend this preoccupation with dogma on other grounds, some of them sound and others specious.[7] During the twentieth century historical theology has been broadened to include the whole development of Christian faith and doctrine rather than merely the record of the official creeds and confessions.[8] Yet the concerns and methods of the history of

[6] Reinhold Seeberg, *Lehrbuch der Dogmengeschichte* (4th ed.; Basel, 1953), I, 20—26.

[7] Gustav Krüger, *Was heisst und zu welchem Ende studiert man Dogmengeschichte?* (Leipzig, 1895).

[8] Walther Köhler has discussed this change in his *Dogmengeschichte als Geschichte des christlichen Selbstbewusstseins* (2d ed.; Zürich, 1943), pp. 1—6.

dogma have continued to dominate the procedures of historical theology. The new interest in the history of Biblical interpretation will bring about a re-examination of the role that exegesis has played in the origins and formulation of the great dogmas of the Christian Church. It will likewise necessitate some reflection on the role that exegesis has sometimes been prevented from playing in the history of dogma because philosophical, political, psychological, and other factors have had such an overriding influence. Both positively and negatively, then, the history of Biblical interpretation has much to contribute to the history of dogma. As Gerhard Ebeling has said, "it will be necessary to correct the one-sided emphasis upon the history of dogma characteristic of previous research in church history, in favor of the history of hermeneutics and Biblical interpretation."[9]

If the history of Biblical interpretation is to illumine the history of dogma, it will have to contend with a serious handicap in the literary sources on which the history of dogma is based.[10] The documents surrounding the conciliar decisions on dogma are principally polemical documents, and in most cases the only documents that were preserved came from the victorious or orthodox party in the dispute. This means, of course, that only with great difficulty and caution can we determine the exact position of the heretical party. Later discoveries of authentic writings by the heretics have sometimes confirmed the reports of the fathers about what the heretics taught, but other discoveries have also thrown doubt upon the accuracy and fairness of some of these re-

[9] Ebeling, op. cit., pp. 25—26.

[10] Walter Nigg summarizes this situation in the epigram: "The heretics maintained that interpretation of the Gospel which went down to defeat in the conflict over ideas. The suppressed interpretation of Christianity comes to voice through them. It is the defeated who are left lying on the field of battle." *Das Buch der Ketzer* (Zürich, 1949), p. 17.

ports.[11] There is even greater difficulty in the effort to determine the exegetical procedures and the Scriptural sources that led the several parties to take the positions that are recounted in the reports of the fathers. When we have no writings by a heretical defendant at all and no exegetical writings by his orthodox prosecutor, how are we to examine the Biblical issues in the controversy and the Biblical grounds for the orthodox solution of the controversy? The answer to that question cannot be unimportant to anyone who seeks to judge Christian doctrine, including church dogma, by the authority of the Bible.

To be sure, there are sources of a specifically Biblical character from the period surrounding some of the controversies, and these can be exploited for a consideration of how exegesis has helped to shape dogma and of how dogma has helped to shape exegesis. One of the most intriguing suggestions put forth in recent years about the mutual influence between Scripture and dogma is the hypothesis that the conflicts over dogma may help to account for some of the textual variants in the manuscripts of the New Testament.[12] In some cases the variants seem to have been produced by

[11] Perhaps the best illustration of this problem is the interpretation of Gnosticism, for which we have been dependent largely on patristic reports until the discovery of Gnostic sources. Cf. Francois M. Sagnard, *La gnose valentinienne et le temoignage de Saint Irenee* (Paris, 1947) for a careful discussion.

[12] "The textual critic . . . should value the readings of his late manuscripts just as he does those of his early manuscripts. All are a part of the tradition; all contribute to our knowledge of the history of Christian thought. And they are significant contributions because they are interpretations which were highly enough thought of in some place and at some time to be incorporated into the Scripture itself. . . . Would it not be better to trace the relationships of manuscripts through their individual readings or, rather, through their reflections of particular doctrines or dogmas?" Merrill M. Parvis, "The Nature and Tasks of New Testament Textual Criticism: An Appraisal," *The Journal of Religion*, XXXII (1952), 172–173.

the dogmatic conflict, while in others the conflict may have come as a result of the textual problem. Students of the New Testament text tend to agree that this suggestion is applicable to certain passages and problems, but that as a generalization it is difficult to substantiate or to refute. Still the chief documents that a student examines for a history of dogma are not Biblical commentaries, much less Biblical manuscripts, but polemical treatises, in which exegetical issues seem, at least at first glance, to have played only a minor role. Hence it is easy for the histories of dogma to dismiss exegesis from consideration and to pursue other explanations of how the dogma came to be.

But it is only at first glance that exegesis seems to have played a minor role. Proceeding from a distorted and atomistic method of Biblical proof, Protestant theologians have sometimes failed to recognize exegesis when they saw it, simply because it did not conform to their definition of exegesis. Frequently a theologian has been engaged in interpreting the Scriptures without even quoting the Scriptures, or at least without quoting them very much. The literary occasion for the controversy between Augustine and Pelagius was Augustine's prayer: "Give what Thou commandest, and command what Thou wilt." [13] It might appear, therefore, that if their conflict over nature and grace was an exposition of any passage, it was a dispute over the interpretation of these words of Augustine rather than over the exegesis of Scripture. Nor would a consideration of how the New Testament used the term "nature" (φύσις) in comparison with how it used the term "grace" (χάρις) serve as a key to the exegeti-

---

[13] Augustine, *Confessions*, Book X, ch. xxix, *Library of Christian Classics*, henceforth abbreviated as *LCC*, VII, 225. On Pelagius' reaction to this prayer of Augustine, *On the Gift of Perseverance*, ch. 53, *Nicene and Post-Nicene Fathers*, henceforth abbreviated as *NPNF-I*, 547; also John Ferguson, *Pelagius* (Cambridge, 1956), pp. 47—52.

cal issues in the Pelagian controversy. Eph. 2:3-5 would seem to be the only place in the New Testament where φύσις and χάρις are juxtaposed.[14]

But a study of how the New Testament uses χάρις itself would be of primary importance for an understanding of the Pelagian controversy. Such a study would show that the New Testament, following good classical precedent, could ascribe "grace" to persons as a quality of their personality or life.[15] So, for example, Col. 4:6 admonishes: "Let your speech always be gracious [ἐν χάριτι]." In this sense it is common English usage to speak of "the Christian graces." More usually, however, χάρις was attributed to God as a quality of His Person; there it meant the favor of God.[16] It did not take an extended amount of musing to make the student of the Scriptures wonder which of these two was the root meaning of χάρις. Was "grace" something in man that merited God's favor, or was "grace" a favor of God that created a man anew and made him pleasing to God? The answer was not as obvious to the church fathers as it is for anyone today who assumes the correctness of Augustinian teaching.[17] But the solution was the examination of χάρις in the context of how the whole of Scripture dealt with the mysterious relation between divine initiative and human responsibility, between destiny and freedom.[18] And this

[14] Cf. Augustine, *On Nature and Grace*, ch. 3, *NPNF*, V, p. 122.

[15] See the many passages cited in G. P. Wetter, *Charis* (Leipzig, 1913), pp. 95—195.

[16] See Wetter's comments, ibid., pp. 212—213, on exegesis.

[17] This was why it was possible for Pelagius to claim that he was following the teaching of the catholic and orthodox fathers; cf. Augustine, *On the Grace of Christ*, Book I, ch. 46—55, *NPNF-I*, V, 233—236.

[18] Augustine therefore sought to set the Biblical view of grace in opposition to both the Manichaean and the Pelagian heresy. See, among other passages, *Against Two Letters of the Pelagians*, Book III, ch. 25, *NPNF-I*, V, 414—415.

solution, cast in the form of dogma, was fundamentally an exegetical decision.[19]

It could indeed be argued that exegetical issues have often been most at stake in those theological controversies that did not deal *ex professo* with exegetical questions. In part the support one is prepared to lend this argument depends on one's own view of what is involved in the exegesis of the Scriptures. The example of both the church fathers and the Reformers indicates that the exegesis of the Scriptures can never properly be less than the interpretation of the total Biblical outlook, even when it is the examination of only one word or passage in the Bible. If this is true, then it has been genuine exegesis when the fathers synthesized the themes as well as when they analyzed the texts of Biblical history and literature.[20]

Certainly it would be difficult to identify the precise passages being debated in the controversy over Monotheletism during the seventh century.[21] Did Jesus Christ have two wills, i. e., one for each of His natures, or did He have only one will, since He was one Person? The answer to this question could not come from mere concordance study; for such study would quickly determine that in the few passages where the New Testament attributes a will (θέλημα) to Christ, it uses the word in the singular. There are only two passages in the entire New Testament — Acts 13:22 and Eph. 2:3 — that employ the plural θελήματα. In the form in which the seventh century raised it this was not a question that con-

[19] See the interesting collection of Biblical materials in Georges de Plinval, *Pélage, ses écrits, sa vie et sa réforme* (Lausanne, 1943), pp. 93—97.

[20] G. L. Prestige has summarized the situation as follows: "It was the heretics that relied most on isolated texts, and the Catholics who paid more attention on the whole to scriptural principles." *Fathers and Heretics* (London, 1948), p. 21.

[21] Joseph Tixeront, *Histoire des dogmes dans l'antiquite chretienne,* III (Paris, 1928), 160—192.

cerned the Biblical writers. A study of individual proof texts would have been inadequate to answer the question. What was at stake theologically in the Monotheletist controversy, as in the Monophysite controversy that preceded it, was the integrity of the human nature of Christ and its continuity with human nature as such.[22] The declaration of the *Ecthesis* of 638 that Christ had only one will (ἓν θέλημα) seemed to the bishops and theologians at Constantinople in 680 to threaten this integrity and continuity, which were the explicit assertion of only a few passages in the New Testament but the implicit presupposition of every passage in the New Testament.[23] The Council of Constantinople was acting in defense of this presupposition when it rejected Monotheletism.[24]

To be sure, the controversy over Monotheletism was not exegetical, or even theological, but political in origin. The external threat to the Byzantine Empire made it politically expedient to invent a formula on which both Monophysites and Chalcedonians could agree, and the notion of "one will" was such a formula. In addition, the specific issue in the controversy lay in the realm of speculative philosophy. Was "will" a predicate of "nature," as this term had been defined and clarified in the Christological controversies of the fifth and sixth centuries?[25] If so, then Christ had to have two wills, one for each nature. Or was "will" a predicate of "person," as this term had been defined and clarified in those

[22] Cf. Werner Elert, op. cit., pp. 133—184.

[23] J. D. Mansi (ed.), *Sacrorum conciliorum nova et amplissima collectio* (Florence, 1759—98), X, 992—997, contains the text of the *Ecthesis*.

[24] Cf. Mansi, XI, 637.

[25] See the passages from Philoxenus of Mabbug (d. 519) in Elisabeth Bergsträsser, *Philoxenus von Mabbug. Zur Frage einer monophysitischen Soteriologie*, in Friedrich Hübner (ed.), *Gedenkschrift für D. Werner Elert* (Berlin, 1955), p. 46.

same controversies? [26] If so, then Christ had to have only one will; for He was one Person. Beyond all these political and philosophical questions, however, exegesis — understood now, not as the interpretation of individual passages but as the exposition of Biblical themes — was still an issue in the conflict. Although the number of Biblical passages expounded in the sources was surprisingly small, we must still conclude that the meaning of the Biblical message was at stake and that, therefore, even the Monotheletist controversy was at least partly an exegetical debate.

This does not mean, of course, that the controversies surrounding the rise and formulation of Christian dogma never dealt explicitly with the interpretation of specific Biblical passages. They often did. Much of ancient dogma was the determination of what a specific passage meant, together with the rejection of other interpretations as heretical. A good illustration is the role played in the Christological and Trinitarian discussion by the words put into the mouth of Wisdom in Prov. 8:22-31: "The Lord created me at the beginning of His work, the first of His acts of old. Ages ago I was set up, at the first, before the beginning of the earth. When there were no depths I was brought forth, when there were no springs abounding with water. Before the mountains had been shaped, before the hills, I was brought forth; before He had made the earth with its fields, or the first of the dust of the world. When He established the heavens, I was there, when He drew a circle on the face of the deep, when He made firm the skies above, when He established the fountains of the deep, when He assigned to the sea its limit, so that the waters might not transgress His command, when He marked out the foundations of the earth, then I was beside Him, like

[26] J. F. Bethune-Baker's *An Introduction to the Early History of Christian Doctrine* (London, 1958), pp. 233–235, is a useful summary of how the word "person" evolved.

a master workman; and I was daily His delight, rejoicing before Him always, rejoicing in His inhabited world and delighting in the sons of men." [27]

The use of this term "Wisdom" as a designation for both Christ and the Spirit in early Christian literature has given rise to the theory of a "Spirit-Christology" in the Ante-Nicene fathers. [28] Some scholars have even suggested that the proper term for the early Christian doctrine of God is not "Trinitarianism" but "binitarianism." [29] Although the case for this interpretation has been vastly overstated by some of its proponents, the fact remains that the early Christian exegesis of the Wisdom literature of the Old Testament and the Apocrypha could not easily decide when the personified Wisdom was the pre-existent Christ and when it was the Spirit. [30] And it certainly is true that some early Christian writers had difficulty with this distinction in their exegesis because the distinction was not very clear in their theology. In this sense it is valid to speak of a "Spirit-Christology" as one of the ways early Christian interpretation of the Old Testament attempted to relate the Scripture to its new-found insight into the meaning of God in Christ.

It was, however, not the identity of Christ and the Spirit but the identity of Christ and the Father that formed the basis for the controversy over the Person of Christ in the early church. This was also the basis for the controversy

[27] Cf. Hermann L. Strack and Paul Billerbeck, *Kommentar zum Neuen Testament aus Talmud und Midrasch*, II (Munich, 1924), 356–357.

[28] Friedrich Loofs, in *Theophilus von Antiochien adversus Marcionem und die anderen theologischen Quellen bei Irenaeus* (Leipzig, 1930), bases much of his literary analysis on this theory; see also K. E. Kirk, "The Evolution of the Doctrine of the Trinity," in A. E. J. Rawlinson (ed.), *Essays on the Trinity and the Incarnation* (London, 1928), pp. 157–237.

[29] Waldemar Macholz, *Spuren binitarischer Denkweise im Abendlande seit Tertullian* (Jena, 1902).

[30] See the passages collected by Harry A. Wolfson, *The Philosophy of the Church Fathers*, I (Cambridge, 1956), 245–256.

over the meaning of the eighth chapter of Proverbs. So prominently did this chapter figure in the Arian debates that it would be possible to write the history of those debates as the development of the exegesis of Prov. 8.[31] Hilary of Poitiers reports that the Arians "strive to prove from it [this chapter] that Christ was created, not born as God, and that, therefore, He shares in the nature of created beings, even though He is superior to them because of the way He was created." Hilary promised, on the other hand, that he would prove from this very chapter that "there is a Wisdom that was born before all things, and there is also a wisdom that is created for special purposes. The Wisdom that is from eternity is one thing, but the wisdom that has come into being during the course of time is quite another." [32] Later on in the treatise he went into a lengthy exegesis of Prov. 8 to establish this latter point.[33] Hilary's great contemporary, Athanasius, was likewise exercised over the Arians' reliance on Prov. 8. Half of his second *Discourse Against the Arians* was devoted to a detailed study of this passage in its context and to a demonstration of its consonance with the Nicene doctrine of the Person of Christ.[34] He was obliged to defend the orthodox exegesis of the passage elsewhere in his writings

[31] "From the very outset," writes Georg Kretschmar, "Wisdom was a cosmic reality; and when the ecclesiological significance of Sophia receded, its application to the creation remained and even received a new emphasis. Thus the co-ordination of creation and redemption finds an echo now in the co-ordination of Wisdom and Logos. . . . In this way Sophia ultimately becomes the heavenly archetype not of the church, but of Christ. This is the sense in which Justin and the Alexandrians employ Proverbs 8 as Scriptural proof. Word and Wisdom apply to Jesus of Nazareth in equal measure." *Studien zur frühchristlichen Trinitätstheologie* (Tübingen, 1956), p. 60.

[32] Hilary of Poitiers, *On the Trinity*, Book I, ch. 36, NPNF-II, IX, 50 (translation my own).

[33] Ibid., Book XII, chs. 35—50, NPNF-II, IX, 226—231.

[34] Athanasius, *Four Discourses Against the Arians*, Discourse II, chs. 19 to 22, NPNF-II, IV, 372—393.

too.[35] This would indicate that the opponents of the Nicene doctrine continued to find in this chapter one of their chief Biblical supports, and that Christians of various theological positions saw in it an important testimony to the meaning of the Person of Christ.

Prov. 8 appears to have figured as such a testimony very early in Christian history. In antithesis to the modalism of Praxeas, Tertullian used this chapter to prove that Christ was not merely an attribute or a manifestation of the Father.[36] His exegesis here seems to reflect the usage of the church at large rather than of his Montanist sect, for the Montanist influence upon this treatise is actually rather slight.[37] The same chapter created difficulties for the exegesis of Origen; but, as Prestige has said: "Origen was not the man to shrink from difficulties, and if Scripture [Prov. 8] said that the Lord created Wisdom, and ecclesiastical tradition identified Wisdom with the Logos, his bold speculative intellect was quite prepared to assert that the Logos was indeed created."[38] In all probability, however, the Christological use of this chapter was considerably older than either Tertullian or Origen. There is reason to believe that echoes of it appear in the New Testament itself.[39] Rendel Harris once suggested, with his usual virtuosity, that John 1:1-3 is a paraphrase of Prov. 8 and that the masculine word λόγος has replaced the

[35] Cf. Guido Müller, *Lexicon Athanasianum* (Berlin, 1952), col. 1642, for a listing of the passages in which Athanasius deals with this chapter; see also ibid., coll. 1342–1343, s. v. σοφία.

[36] Tertullian's use of this chapter is carefully summarized in Ernest Evans (ed.), *Tertullian's Treatise Against Praxeas* (London, 1948), pp. 216 to 219.

[37] Cf. Jaroslav Pelikan, "Montanism and Its Trinitarian Significance," *Church History*, XXV (1956), 99–109.

[38] G. L. Prestige, *God in Patristic Thought* (2nd ed.; London, 1956), p. 134.

[39] Oscar Cullmann, *Die Christologie des Neuen Testaments* (Tübingen, 1957), p. 263, with bibliographical notes.

feminine σοφία because of the identification of Wisdom with Jesus Christ.[40] Even though this explanation may seem far-fetched at first reading, the affinities between the two chapters are so pronounced as to suggest some direct lineage.[41] This suggestion is reinforced by a consideration of how Wisdom was being interpreted in Jewish thought.[42] If the Christological exegesis of Prov. 8 was not part of the New Testament, it must have belonged to that broad tradition of early Christian teaching and exegesis about the existence of which in the second (and perhaps in the first century) we are now beginning to learn so much.[43] So this exegesis went into the later exegetical tradition of the church, influencing not only the church fathers but interpreters like Martin Luther.[44]

If the history of the Christological and Trinitarian dogmas is to be faithful to its materials, therefore, it must develop a far greater sensitivity to the exegetical problems being debated by the church fathers. Yet it is not true that the fathers who formulated the ancient dogma faced one another, Bibles in hand, and forgot everything in the world but the Word. For the history of dogma is not only — as the historians of dogma like Harnack have often neglected to show — the history of the interpretation of the Scriptures. It is also — as the orthodox theologians of past and present have

[40] Rendel Harris, *The Origin of the Prologue to St. John's Gospel* (Cambridge, 1917), p. 18.

[41] The affinities to Rev. 3:14 are even more obvious and help to support the suggestion that Prov. 8 was being applied to Christ in the first century.

[42] See Paul Heinisch, *Die persönliche Weisheit des Alten Testaments in religionsgeschichtlicher Beleuchtung* (Münster, 1923), especially pp. 58 to 62.

[43] Jean Danielou's *Sacramentum futuri* (Paris, 1950), pp. 152–176, is one discussion of this tradition. For a sympathetic critique of Danielou's concept of the exegetical tradition see R. P. C. Hanson, *Allegory and Event* (London, 1959), pp. 97–129.

[44] *Lectures on Genesis* (1535–45), W, XLII, 11; *Luther's Works*, 1, 13.

often neglected to realize — the history of how theology has sometimes avoided or even abused the interpretation of the Scriptures in the defense of a personal theological whim or of an ecclesiastical party line. A study of the history of theology reveals that the exegesis of the Scriptures has profoundly influenced Christian thought, but it also shows that many theologians have been unable to hear the testimony of the Scriptures because their personal or denominational prejudices have foreclosed the possibility of any exegesis that would change their minds about anything.

Helping to foreclose such a possibility is the polemical stance of many theologians. The press of polemics has often helped a theologian to a more profound understanding of a Biblical text which he had been taking for granted or interpreting in a superficial and conventional manner. Later chapters of this book will provide numerous illustrations of this generalization from the polemical exegesis of Luther. Those same chapters will also raise the question whether the polemical context of Luther's exegesis — or of anyone else's exegesis — may not have forced him to an extreme position or at least to an extreme formulation of his position, which he might have modified in the more sober moments of exegetical reflection. In short, polemics has helped theologians to see deeper meanings in a text; but it has sometimes helped them to see meanings that were not in the text or to overlook meanings that were.

For this reason it is also wholesome to compare what the church eventually adopted as the orthodox answer to a theological question with the polemical viewpoints previously espoused by the theological parties in the controversy. Such a comparison suggests that frequently the exegetical and liturgical sobriety of the church won out over the polemical extravagances of the theologians on both the left and the right wing of the controversy. At the same time the orthodox answer itself carried the scars of the battle. Especially was this true in those instances — and they were more than frequent enough — when considerations of ecclesiastical or secular politics helped to dictate the terms of the dogmatic settlement. Although it is a mistake, for example, to ascribe the settlement at Chalcedon in 451 exclusively to such political considerations, it would also be historically dishonest to imagine that only piety and exegesis were at stake there. The history of Chalcedon or of the Fourth Lateran Council is partly the history of Biblical interpretation, but the historians of these councils must continue to learn from Harnack and others to look for the "nontheological" factors alongside the theological and the exegetical.[45] Otherwise their accounts of the history of dogma will inevitably distort the story.

If the scope of the history of dogma is widened to include not only the account of the rise of dogma but also the record of what happened to the dogma after its official formulation, this introduces another interesting twist. As the fourth chapter of this book will show at some length,[46] it has sometimes fallen to later generations to discern exegetical motifs that had indeed been involved in the original formulation of dogma but had frequently been left undeveloped. Later theology has sometimes had to make explicit the exegesis that was only implicit in the dogma. For example, the conclusion of the Chalcedonian formula makes the claim that it teaches "even as the prophets from of old

[45] As Adolf Harnack says of the period after Chalcedon: "The historian is interested only in the things that matter in history. After about 444, therefore, the political historian replaces the historian of dogma almost everywhere." *Lehrbuch der Dogmengeschichte*, II (5th ed.; Tübingen, 1931), 373. Unfortunately, this judgment is marred by Harnack's own theological bias; but the "nontheological factors" were certainly prominent enough.

[46] See pp. 78—84.

[have spoken] concerning Him [Christ], and as the Lord Jesus Christ Himself has taught us, and as the Symbol of the Fathers has delivered to us." [47] The Council of Chalcedon thus declares that its doctrine accords with both Scripture and tradition, but it does not identify the particular Biblical statements in accordance with which it professes to be speaking.

Starting with the Chalcedonian formula as a basis, the theologians and exegetes of the church have supplied the formula with the Biblical support to which the fathers had appealed. Far from being "the grave-clothes of the historical Jesus," as Albert Schweitzer maintains,[48] the *Chalcedonense* has provided the framework within which the Christian study of the historical Jesus could be carried on without some of the excrescences which appeared in the centuries, both before and since, when that framework was missing.[49] The recurring emphasis of Christian piety and theology upon the true humanity of Jesus Christ has not been a tacit revolt against Chalcedon and its dogma of the two natures. On the contrary, it has been an exegetical and devotional repossession of that which the Chalcedonian dogma of the two natures had sought to circumscribe. The primary purpose of this dogma was not to give an account of the content of Christ's humanity but only to fix the limits beyond which worship of Him and speculation about Him could not be permitted to wander without sacrificing its orthodoxy. Thus the task of the dogma was not to describe but to "define" — to "define," not in the sense of determining the essential

[47] R. V. Sellers, *The Council of Chalcedon* (London, 1953), p. 211.

[48] Albert Schweitzer, *The Quest of the Historical Jesus*, tr. by W. Montgomery (London, 1911), p. 3.

[49] Jaroslav Pelikan, "Chalcedon After Fifteen Centuries," *Concordia Theological Monthly*, XXII (1951), 926–936.

qualities of divinity and humanity but in the sense of establishing the boundaries of thought and devotion.[50]

When the church's exegesis found the figure of the Elder Brother in the Gospels, therefore, it was only filling in the content of what the church had previously "defined" as His humanity. Thus the Christological dogma has not necessarily been a hindrance to genuine historical exegesis, as the Enlightenment and nineteenth-century liberalism maintained. Nor is the Christological dogma a compensation for the loss of meaning in the exegesis of eschatological passages of Scripture, as Martin Werner has sought to prove.[51] On the contrary, since both dogma and exegesis have been functions of the teaching and worshiping church, they have provided mutual enrichment. At times the dogma has been obliged to carry Christology; for exegesis has been either too shallow to give any content to Christology or too complex and controversial to give it any clarity. At other times exegesis has moved to the fore when fresh movements in the life and thought of the church have given the theologians a new insight into the terms of Scripture and of dogma. The period of the Enlightenment is a good illustration of how dogma has sometimes had to preserve the church's faith in opposition to exegesis; the Franciscan revival and the Reformation, each in its unique way, demonstrate how the apparently sterile dogma about the two natures in Christ can give birth to an exegesis of the Gospels in which our Lord Jesus Christ is truly flesh of our flesh and bone of our bone.

Recent attention to the history of Biblical interpretation

[50] As Alan Richardson has put it, "When the formulations were undertaken, they were usually drawn up with a view to excluding heretical views rather than with the intention of limiting men's freedom of thought upon the mysteries of the Christian faith." *Creeds in the Making* (2nd ed.; London, 1951), p. 82.

[51] In Jaroslav Pelikan's "The Eschatology of Tertullian," *Church History*, XXI (1952), 108—122, there is an examination of Werner's thesis.

thus promises to be a fruitful resource for the history of dogma. Another area of historical theology that will benefit from such attention is the history of the great theological systems. For not only has the historical scholarship of the past century underemphasized the exegetical basis of dogma, it has also tended to minimize the role that exegesis has played in the creative and systematic thought of the makers of Christian theology. As a consequence, these systems have been fearfully oversimplified in modern handbooks. The propositional clarity and simplicity of dogmatics has replaced the fecundity and complexity of exegesis as the fundamental point of interpretation. The rubrics for the history of theology have usually come from dogmatics rather than from exegesis. There is historical research into the real presence or the two natures, but not into the Christian interpretation of the Exodus or of Abraham.[52] Once the importance of exegesis in the theological systems of the past centuries has been recovered, it may prove more difficult to interpret these systems. In addition, the interpretation itself may be less tidy; but it may also do more adequate justice to the systems themselves — if this word is still applicable at all.

There is a close analogy between the problem besetting the interpretation of the great theological systems and that involved in the study of the history of dogma. The discovery of "the Hellenization of Christianity" — usually associated with the name of Adolf Harnack but going back to J. L. Mosheim (1694—1755), the Enlightenment, and even earlier [53] — has obscured the complex and subtle interrelation

[52] David Lerch's *Isaaks Opferung christlich gedeutet* (Tübingen, 1950) contains the beginnings for a history of Abraham as the father of believers.

[53] Walther Glawe's *Die Hellenisierung des Christentums in der Geschichte der Theologie von Luther bis auf die Gegenwart* (Berlin, 1912) traces the development of this notion in the polemical and historical literature of Protestantism.

between philosophical and theological elements in the history of Christian thought. Karl Barth has summarized the way this process of obscuring took place: "Since they themselves [the historians of dogma, etc.] were actually philosophizing when they supposed that they were theologizing, they could no longer grasp or understand that perhaps others may actually have been theologizing when they seemed so obviously to be philosophizing." [54] For example, the controversial term ὁμοούσιος in the Trinitarian and Christological controversies gives every appearance of being a piece of alien metaphysics blatantly smuggled into the church's theology, and in the historical and systematic theology of the past century it has often been interpreted as just that.[55] Actually, as Werner Elert has put it, "by its dogma the church threw up a wall against an alien metaphysics." [56]

On the other hand, the theologians of the church have sometimes been thinking philosophically as well as theologically when they seemed to be speaking only theologically and exegetically. A splendid illustration would seem to be the history of the Christian exegesis of Ex. 3:14: "I am who I am." [57] Oskar Grether has described the theological and metaphysical implications of this passage in the history of the Israelitic view of God.[58] In the history of the Christian view of God this passage has enabled theologians to employ Biblical speech as a vehicle for the expression of Greek metaphysics. To Clement of Alexandria the passage means that

[54] Karl Barth, *Die protestantische Theologie im 19. Jahrhundert* (Zürich, 1947), p. 132.

[55] J. F. Bethune-Baker's *The Meaning of Homoousios in the 'Constantinopolitan' Creed* (Cambridge, 1901) is still an able defense against this interpretation; see also Prestige, *God in Patristic Thought*, pp. 197—218.

[56] Elert, *Ausgang*, p. 14.

[57] Cf. the excursus in Emil Brunner, *Dogmatik*, I (Zürich, 1946), 134 ff.

[58] Oskar Grether, *Name und Wort Gottes im Alten Testament* (Giessen, 1934).

"God is one, and beyond the one, and above the Monad itself." [59] His pupil Origen took it to imply that "in Him who truly exists and who said by Moses, 'I am who I am,' all things, whatever they are, participate; which participation in God the Father is shared both by just men and sinners, by rational and irrational beings, and by all things universally which exist." [60] Both of these fathers, though not unaffected by Greek patterns of thought, are actually drawing a valid and necessary inference from the passage.

The later history of the passage in Christian exegesis is more impressive. When Paul Tillich attempts to show that Biblical religion and the metaphysical search for ultimate reality are finally congruent,[61] he is reiterating what a theologian like Gregory of Nazianzus said on the basis of this passage. The Biblical words "I am who I am" confirmed for Gregory what his theological and philosophical thought had discovered, that ὁ ὤν was the most precise and fitting term for God.[62] Apparently without a knowledge of Gregory, Augustine employed the same passage in support of virtually the same contention, namely, that the term *essentia* could be used *proprie* about God, while the term *substantia* might be used only *abusive*.[63] From these two leading fathers of the East and West respectively the consideration of this passage passed over into the theological tradition of both sections of Christendom. John Scotus Erigena used it to refute the predestinarianism of Gottschalk, but the ontological framework of his refutation made his position more dangerous to

[59] Clement of Alexandria, *The Instructor*, Book I, ch. 8, *Ante-Nicene Fathers*, henceforth abbreviated as *ANF*, II, 227.

[60] Origen, *De principiis*, Book I, ch. 3, *ANF*, IV, 253—254.

[61] Paul Tillich, *Biblical Religion and the Search for Ultimate Reality* (Chicago, 1955).

[62] Gregory of Nazianzus, *The Theological Orations*, Oration IV, ch. 18, *LCC*, III, 189.

[63] Augustine, *On the Trinity*, Book VII, ch. 6, *NPNF-I*, III, 111.

the Catholic faith than even Gottschalk's was.[64] The theological tradition of the East found one of its most authoritative spokesmen in John of Damascus, to whom the word
from the burning bush meant that "He keeps all being in
His own embrace, like a sea of essence infinite and unseen." [65]
The spokesman for the theological tradition of the West,
Thomas Aquinas, used this word to validate his proofs for
the existence of God.[66] John of Damascus and Thomas
Aquinas have become textbooks of theology for much of the
church, and their use of "I am who I am" set the pattern
for later Eastern Orthodox, Roman Catholic, and even Protestant theology.[67]

These citations illustrate the prominent role which the
exegesis of Ex. 3:14 has played in the history of the Christian
doctrine of God. They also show how subtle and unconscious
are the elisions from theology to philosophy and back again.
The mere citation and multiplication of Biblical passages is
no guarantee that a theology is Biblical. The dogmatics of
Protestant orthodoxy and fundamentalism may act as though
philosophy were unimportant to it, but it often philosophizes
in spite of itself.[68] On the other hand, the absence of explicit
Biblical quotations or references is no sign that a theologian
has ignored the Bible in his thought. Neglect of this subtle
interrelation between philosophy and exegesis has given rise
to the notion, so widely circulated today, that to understand
any theology it is necessary first to isolate its philosophical
presuppositions — among which the method of interpreting

[64] John Scotus Erigena, *De praedestinatione*, IX, 4, *Patrologia, Series Latina*, CXXII, 391.

[65] John of Damascus, *Exposition of the Orthodox Faith*, Book I, ch. 9, *NPNF-II*, IX, 12.

[66] Thomas Aquinas, *Summa theologica*, I, Q. 2, Art. 3, *LCC*, XI, 54.

[67] See, for example, Johann Gerhard, *Loci theologici*, Locus III, ch. 2, ed. by Ed. Preuss, I (Berlin, 1863), 388—389.

[68] Jaroslav Pelikan, *From Luther to Kierkegaard* (Saint Louis, 1950), pp. 49—75.

Scripture *may* be one. Once these presuppositions are isolated, the theologian will be seen to think, not as he wishes
or as his Biblical material directs, but as his philosophical
premises permit. Thus the angularity of an exegetical theology is cut to fit what the historian has isolated as its hidden
assumptions. Under such a method it is little wonder that
the exegetical judgments, and sometimes even the exegetical
writings, of a theologian have been treated as mere rational-
izations of his "theological" position, i. e., of the position
reflected in his dogmatic and apologetic writings.

How this method can distort historical theology is perhaps best illustrated in the interpretation of Origen. The
picture of Origen's theology dominating many histories of
early Christian thought is based largely, if not exclusively,
on two works, *De principiis* and *Contra Celsum*.[69] The former
was a more or less systematic exposition of the Christian
faith, the latter a defense of the faith against an outstanding
pagan critic. Historians have particularly fastened upon the
occasional speculations in *De principiis* and the occasional
concessions in *Contra Celsum* to find in these the true
Origen.[70] This would be almost like trying to discover the
theology of Paul from the sermons in Acts, with special
reference to the discourses addressed to the cultured despisers of Christianity in the fourteenth and the seventeenth
chapters. In presenting this picture of the true Origen many
historians have also ignored what Bigg calls his "doctrine
of reserve."[71] When he advanced his speculations, Origen

[69] For a criticism of earlier treatments of Origen's philosophy see Hal
Koch, *Pronoia und Paideusis* (Leipzig, 1932).

[70] Cf. the balanced estimate by Robert M. Grant, *The Bible in the
Church* (New York, 1948), p. 70: "While Origen constantly tries to express
what he regards as the orthodox Christian faith, the philosophical aids to
faith with which he is so much occupied tend to alter the content of that
faith."

[71] Charles Bigg, *The Christian Platonists of Alexandria* (Oxford, 1886),
pp. 144—145.

very carefully distinguished them from his expositions of the church's faith, setting them forth as merely suggestions rather than as his firm conclusions. For these suggestions Origen has acquired a reputation in the history of Christian eschatology for a definiteness he did not pretend to have. Origen realized that in eschatology there are some things we know and some things we do not know; where we do not know, he believed he had the right to wonder.

Yet it is because of this wondering that Origen was condemned as a heretic centuries after his death,[72] and that he has been interpreted as primarily a speculative theologian ever since. As the story of Rufinus and Jerome shows, his friends have sometimes done him more harm here than his enemies.[73] Yet how different Origen looks when viewed through his exegetical works! Though it was precisely these that Luther condemned, because of their allegorical extravagance,[74] Origen the exegete is beginning just now to emerge as the spokesman for the church's faith and as the church's faithful servant.[75] As an exegete, too, he spent some time wondering about questions that the text left unanswered. What exegete does not? But he did not devote his primary

[72] On the historical and canonical problems connected with this see Cyril C. Richardson, "The Condemnation of Origen," in *Church History*, VI (1937), 50—64.

[73] R. P. C. Hanson, *Origen's Doctrine of Tradition* (London, 1954), pp. 40—47: "Origen's Translators."

[74] "The bare allegories, which stand in no relation to the account and do not illuminate it, should simply be disapproved as empty dreams. This is the kind which Origen and those who followed him employ." *Lectures on Genesis* (1535—45), *Werke* (Weimar edition), henceforth abbreviated as W, XLII, 173; *Luther's Works*, 1, 233.

[75] Henri de Lubac has a very cordial chapter on "Origen, the Man of the Church" in his *Histoire et esprit* (Paris, 1950), pp. 47—91. Jean Danielou declares: "Origen was first and foremost a faithful son of the Church," *Origen*, tr. by Walter Mitchell (New York, 1955), p. 27. See the caveat of Hans von Campenhausen, *The Fathers of the Greek Church*, tr. by Stanley Godman (New York, 1959), p. 166.

attention to the pre-existence of the soul or to the theory of the restoration of all things — the two notions for which he is perhaps best remembered. Rather he gave minute, almost microscopic, attention to the meaning of the text. The man who compiled the *Hexapla* was no Prometheus whose speculations defied the heavens. He was a sober and responsible student of the Scriptures. To be sure, the Neoplatonic thought responsible for notions like pre-existence and restoration also shaped the course of his exegesis. In interpreting St. Matthew, for instance, he treated the historical life of our Lord as less significant for the truly spiritual Christian than for the psychic Christian. He did seem to make the historical Jesus almost a crutch which the mature Logos mystic could discard.[76] One could find other instances where his exegesis suffered because of his reliance on extra-biblical sources.[77] Even these do not obscure, but rather emphasize, the predominantly exegetical cast of Origen's theology.

What was true of Origen applied in varying degrees to other theologians as well. It applied to Augustine. As Prof. Outler has put it, we must "appeal from a worse Augustine, in his abstract and speculative moods, to a better Augustine, in his constructive, evangelical moods," to Augustine, the student of the Scriptures and the servant of the church.[78] In his speculations on the nature of being, for example, Augustine frequently spoke in a manner in-

[76] Aloisius Lieske's *Die Theologie der Logosmystik bei Origenes* (Münster, 1938) is a careful investigation of this facet of Origen's thought.

[77] W. Völker, *Das Vollkommenheitsideal des Origenes* (Tübingen, 1931). See the useful bibliography in Henry Chadwick (ed.), *Origen Contra Celsum* (Cambridge, 1953), pp. xxxv—xl.

[78] Albert C. Outler, "The Person and Work of Christ," in Roy W. Battenhouse (ed.), *A Companion to the Study of St. Augustine* (New York, 1955), p. 365.

distinguishable from Neoplatonic ontological discussions.[79] But in his minute commentary on the early chapters of Genesis he penetrated into the Biblical view of creation and its contrast with the ontological discussions of the Neoplatonists.[80] Still it is easy to find many present-day discussions of Augustine's Neoplatonism, especially as a consequence of the debate launched by Boyer and others; but it is hard to find an adequate discussion of Augustine's doctrine of creation. It is perhaps a commentary on the state of affairs in the handling of the church fathers that Whitney Oates could omit almost all the exegetical material from his edition of Augustine's treatise on the Trinity in *The Basic Writings of St. Augustine,* while he included the early Neoplatonic essays without omission.[81] More recently John Burnaby has done the same in "The Christian Classics." [82] Yet in the *De Trinitate* Augustine thought he was expounding a Biblical theology! Even if a historian concludes that this was not a Biblical theology,[83] the treatise deserves to be judged on the grounds which it itself cites. From the truncated editions now available one would have to conclude that the basic approach of the treatise is speculative rather than exegetical, even though Augustine explicitly founds his speculation on exegesis.[84]

Such instances of how an examination of exegesis can

[79] See *The City of God,* Book VIII, ch. 11, *NPNF-I,* II, 152, which compares the Biblical and the Platonic views of being. On Augustine's doctrine of being see Irenee Chevalier, *S. Augustin et la pensee grecque. Les relations trinitaires* (Fribourg, 1940), pp. 74—75.

[80] See William A. Christian, "The Creation of the World," in Battenhouse, pp. 316—342, for a brief but incisive interpretation.

[81] Whitney J. Oates (ed.), *Basic Writings of Saint Augustine,* II (New York, 1948), 667—878.

[82] John Burnaby (ed.), *Augustine: Later Works, LCC,* VIII, 38—181.

[83] Such is the conclusion drawn by Cyril C. Richardson, *The Doctrine of the Trinity* (Nashville, 1958).

[84] *On the Trinity,* Book I, ch. 2, *NPNF-I,* III, 19.

affect historical theology would be easy to multiply, but those which we have cited should demonstrate that the history of dogma and of systematic theology has neglected an important resource when it has overlooked Biblical exegesis. The studies in the history of Biblical interpretation that have already appeared are beginning to enrich — and to confuse — the history of theology. As they increase, we shall have a much more adequate conception of many issues in the history of theology. For example, it seems evident already that the continuity in that history will stand out even more than it has heretofore; for exegetes have almost always stood on the shoulders of their predecessors. This, in turn, will raise the problem of Scripture and tradition in a new way. Although the present volume is concerned with only one chapter in the history of Biblical interpretation, it attaches itself to this growing interest in that history as a whole. Our method and our very problem have been shaped by recent studies in the history of patristic exegesis as well as by the studies of Luther's exegesis that have made their appearance. This study of Luther's exegesis, on the other hand, may be useful to students of exegetical history whose primary area of interest lies in other periods than the Reformation. Its primary contribution, however, should be its illumination of the problems in Luther's theology itself.

CHAPTER TWO

Luther as a Biblical Theologian

As the study of the history of theology begins to pay new attention to the history of exegesis, it will revise and reconsider many of its earlier judgments. New affinities and new contrasts will become evident in the development of Christian thought, and many leading figures in that development will begin to assume different proportions. It is probable that among these figures few will receive more detailed attention than Martin Luther.

The study of Luther is bound to figure prominently in the history of exegesis, not only because he himself was so predominantly an exegete, as we shall see in the main body of this book, but also because the study of Luther and of his theology has always been a factor of decisive significance in Protestant theology. It has been simultaneously cause and effect in the development of Protestant thought since the Reformation. Thus, for example, John Dillenberger has been able to write the history of the idea of revelation in the Protestant thought of the past century from the standpoint of Luther's view of the *Deus absconditus.*[1] In the same vein Edgar Carlson has shown how the themes of Luther's thought have determined the course of Swedish theology, and how the course of Swedish theology has, in turn, determined the interpretation of the themes of Luther's thought.[2] Every age

[1] John Dillenberger, *God Hidden and Revealed* (Philadelphia, 1953).

[2] Edgar M. Carlson, *The Reinterpretation of Luther* (Philadelphia, 1948), p. 28: "It might be said that the history of theology in Sweden is a history of Luther research."

[32]

in the history of Protestant theology has had its own picture of Luther and of his thought.[3] The variety of these pictures, as described in a recent book by Heinrich Bornkamm, corresponds to the variety in the history of German Protestant theology itself.[4] From the Luther of high Lutheran orthodoxy (who had a special call from God)[5] to the Luther of nineteenth-century German idealism (who discovered the categorical imperative of Kant three centuries before Kant)[6] the figure of the Reformer has cast its shadow over Protestant theological discussion, especially in Germany, and it still does.

It is, therefore, true, as Ernst Zeeden says in his biased and yet perceptive *The Legacy of Luther,* that "in Germany, the changing picture of Luther through the decades and centuries has one constant factor, in that it is a reflex of religious ideas. The changes are indications of spiritual evolutions, and if it is indeed true that a nation's religious movements tell its innermost history, then light on the successive transformations undergone by Luther and the Reformation, in the minds of successive generations, is bound to show some portion of the road along which the German nation — or part of it — travelled."[7] The twentieth century has continued this interpretation and reinterpretation of Luther. To the gallery of earlier portraits our century has added Luther the Nazi, Luther the Kierkegaardian, and Luther the Barthian, while some American Protestants, in mistaken zeal, have tried to

[3] Horst Stephan, *Luther in den Wandlungen seiner Kirche* (2nd ed.; Berlin, 1951).

[4] Heinrich Bornkamm, *Luther im Spiegel der deutschen Geistesgeschichte* (Heidelberg, 1955).

[5] Johann Gerhard, *Loci Theologici,* Locus XXIII, ch. 8, ed. by Ed. Preuss, VI (Berlin, 1868), 83–90.

[6] Otto Wolff's *Die Haupttypen der neueren Lutherdeutung* (Stuttgart, 1938), is a careful delineation of modern pictures of Luther.

[7] Ernst Walter Zeeden, *The Legacy of Luther,* tr. by Ruth Mary Bethell (London, 1954), pp. xi–xii.

draw a picture of Luther the Jeffersonian.[8] If, as has been waggishly suggested, a theology can prove itself today only if it is "ecumenical, existential, and eschatological," then Luther's theology has certainly proved itself; for it is now being lauded for all three of those qualities.

Contemporary theological discussion is influencing the study of Luther's theology in at least two ways. In the first place, Luther's doctrine of the church has occupied a place of central importance in current theological thought and research.[9] This is because the doctrine of the church loomed so large in his own thought and because the doctrine of the church has assumed such overwhelming significance in the present theological scene; the interrelation between these two factors is itself deserving of study.[10] The second point at which the study of Luther reflects modern trends in theology is the subject of this book. For it is certainly no coincidence that scholars should be turning to a consideration of Luther's exegesis just at a time when, through the work of a generation of Biblical scholars, the problems of Biblical hermeneutics are once more receiving so much attention on all sides.[11] In the first volume of essays evoked by the programmatic essay of Rudolf Bultmann on myth and the New Testament there was a study of Luther's significance for this issue.[12] The

[8] Cf. Walther von Loewenich, *Lutherforschung in Deutschland*, in Vilmos Vajta (ed.), *Lutherforschung heute* (Berlin, 1958), pp. 150–171, with an extensive bibliography.

[9] See the excellent summary of this research in Gordon Rupp, *The Righteousness of God* (New York, 1953), pp. 310–343.

[10] It is indeed deserving of study to ask whether the current significance of the doctrine of the church is due to the recovery of the sense of the corporate characteristic of so much in contemporary thought and life.

[11] Wolfgang Schweitzer's *Schrift und Dogma in der Oekumene* (Gütersloh, 1953) is a provocative discussion of the hermeneutical problem from an ecumenical perspective.

[12] Friedrich Karl Schumann, *Gedanken Luthers zur Frage der Entmythologisierung*, in *Festschrift Rudolf Bultmann zum 65. Geburtstag überreicht* (Stuttgart, 1949), pp. 208–220.

relative authority of Scripture and of tradition was a subject which Luther debated fiercely against his Roman Catholic opponents; it is also a subject with which present-day theology is obliged to deal, partly because of current emphases in the study of both the Old Testament and the New Testament.[13] As chapter four makes evident, Luther's own stand on this question was much more ambiguous than it is usually said to have been. That chapter shows also that current attention to the question cannot simply repeat his polemical declarations regarding Scripture and tradition without taking note of how he actually handled both Scripture and tradition.

Most of this volume will be concerned with the interpretation of Luther the expositor, as recent trends in Luther research have shaped it. Examination of the bibliography in the notes of this volume will show how much of this research there has been since Karl Holl's decisive essay of November 11, 1920, on "Luther's Significance for the Progress of the Art of Interpretation."[14] In the four decades beginning with that lecture many individual aspects of Luther's work on the Bible have received the attention of scholars. The most impressive volume to emerge from this research is unquestionably Gerhard Ebeling's monograph on the exegesis of the Gospels.[15] The influence of Ebeling's work will be visible throughout this book. But there have also been studies of how Luther interpreted the figure of Samson,[16] of how his exposition of St. John differed from his exegesis

13 See pp. 71—88.

14 Karl Holl, *Luthers Bedeutung für den Fortschritt der Auslegungskunst,* in *Gesammelte Aufsätze zur Kirchengeschichte,* I, *Luther* (7th ed.; Tübingen, 1948), 544—582.

15 Gerhard Ebeling, *Evangelische Evangelienauslegung* (Munich, 1942).

16 Rudolf Hermann, *Die Gestalt Simsons bei Luther* (Berlin, 1952).

of the Synoptic Gospels,[17] of how he probed the meaning of
the sacrifice of Isaac,[18] and of other themes and issues in his
Biblical theology.[19] While this entire volume will be sum-
marizing much of this research and supplementing or cor-
recting it from independent study of Luther the expositor,
this chapter is intended to suggest what the new emphasis
upon Luther's exegesis may come to mean for the portrayal
of his theology as such.

During most of the centuries since the Reformation the
interpretation of Luther the man and of Luther the theologian
has been dominated by the polemical aspect of his career.
There are several possible reasons for the dominance of this
side of Luther in the literature. One reason is certainly the
fascination that a conflict of any sort holds for people, for
historians no less than for others. Everybody enjoys a fight,
even though he may condemn the fighters as vulgar rowdies.
Even today much of the history of nations and cultures is the
history of warfare. From Thucydides' *History of the Peloponnesian War* to Winston Churchill's *The Second World
War* the historiography of the West has been preoccupied
with the record of the conflicts in which men and nations
have achieved greatness or met their end. The emphasis of
recent historians upon "social history" as the record of the
more peaceful pursuits of man has frequently managed only
to replace the bloody chronicle of war with bloodless tales

[17] Walther von Loewenich, *Luther und das johanneische Christentum*
(Munich, 1935); Carl Stange, *Der johanneische Typus der Heilslehre
Luthers im Verhältnis zur paulinischen Rechtfertigungslehre* (Gütersloh,
1949); James Atkinson, *Luthers Einschätzung des Johannesevangeliums,* in
Vajta, op. cit., pp. 49—56.

[18] David Lerch, *Isaaks Opferung christlich gedeutet* (Tübingen, 1950),
pp. 156—202.

[19] A recent study is Eberhard Wölfel's analysis of Luther's *Commentary on Ecclesiastes* of 1526, *Luther und die Skepsis* (Munich, 1958). In
addition to its intrinsic value as a careful study of Luther's exegesis of
this one book, Wölfel's monograph contains an exhaustive bibliography
on Luther's exegesis.

about weaving, dairying, and children's games; these, in turn, serve to illustrate the boredom that drove men to war! Victory and defeat in warfare bring out the best and the worst in men. Hence the themes of victory and defeat are always exciting to both participant and spectator, even when the spectator watches from a vantage point several centuries away.

This is no less true of victories and defeats in theology. The very organization of chapters in the textbooks of historical theology gives evidence of this same excitement. And when the combatant was a theologian who combined the finesse of Gene Tunney with the violence of Jack Dempsey, as Luther uniquely did, the fight is so interesting that no one cares very much about how the fighter used to spend his more placid and reflective moments. Luther's severest critics are obliged to concede that his polemical writings are masterpieces of German and Latin prose — not because he was always fair or even accurate in his treatment of his opponents, for he was not, but because he responded to attack with such vehemence that there is rarely a dull moment in these treatises. One is sometimes disappointed, often irritated, but seldom bored by Luther's controversial writings. They are probably the most interesting books Luther ever wrote.

They may also be the most important. Even in a volume like this one, which is dedicated to a study of Luther's exegesis, it must be kept in mind that Luther's historic achievement was the Reformation. For that reason, too, we shall devote the second half of this book to the exegetical bases of the eucharistic controversy; for only in this way can we take the measure of Luther's work as an expositor of the Scriptures. There have been innumerable expositors of the Scriptures both before and since Luther, but it was Luther who brought on the Reformation and who changed the map of Christendom. And while his exegetical writings are not without significance for the interpretation also of his reformatory work, as this volume will seek to demonstrate, the fact remains that not his works on the Bible but his works against Eck and Emser, Carlstadt and Zwingli were the ones in which the program of his reformatory work was most clearly and most fully articulated. Much of Luther's exegesis was undistinguished, and even more of it was a product of the exegetical tradition that preceded him. If his reputation and influence depended solely upon his exegesis, he might be nothing more than one in a series of exegetical masters — more of a virtuoso than most, to be sure, but not the Reformer of the Christian Church.

Yet it was as the Reformer of the Christian Church and, therefore, as the founder of Protestantism that Martin Luther made history. It is, moreover, as the founder of Protestantism that he has had to be defended against his accusers and detractors. The confessional polemics of the sixteenth, seventeenth, and eighteenth centuries consisted very largely of attacks upon, and apologies for, Luther the Reformer. In an interesting and illuminating study of Roman Catholic polemical literature Adolf Herte has shown that the character assassination perpetrated by Johann Cochlaeus' biography of Luther continued to pass from one Roman Catholic writer to another for centuries after the Reformation, making an objective assessment of Luther and his work almost impossible.[20] On the Lutheran side objectivity was also difficult, for the discussion of Luther's personal virtues and vices was more often a confessional issue than a biographical one. Lutheranism was defending itself, but in so doing it was defending Luther.

---

[20] Adolf Herte, *Das katholische Lutherbild im Bann der Lutherkommentare des Cochläus* (3 vols.; Münster, 1943).

Such a congruence between the biographical issue and the confessional issue was due in part to the circumstance that Lutheranism was — or at least thought it was — faced with the same set of opponents against whom Luther had contended. The Roman Catholicism with which it had to deal was post-Tridentine both chronologically and theologically, and the Reformed thought it confronted was Calvinistic rather than Zwinglian. Both of these transformations should probably have brought about a revision of Luther's judgments; in any case there is considerable ground for such a contention.[21] But most confessional theologians continued to interpret Trent in the light of Luther's Roman Catholic antagonists and to read both Calvin and Beza as Zwinglians. Engaged as it was in this confessional polemic during the centuries following the Reformation, Lutheranism tended to develop a stereotype of Luther as well as of his opponents. Luther at Worms was its answer to Rome; Luther at Marburg, its answer to Geneva. And against both Rome and Geneva Lutheranism continued to hurl many of the charges Luther had voiced at Worms and Marburg.[22] Since the attacks upon Lutheranism from both Rome and Geneva were often aimed against Luther's character and career, it was to the polemical accents of his career that his defenders continued to turn. Thus Luther acquired the title of "Reformer." Less often did his defenders point out that he deserved the title of "doctor of the church" as well. To justify his right to the latter title, one would have to turn primarily to his expository writings.

During the past century the interpretation of Luther and of his theology has succeeded in disengaging itself from

[21] Cf. Hans Grass, *Die Abendmahlslehre bei Luther und Calvin* (2nd ed.; Gütersloh, 1954), pp. 193—212.

[22] Jaroslav Pelikan, *From Luther to Kierkegaard* (Saint Louis, 1950), pp. 24—48, on "Melanchthon and the Confessional Generation."

the older type of confessional polemics.[23] This was partly because so many of the theologians and historians who took the lead in Reformation scholarship were the theological descendants of Albrecht Ritschl. Recent study of Luther has devoted much — probably too much — of its attention to the figure of the young Luther.[24] The scholarship of confessional polemics was principally concerned with the Luther of the 1520's, from Worms in 1521 until Marburg in 1529; and it interpreted Augsburg in 1530 as the summary of what was truly permanent in Luther's reformatory thought and work. But the scholarship of the so-called "Luther-renaissance" has concentrated upon the Luther of the decade closing at Leipzig in 1519. It has carefully examined the course of Luther's development in that decade, which opened with Luther safely within the Augustinian Order and closed with him on the brink of excommunication and the ban of the empire. Scholars have sought to assess the internal and external influences upon that development, debating the validity of terming Luther an Occamist, the role of sexual conflict in Luther's struggles with guilt, and similar questions.[25] Of particular interest has been the doctrine of justification, as developed in Luther's early lectures on Romans.[26]

[23] "It should be recognized that the 'Luther Renaissance' and the 'Calvin Renaissance' are the direct result of the peoccupation of historically minded liberal theologians with the Reformation." Wilhelm Pauck, *The Heritage of the Reformation* (Boston, 1950), p. 277.

[24] Cf. Gerhard Belgum (ed.), *The Mature Luther* (Decorah, 1959), in which Theodore Tappert, Willem Kooiman, and Lowell Green attempt to redress this overemphasis on the young Luther.

[25] The two outstanding summaries of this scholarship are Heinrich Boehmer, *Road to Reformation,* tr. by John W. Doberstein and Theodore G. Tappert (Philadelphia, 1946); and Otto Scheel, *Martin Luther. Vom Katholizismus zur Reformation* (2 vols.; Tübingen, 1917, and later editions), which has, unfortunately, never been translated.

[26] Uuras Saarnivaara, in *Luther Discovers the Gospel* (Saint Louis, 1951), summarizes the previous discussion of Luther's doctrine of justification and adds his own interpretation.

Just when did Luther come to the truly "Lutheran" view of justification and of righteousness? And for that matter, what was this truly Lutheran view? [27] In these and related problems much of the research into the theological development of the young Luther has centered, with results that have permanently changed the interpretation not only of Luther but of the entire Reformation.

Neither the study of Luther's polemics nor the study of his early development could ignore his exegetical work. After all, what he was defending against the theologians of Rome was a particular interpretation of the Scriptures, together with his right to maintain such an interpretation. And the conflict with Zwingli did involve somewhere near its core the question of how the church was to understand the meaning of the words of Scripture. Luther's polemical works, therefore, were inextricably bound up with his conception of what the Bible meant. Similarly, the sources for the study of his early development were almost exclusively his Biblical commentaries. It was, in fact, the discovery of several of these that helped to set off the new interest in that development.[28] No one could study the young Luther, therefore, without exposing himself to Luther's expository activity.

But the curious fact is that both methods of Luther-study could practically ignore Luther the expositor even while studying Luther's expositions. In rehearsing Luther's stand at Marburg in opposition to Reformed theology, Lutheranism only rarely sought to show the implications of Luther's stand for the whole of the exegetical task. Even if one does not agree with Franz Hildebrandt that *Est* is "*the* Lutheran

[27] This was the question over which Karl Holl and Wilhelm Walther clashed a generation ago; cf. Rudolf Hermann, *Zu Luthers Lehre von Sünde und Rechtfertigung* (Tübingen, 1952), for a clear and profound discussion.

[28] Cf. Johannes Ficker's detailed account of these discoveries in the Introduction to W, LVI.

principle," [29] it is clear that Luther's interpretation of the words of institution represented a hermeneutical stance with the most far-reaching consequences; more of this in Part Two. Similarly, it should not be a matter of indifference to interpreters of Luther's thought that the documentation for his early development comes almost completely from his Biblical lectures. At the risk of sounding naive, one could ask whether some of the interpreters of Luther's early development adequately considered the possibility that he derived some of his ideas from the Scriptures rather than from Augustine, Occam, Lyra, Hugo Cardinal, or his own virtuosity. At least that was what he claimed, and the claim would seem to deserve some consideration in an assessment of the several elements converging to produce Luther's theology. In both cases more attention to the exegetical aspect would have revised or modified the interpretation of Luther's theology.

Accompanying both these interpretations, with monotonous regularity, has been the gratuitous explanation, "But, of course, Luther was not a systematic theologian." [30] This explanation proceeded on the assumption that the speaker knew exactly what a systematic theologian was, and that by this definition Luther simply would not qualify. While further attention to Luther's exegesis would bring him no nearer to qualifying under the terms sometimes dictated by this definition, it might lay serious and necessary strictures upon the adequacy of the definition itself. As one systematic theologian has put it, "There is, to be sure, a sense of the term *systematic thinker* before which Luther would not qualify — which in fact he would not understand. If, that is, the connotation of system which is proper to propositional logic is

[29] Franz Hildebrandt, *EST. Das Lutherische Prinzip* (Göttingen, 1931), an unusual mixture of historical and speculative elements.

[30] See Karl Holl, op. cit., p. 117, note 2.

made absolute, then Luther was not systematic. But we must decidedly reject any such presumption. There is a system proper to the dissection of the dead; and there is a system proper to the experience and description of the living. There is a system proper to the inorganic; and there is a system proper to an organism. A crystal has a system. But so does a living personality in the grip of a central certainty. If, then, by system one means that there is in a man's thought a central authority, a pervasive style, a way of bringing every theme and judgment and problem under the rays of the central illumination, then it must be said that history shows few men of comparable integration." [31] A consideration of Luther's exegesis would thus restore to Luther's theology a balance and comprehensiveness that it does not appear to possess if one concentrates exclusively upon either the polemical Luther or the young Luther.

Although Luther's polemical writings appear to disqualify him as a systematic theologian, his exegesis frequently corrected the overemphases caused by his polemics. Perhaps the best example is the eucharistic controversy, analyzed in some detail by later chapters of this book. If one contrasts Luther's doctrine of the Lord's Supper with those of both the New Testament and the church fathers, the most striking difference is that between the richness of sacramental motifs in the Biblical and patristic literature and the singleness of emphasis in Luther's polemics against Oecolampadius, Carlstadt, and Zwingli. [32] Because these men had attacked his doctrine of the real presence and, in so doing, had assigned to other motifs much of the power that, according to Luther,

[31] Joseph Sittler, *The Doctrine of the Word in the Structure of Lutheran Theology* (Philadelphia, 1948), pp. 3—4.

[32] Yngve Brilioth's *Eucharistic Faith and Practice, Evangelical and Catholic* (New York, 1934) is in part an examination of this singleness of emphasis.

should have been assigned to the real presence,[33] it was to the defense of the real presence that Luther addressed himself. All the other themes and ideas of the Lord's Supper almost seemed to be attached as mere corollaries to the doctrine of the real presence. Entirely apart from the important question whether Luther's approach was Biblically justifiable, it should be pointed out that when he came to deal with the texts involved exegetically and not only polemically, he often assigned much more prominence to other motifs and themes in the doctrine of the Lord's Supper. Therefore the view of the Sacrament contained in his exegetical and homiletical discussions, like that of the texts with which he was working, spanned an entire complex of emphases — some of which are recounted at length in Part Two of this book — and not merely the narrower range of emphases which he defended against his opponents.

In other words, an interpretation of Luther's doctrine of the Lord's Supper dare not be based exclusively on his polemical statements against Carlstadt, Zwingli, and others, as many interpretations, both sympathetic and critical, have been.[34] Such interpretations single out certain aspects of Christian eucharistic theology and minimize others, thus giving the impression that Luther was, of course, no systematic theologian but a theological journalist who improvised his thought and language as the polemical situation seemed to require. On the other hand, if the interpretation of Luther's teaching on the Lord's Supper made use also of his exegetical and homiletical works, it would begin by setting forth the complex of sacramental themes and motifs which Luther the exegete tried to hold together; and it would seek to identify the ways in which he co-ordinated these several themes and motifs. Then it would examine

[33] Cf. pp. 192—194.
[34] Cf. pp. 205 ff.

the controversy with Zwingli, Carlstadt, and Oecolampadius, to determine which of these motifs were under threat in that controversy and why Luther reacted to the threat as he did in his polemical writings. In addition, as chapter seven will indicate, the interpretation of Luther's eucharistic doctrine must also examine the exegetical and hermeneutical issues at stake in the conflict.

The Luther to emerge from such an interpretation would still not be a systematic theologian after the fashion of those for whom systematic theology is "the only truly exact science." But he would emerge as less chaotic a thinker than he has often been portrayed. Clearer than ever before would be the central base of operations from which he worked both as a commentator and as a controversialist. Not merely the left flank or the right flank, but the main column of his thought would thus come into view. This was not a random mob of ideas, united only by the fact that, in some mysterious fashion, one man could believe all these things at the same time. Yet these were not tin soldiers either, who stayed in line because they were tin and had no life. These were living ideas, deployed in as orderly a fashion as their military purpose required, held together by the discipline of a common source and a common Master. If this was not systematic theology, we may well need another and a better term.

It would seem, therefore, that before any summary presentation of Luther's theology becomes possible, it will be necessary to make it clearer than Luther scholars have made it in the past that, systematic theologian or not, Luther was a Biblical theologian. In a familiar bon mot of Heinrich Bornkamm, if Luther belonged to a modern theological faculty, he would not be a professor of systematic theology or dogmatics; to judge from his actual work in the lecture hall, he would not even be a professor of New Testament exegesis, but of Old Testament exegesis.[35] Thus the most ironic feature of the reinterpretation of Luther's thought on the basis of his exegetical work is that this rediscovery of Luther as a Biblical theologian will bring Luther scholarship back into line with Luther! For it was as a Biblical theologian that Luther understood himself and wanted others, both his friends and his enemies, to understand him.

"Biblical theologian" would, in fact, be a pretty good translation of the title *Doctor in Biblia,* which Luther acquired at the urging of Johann Staupitz in 1512.[36] The title "doctor" summarizes more adequately than does any other Luther's own sense of vocation and mission. To the question, "Why do you publicly attack the pope and others, instead of keeping the peace?" Luther replied: "I have the commission and charge, as a preacher and a doctor, to see to it that no one is misled." [37] And it was more as a doctor than as a preacher that he felt called to do this; for elsewhere he argued that a preacher had no right to thrust himself upon a parish where he had not been called to preach, even if that parish were served by "a papistic or heretical pastor." [38] But a doctor of theology had a different and more universal vocation. If someone were to ask Luther, "Why do you, by your books, teach throughout the world, when you are only preacher in Wittenberg?" he would answer: "I have never wanted to do it and do not want to do it now. I was forced and driven into this position in the first place when I had to become Doctor of Holy Scripture against my will.

[35] Heinrich Bornkamm, *Luther und Das Alte Testament* (Tübingen, 1948), p. 6.

[36] Cf. Hermann Steinlein, *Luthers Doktorat* (Leipzig, 1912), for a study of what Luther's doctorate meant to him.

[37] *The Sermon on the Mount* (1530), W, XXXII, 334; *Luther's Works,* 21, 44.

[38] *Commentary on Psalm 82* (1530), W, XXI-I, 211; *Luther's Works,* 13, 65.

Then, as a doctor in a general free university, I began, at the command of pope and emperor, to do what such a doctor is sworn to do, expounding the Scriptures for all the world and teaching everybody. Once in this position, I have had to stay in it, and I cannot give it up or leave it yet with a good conscience." [39]

From statements like this it is clear that for Luther himself the polemical assignment of the theologian had to be subordinated to his exegetical assignment. Even in carrying out the former, Luther strove to keep the discussion on an exegetical plane. Although he was often no more successful in this than his opponents were, it does seem an injustice to both him and his opponents if historians and biographers ignore the exegetical bent of their writings. In chapter six we shall return to this theme, but in the present context it is important to see the title "Biblical theologian" as an integral part of Luther's sense of calling. It was as a Biblical theologian that he took up polemics. In fact, it was as a Biblical theologian that he became the Reformer. And it is as a Biblical theologian that he deserves to be interpreted.

[39] Ibid., W, XXXI-I, 212; *Luther's Works*, 13, 66.

CHAPTER THREE

The Bible and the Word of God

THE theology of Martin Luther was a theology of the
Word of God.[1] "The Word they still shall let remain,
Nor any thanks have for it; He's by our side upon the plain
With His good gifts and Spirit"[2] — this is not only the con-
cluding stanza of Luther's hymn, "A Mighty Fortress Is Our
God"; it is the theme and the motto of his whole life and
thought. He lived *by* the Word of God; he lived *for* the
Word of God. It is no mistake, then, when interpreters of
Luther take his doctrine of the Word of God as one of the
most important single keys to his theology.[3] "My conscience
is captive in the Word of God," he is reported to have said
in 1521 at the Diet of Worms.[4] And whether he really said
it or not, the important thing is that he believed his conscience captive to the Word of God at Worms in 1521 and
throughout the quarter-century that followed until his death
in 1546.

But the theology of Martin Luther was also a theology
of the Holy Scriptures. His rediscovery of the Gospel came
to him not by private revelation — this he would have spurned
as a manifestation of the devil[5] — but by the study of the
Bible. His works on the Scriptures occupy more than half

[1] The most satisfactory treatment of this subject is the monograph
by Heinrich Bornkamm, *Das Wort Gottes bei Luther* (Munich, 1933).

[2] W, XXXV, 457.

[3] Philip S. Watson, *Let God Be God!* (Philadelphia, 1949), pp. 149
to 189.

[4] Cf. *Luther at the Diet of Worms, Luther's Works*, 32, 112.

[5] See p. 103, note 76.

of this American edition of *Luther's Works,* and what we are
including here is by no means all of Luther's works on the
Scriptures.[6] He translated the entire Bible into German;
then he revised and polished that translation throughout
his life.[7] He was so saturated with the language and thought
of the Bible that he often quoted it without even being
conscious of it.[8] In 1512 he received the degree of *Doctor
in Biblia.* And as the preceding chapter sought to show, this
degree, even more than his ordination to the priesthood, was
his authorization for carrying out his reformatory work.[9]

The centrality of the Scriptures in Luther's thought and
the primacy of the Word of God in Luther's thought came
together in his exegesis. For the doctrine of the Word of
God was one of the components of Luther's work as an
expositor. This chapter and the three chapters that follow
it will attempt to isolate four such components: the Word
of God, the tradition, the church, and the role of polemics.
For Luther the expositor, of course, these four components
were continually being blended. Thus it was in response
to a polemical challenge that Luther, as a man of the church,
took the Word of God in the Scriptures to mean what the
tradition of the church had been saying. Again, it was in
the name of the Word of God that Luther defied the tradition
and sought to rescue the church from the tradition. Nevertheless, these constituent elements of Luther's work as an
expositor, while never separated in the actual practice of
his exegesis, need to be distinguished in a systematic inter-

---

[6] We have, for example, included only part of Luther's *Works on the
Psalms, Luther's Works,* 14, 281–349.

[7] M. Reu's *Luther's German Bible* (Columbus, 1934) is still an emi-
nently useful guide.

[8] Karl August Meissinger, *Der katholische Luther* (Munich, 1952),
pp. 82–84. As Meissinger points out, p. 78, there can be no complete study
of Luther the expositor until there is an index to the Biblical passages in
the Weimar edition.

[9] See pp. 46–47.

pretation of that exegesis. And among them the Word of God certainly deserves first place. Research into Luther's exegesis depends upon clarification of what he meant by the "Word of God." For sometimes he meant the Bible by this term; at other times, he, like the Bible itself, meant something other than the Bible. This discussion will analyze the several meanings which Luther the expositor of the Bible found in the Biblical phrase "Word of God."

The "Word of God" was the speech of God, and "the God who speaks" would be an appropriate way to summarize Luther's picture of God.[10] It was characteristic of the God of the Bible that He not only created by His power and redeemed by His love, but that both His creating power and His redeeming love proceeded from Him through His speaking. Luther frequently warned against a picture of God that would paint Him in remote and self-contained isolation.[11] It was in the very nature of God to want to speak and to be able to speak, and therefore by definition God was never speech-less. The Speech of God was as eternal as God Himself, and was God Himself. The God of Christian faith was one who had a voice, an eternal Speech. This voice and eternal Speech of God was the cosmic sense of the term "Word of God."

This was the "cosmic" sense of the term because the Scriptures use it to speak of the creation of the cosmos,

[10] H. Ostergaard-Nielsen's *Scriptura sacra et viva vox* (Munich, 1957) summarizes and interprets the appropriate passages.

[11] "The people of Israel did not have a God who was viewed 'absolutely,' to use the expression, the way the inexperienced monks rise into heaven and think about God as He is in Himself. From this absolute God everyone should flee who does not want to perish, because human nature and the absolute God . . . are the bitterest of enemies. . . . Let no one, therefore, interpret David as speaking with the absolute God. He is speaking with God as He is dressed and clothed in His Word and promises, so that from the name 'God' we cannot exclude Christ, whom God promised to Adam and the other patriarchs." *Commentary on Psalm 51* (1532), W, XL-II, 329; *Luther's Works*, 12, 312.

ascribing its origins and its continuance to the speaking of God. If anything may be said to be the central emphasis of Luther's lengthy comments on the first two chapters of Genesis, it is this fundamental importance of the Word of God in the creation.[12] According to Luther, when the Scriptures asserted that the creation was derived from the Word of God, they were saying something about the cosmos; but they were also saying something about God. By employing His speech or Word to create the world, God had made His Word the essential and constitutive element in all His dealings with the world. Luther contended that whatever God might be in and of Himself apart from the created world, in the creation He had put relations between Himself and the world upon the foundation of the Word of God.[13]

But the Word of God was so central in Luther's thought that even God in and of Himself, apart from the created world, was a God of the Word for Luther. Luther preached on the first chapter of John about two years after lecturing on the first chapter of Genesis. In both texts he found the teaching that the Word of God in creation preceded creation. The sermons on St. John, perhaps because they were addressed to the common people of Wittenberg, gave an espe-

[12] "This, therefore, is sufficient for the confirmation of our faith: that Christ is true God, who is with the Father from eternity, before the world was made, and that through Him, who is the wisdom and the Word of the Father, the Father made everything. But in the passage referred to (2 Cor. 4:6) this point should also be noted: that Paul regards the conversion of the wicked — something which is also brought about by the Word — as a new work of creation." *Lectures on Genesis* (1535—45), W, XLII, 14; *Luther's Works*, 1, 17.

[13] "Everything was created and is preserved through the Word. Moses employs such language in order to give prominence to the greatness of the Person who with one word destroys and establishes all things. What appears to be more meaningless than a word? And yet when God speaks a word, the thing expressed by the word immediately leaps into existence." *Commentary on Psalm 90* (1534—35), W, XL-III, 522; *Luther's Works*, 13, 99.

cially striking interpretation of this teaching.[14] God, said Luther, was like a man who walks along the street holding a conversation with himself. A man may be mumbling and discussing, but one cannot hear or understand what he is saying. All of a sudden he stops and shouts, and everyone is startled to hear him speak. What he shouts is what he has been saying to himself all along, but now he says it for others to hear too. "God, too, in His majesty and nature, is pregnant with a Word or a conversation in which He engages with Himself in His divine essence and which reflects the thoughts of His heart. This is as complete and excellent and perfect as God Himself. No one but God alone sees, hears, or comprehends this conversation. . . . God is so absorbed in this Word, thought, or conversation that He pays no attention to anything else."[15] But it was only when He spoke His Word out loud that men could hear what He had been saying since the creation of the world and even before the creation of the world. When God spoke His Word in Christ, therefore, it became possible to hear His Word in the creation and to know that the Word of God now vocal in Christ had always been with God.

Because Luther's theology was a theology of the Word of God, it is also a Trinitarian theology: the "Word of God" in the cosmic sense was the Second Person of the Trinity.[16] There is in Luther's writings very little speculation about the inner life of the Holy Trinity, which had been a favorite subject among theologians.[17] He had surprisingly little to

[14] "We must realize that this Word of God is entirely different from my word or yours." *Sermons on the Gospel of St. John: Chapters 1–4* (1537–39), W, XLVI, 543; *Luther's Works*, 22, 8.

[15] Ibid., W, XLVI, 544–545; *Luther's Works*, 22, 9–10.

[16] Regin Prenter, *Spiritus Creator*, tr. by John M. Jensen (Philadelphia, 1953), pp. 173–184.

[17] See, for example, his rather coy remarks in the *Lectures on Genesis* (1535–45), W, XLII, 37–38; *Luther's Works*, 1, 50.

say even about Christ as the Second Person of the Trinity apart from Jesus Christ in the flesh. Yet when the Biblical text seemed to require it, as in the prolog to St. John, Luther did discuss the Trinity and the pre-existent Christ. But because the central emphasis of these discussions was the Word of God, Luther used them to delineate the congruence between God as He is and God as He speaks. From the Word of God in Jesus Christ one could know the Word of God as the Second Person of the Trinity, but not vice versa.[18] Luther's doctrine of the Trinity was centered in Christ, but his doctrine of Christ was centered in the Word of God spoken through Christ by the Father. On this ground he maintained that the Word of God, the Logos, was indeed eternal, both before creation and before redemption.

For the ears of faith, however, the Word spoken in redemption made audible the Word spoken in creation; and the Word spoken in both made audible the eternal Word of God as the Second Person of the eternal Trinity. One of the primary functions served by Luther's doctrine of Christ as the Logos-Word of God was to prevent either an identification or a separation of the creating Word and the redeeming Word.[19] The Word of God in creation could not be simply identified with the Word of God in redemption, because the redeeming Word was the historical figure of Jesus Christ of Nazareth. But they could not be separated either, as though creation were beneath the dignity of the God who redeemed men through the Word that was in Christ; for the cosmic Word of God had become flesh in Jesus of Nazareth.

[18] Therefore Prenter can say, p. 179: "All piety which is not *theologia crucis* is an attack on the trinitarian faith in God."

[19] Johann Haar's *Initium creaturae Dei* (Gütersloh, 1939) is a helpful examination of the relation between creation and redemption in Luther through his idea of the new creation.

Thus it is clear that the idea of the cosmic "Word of God" was not as prominent in Luther's theology as it had been in the theology of the early Greek fathers.[20] It was rather the "Word of God" in the historical sense that predominated in Luther, for his theology was one in which history came into its own.[21] This means that the basic category for Luther's doctrine of the Word of God was not the category of "being" but the category of "deed."

For Luther, then, the "Word of God" in the historical sense was a deed of God.[22] Compelled as he was by his work as an expositor of the Old Testament to dig into the root meanings of Hebrew vocables, Luther saw that one of the Hebrew terms for "word," the term דָּבָר, meant not only the spoken word but also that to which the spoken word referred. He also recognized that this Hebrew way of speaking had influenced the language of the New Testament.[23] For the understanding of Luther's doctrine of the Word of God this means that he interpreted the Word as the concrete action of God. The concrete things of the created world were all words of God, because each of them owed its existence to God's creating deed. The concrete events of human history were all words of God, because, in the mystery of divine providence, each of them was a deed of God.

To qualify as a "Word of God" in the historical sense, however, a concrete thing of the created world or a concrete event of human history had to be special. Not all concrete things and concrete events were the "Word of God" in this special sense. Not that God had not created them or was not at work in them; as Luther often stressed, "the earth

[20] On the similarities and differences cf. Walther von Loewenich, *Luther und das johanneische Christentum* (Munich, 1935), p. 36—38.

[21] Cf. H. Zahrndt, *Luther deutet Geschichte* (Munich, 1952).

[22] See p. 58, note 39.

[23] *Lectures on Genesis* (1535—45), W, XLII, 13; *Luther's Works*, 1, 16.

is the Lord's and the fullness thereof." [24] But there were certain specific things and certain particular events to which the title "Word of God" in the strict sense applied. How did they earn this title? Luther frequently pointed out that they did not earn it at all but had it simply because God had chosen to attach it to them. There was nothing about the people of Israel that prompted God to make them His people and to speak His Word to them and through them. He had done so simply because such was His free and sovereign will.[25] Sometimes, as in his discussion of the Jews, Luther emphasized the arbitrary character of this divine choice.[26] At other times, as in his discussion of Jesus, he could find a basis for the choice in the character of the one chosen.[27] But even when he discussed Jesus, Luther emphasized that Jesus was the chosen Christ of God, with the emphasis on the divine act of choosing.

When God chose these special deeds to be the Word of God, He had, according to Luther, a twofold purpose, namely, redemption and revelation.[28] A Word of God was a deed through which God chose to act redemptively. The God who chose special deeds as His Word did indeed act redemptively apart from those deeds too. In some places Luther went so far as to say that God had built the redemption into the very structure of the universe, so that trees and birds spoke of forgiveness.[29] But a deed was the Word of

[24] Hanns Lilje, *Luthers Geschichtsanschauung* (Berlin, 1932).

[25] See pp. 99 ff.

[26] See pp. 93—95.

[27] Christ "was to assume the form of an accursed and damned man, yes, of a serpent, and become the Savior of the world. The world seeks to be saved by good works, but it pleased God to help mankind in this way. The world would regard His Son as a vile worm, but He would nevertheless save all who believed in Him." *Sermons on the Gospel of St. John: Chapters 1—4* (1537—39), W, XLVII, 70; *Luther's Works*, 22, 343.

[28] John Dillenberger, *God Hidden and Revealed* (Philadelphia, 1953).

[29] See p. 163, note 22.

God if through it God conferred the forgiveness of sins. Did the deed cause God to confer forgiveness? To this question Luther, like the Scriptures, replied both ways. On the one hand, the redemptive purpose of God had selected certain events as the channels of redemption.[30] On the other hand, these events called forth from God the response of redemption.[31] The grace of God caused Christ to come, and Christ caused the grace of God to come. Neither of these statements without the other would correctly represent Luther's teaching. For he saw that in the deeds of redemption the purpose of God and the nature of the deed were finally one; that is what made such deeds the Word of God.

The "Word of God" was a deed, but it still remained a word. Therefore its redemptive purpose was also to reveal God as Lord and Savior. Because man was finite, he could not grasp God; because man was sinful, he could not face God.[32] Therefore God remained the hidden God, and no amount of investigation from man's side would extort His secret from Him. It was necessary for Him to give up that secret Himself. But because a man could not look upon the Almighty and live, God gave this secret in the mask of a Word of God. When Moses asked to see the face of God in Ex. 33, God forbade it; but He did permit Moses to see His back after He had passed by. So, said Luther in his comments on this story, man could not look at the glory of God; but God did permit man to see His deeds after He

---

[30] *Sermons on the Gospel of St. John: Chapters 1—4* (1537–39), W, XLVII, 65; *Luther's Works*, 22, 339.

[31] In the sermon, after the words referred to in the preceding note, Luther said: "Looking at the serpent and looking at the Lord Christ are not one and the same thing. For we find it stated here that we are not merely to look at Christ the Son of God, but to believe in Him"; for Christ was more than a sign of the redemptive purpose of God. Ibid., W, XLVII, 74; *Luther's Works*, 22, 348.

[32] Jaroslav Pelikan, *Fools for Christ* (Philadelphia, 1955), pp. 111—112.

had passed by.[33] These special deeds of divine revelation and redemption were the Word of God.

Since the Word of God was a special redemptive deed of God, Luther found the Word of God in the Old Testament.[34] For, as he never tired of pointing out in his commentaries on the Old Testament, the God of the Old Testament, the God of the covenant, was the Redeemer-God of the New Testament.[35] Of course, Luther accepted the Old Testament as Christian Scripture because it was part of the tradition which he had inherited; but his attention to the Word of God caused him to repossess and to reinterpret that tradition. His repudiation of the legalism which he saw in previous interpretations of the Old Testament — as though the Old Testament were only Law, still binding upon Christians, and the New Testament were only Gospel — enabled him to discern the redemptive theme in Old Testament history. Because he did not identify the Old Testament with the Law, he was able to find the Word of God as Gospel in the Old Testament.

The Word of God in the Old Testament were the redemptive deeds of God recorded there. Some were deeds of redemption addressed to particular individuals. With an unforgettable vividness Luther described how the Word of God came to Abraham, how he struggled with his doubts and fears, and how he was comforted, not by discovering

[33] "The man who deserves to be called a theologian is not the one who seeks to understand the invisible things of God through the things that are made (Rom. 1:22) but the one who understands that the visible things and the hind parts of God are seen through suffering and the cross." *Heidelberg Theses* (1518), W, I, 361—363; cf. *Luther's Works*, 22, 157.

[34] Heinrich Bornkamm, *Luther und das Alte Testament* (Tübingen, 1948), pp. 69—184.

[35] "The appellation 'the God of Israel' signifies that our God is none other than the one whom the Israelites once had. It is Christ, whom the Israelites once possessed and of whom we now also say: He who does these things is no longer only Israel's God but the God of the whole world." *Commentary on Psalm 68* (1521), W, VIII, 35; *Luther's Works*, 13, 37.

his hidden resources from within but "continually clinging to the promise or Word of God." [36] Thus Abraham became the father of believers, because to be a believer meant to rely on the redemption of which the Word of God testified.[37] As an expositor of the Old Testament, Luther had frequent occasion to describe the workings of the Word of God in the lives of Old Testament saints. David was the prototype of those to whom the Word of God came as judgment in order to come as redemption.[38] The prophets "learned from Moses to speak correctly of the acts of God. For they saw that in the case of God to speak is to do, and that the word [of God] is the deed." [39]

Yet the redemptive deeds of God in the Old Testament were addressed, not to individuals primarily but to the people of God.[40] Specifically, the focal point of the Word of God as redemptive deed in the Old Testament was the Exodus of Israel.[41] To it all the preceding narratives pointed; from it all the subsequent narratives and declarations of the Word of God derived their meaning. As Luther commented in his exposition of Hab. 3:2, the prophets "exalt this history of the Exodus from Egypt as the high point of all the other histories, making frequent mention of it, developing it in detail, and arranging other histories on the basis of it. The prophet Habakkuk is doing that very thing here. Because he is asking for redemption, he first calls attention to this wonderful deed of God, weaving it as a sort of canvas on which he portrays the many various deeds and wonders of

[36] *Lectures on Genesis* (1535–45), W, XLIII, 103.

[37] *Lectures on Romans* (1515–16), W, LVI, 45–46.

[38] That is the theme of the *Commentary on Psalm 51* (1532), W, XL-II, 315–470; *Luther's Works*, 12, 303–410.

[39] *Commentary on Psalm 2* (1532), W, XL-II, 231; *Luther's Works*, 12, 33.

[40] See chapter five.

[41] Cf. *Sermons on Exodus* (1524–27), W, XVI, 188.

God." [42] The Exodus was the Word of God in the Old Testament according to the strictest sense of the term "Word of God"; for in the Exodus God acted redemptively, and through the Exodus God spoke that Word of revelation which made all His other deeds meaningful.

Even the Exodus, however, was not the ultimate Word of God, just as it was not the ultimate redemption. Luther found support for this in the Pentateuch itself, in the words of Moses in Deut. 18:15: "The Lord your God will raise up for you a Prophet like me from among you, from your brethren — Him you shall heed." Following the lead of the Book of Acts, Luther applied this passage to Christ, using it to show that the God who had spoken His redemptive Word through Moses and the Exodus had yet another Word to speak. [43] Therefore the Word of God in the Old Testament was not only the Exodus as such but the anticipation by the Exodus of God's ultimate redemptive deed in Jesus Christ. For this reason Luther so often equated the Old Testament term "Word of God" with "promise" [44]; for when God spoke His redemptive Word to Israel, the redemption which this Word wrought and brought was the redemption ultimately accomplished in Christ. By this profound insight Luther was able to go beyond the "Messianic prophecies" of the Old Testament to a recognition of the Word of God in the Old Testament even in those passages where the Messiah was not mentioned. It must be added, of course, that Luther found the Messiah mentioned in many passages where very few modern students of the Old Testament would find Him. [45] In any case, it was as an expositor of the Old Testament that

[42] *Lectures on the Minor Prophets* (1524—26), W, XIII, 440.

[43] "This is the chief passage of this whole book and clearly an express prophecy of Christ, the new Teacher. Hence the apostles also vigorously allude to this passage." *Notes on Deuteronomy* (1525), W, XIV, 675.

[44] See p. 58, note 36, for one example.

[45] Heinrich Bornkamm, *Luther und das Alte Testament*, pp. 86—103.

Luther came to understand the Scriptural meaning of the Scriptural term "Word of God," and he applied his understanding to the use of the term "Word of God" in the New Testament.

When Luther referred to the "Word of God" in the New Testament, therefore, he did not mean merely that the writings of the apostles in the New Testament possessed a unique authority, although he meant that as well. He meant primarily that the New Testament spoke a Word of God which had been audible already in the Old Testament, but which could be heard through the New Testament in a special manner and to a special degree. If the Word of God in the Old Testament was a redemptive deed together with its anticipation of the ultimate redemption, then the "Word of God" in the New Testament was likewise a redemptive deed, but the ultimate one. In short, as the "Word of God" in the cosmic sense was the eternal Christ, and as the "Word of God" in the Old Testament was finally the anticipated Christ, so the "Word of God" in the New Testament was essentially the historical Christ.

When God spoke His Word in Christ, He did so through both words and deeds. Luther's sermons on the Gospels gave him an opportunity to examine the sayings of Jesus and the stories about Jesus with a view to discerning the Word of God in them.[46] He cherished the Gospel of John so highly because it concentrated upon the discourses of the Lord rather than upon His miracles.[47] Unlike many of his predecessors, who interpreted the parables of Jesus as illustrations of common-sense morality, Luther took seriously the formula that introduced most of the parables: "The kingdom

[46] See, for example, his exegesis of "pure in heart" in the *Commentary on the Sermon on the Mount* (1530—32), W, XXXII, 328—329; *Luther's Works*, 21, 34—35.

[47] See the works referred to on p. 36, note 17.

of God is like. . . ." He therefore read them as descriptions of the ways of God in His kingdom, where God spoke His Word by means that man could neither control nor predict.[48] The Word of God in the teachings of Jesus was, therefore, a redemptive Word, not just good advice about human problems. Because he regarded them from this perspective, Luther could set the parables into the matrix of Old Testament prophecy, recognizing both the continuity and the novelty in the words of Jesus. His opponents made the Sermon on the Mount a new morality of so-called "evangelical counsels," possible only for monks and other religious athletes.[49] Luther's interpretation of the Sermon on the Mount sounded the redemptive note in these chapters and could, therefore, apply them to the everyday needs and problems of his hearers in Wittenberg.[50]

As Luther thus heard the Word of God in the teachings of Jesus, so he also found the Word of God in the acts of Jesus. Sermons based on the miracle stories in the Gospels have often had the effect of making later hearers feel deprived because they were obliged to bear their illnesses while the contemporaries of Jesus could have theirs disposed of in this extraordinary manner.[51] Or, in Luther's day, these stories could become the basis for tales about the even more extraordinary cures wrought by the relics of the saints.[52]

[48] Walther von Loewenich, *Luther und die Gleichnistheorie von Mk. 4, 11 ff.*, in *Theologische Literaturzeitung*, LXXVII (1952), 483—488; Prof. Loewenich has expanded this material in his detailed study, *Luther als Ausleger der Synoptiker* (Munich, 1954).

[49] Cf. Karlmann Beyschlag, *Die Bergpredigt und Franz von Assisi* (Gütersloh, 1955), pp. 217—226.

[50] *Commentary on the Sermon on the Mount* (1530—32), W, XXXII, 299—544; *Luther's Works*, 21, 3—294.

[51] Johannes Wendland's *Miracles and Christianity*, tr. by H. R. Mackintosh (New York, 1911), pp. 66—68, summarizes Luther's comments on this problem.

[52] Gerhard Ebeling's *Evangelische Evangelienauslegung*, p. 449, note 405, contrasts Luther's exegesis with that of his predecessors.

Luther, however, used the miracle stories to speak about the Word of God. They showed him, first, that when God addressed His Word to men, it healed and saved them; they showed him, secondly, that though the extraordinary deeds of Christ may have been great, the greatest of all miracles was faith, called into being by the Word of God.[53]

But the deed through which the Word of God in Christ was spoken most clearly was the crucifixion and resurrection. Taken together, as Luther consistently took them, these two deeds spoke God's Word of redemption to man. God wounded in order to heal, He crushed in order to raise up, He killed in order to grant life — all these themes Luther found in the crucifixion and resurrection, where faith was enabled by the Holy Spirit to hear the Word of God.[54] Christ was not primarily an Example for men to imitate through their moral obedience, but the Exemplar in whom God had manifested His work and His Word.[55] It is not what Christ did that believers must do, but what was done to Christ is what believers must learn to recognize as being done to them as well. Thus the deed of God in Jesus Christ crucified and risen fits Luther's definition of the Word of God; for it accomplished the redemption of mankind, and it revealed the way and will of God to mankind.

Nevertheless, the Word of God in Christ was not merely a deed in history for Luther. As the Word of God in the age of the Old Testament had pointed forward by anticipation to the ultimate redemptive deed in Christ, so in the age of the New Testament the deed of God in Christ was continually being remembered and recited in the redemptive community of the church; and this remembering and recital,

[53] *Commentary on the Ninth Chapter of Isaiah* (1543—44), W, XL-III, 665—666.

[54] Erich Seeberg's *Christus. Wirklichkeit und Urbild* (Stuttgart, 1937) is an exposition of this theme.

[55] See *Luther's Works*, 22, 117, note 90.

too, was the Word of God.[56] It was not another Word of God than that spoken in Christ. When the church made pretensions to possessing another Word of God or a supplementary Word of God, it became Antichrist in Luther's eyes.[57] No, the Word spoken in Christ was identical with the Word of God now being spoken in the church. By means of this Word of God the church became and remained a community of redemption; in Luther's doctrine of the church this meant both a community of those who were redeemed and a community which communicated redemption.[58] The redemptive deed of God in Christ thus became an act of redemption now, as the Word of God in the church made that deed contemporary. Despite his stress on the Scriptures, Luther recognized that the church had been doing this ever since it received the command to proclaim the Word, and that this had happened before the books of the New Testament were written and much before they were collected into a canon.[59]

The Word of God in the church usually took the form of the oral Word, the Word of preaching.[60] Throughout his career Luther emphasized the centrality of this oral Word in the life and work of the church. "Christ did not command the apostles to write, but only to preach."[61] Again he said: "The church is not a pen-house but a mouth-house."[62] And yet again: "The Gospel should not be written but

[56] Cf. chapter 11.

[57] "The pope boasts that the Christian Church is above the Word of God. No, this is not true! We must be pupils and not aspire to be masters." *Sermons on the Gospel of St. John: Chapters 6—8* (1530—32), W, XXXIII, 366; *Luther's Works*, 23, 231.

[58] See chapter five.

[59] On Luther's attitude toward the canon cf. pp. 86—88.

[60] Regin Prenter, "Luther on Word and Sacrament" in Gerhard Belgum (ed.), *More About Luther* (Decorah, 1958), pp. 73—74.

[61] *Church Postil* (1522), W, X-I-1, 626.

[62] Ibid., W, X-I-2, 48.

screamed." [63] When one meets the phrase "Word of God" in Luther's writings, it usually has reference to this oral Word of proclamation. In part Luther's emphasis on the oral rather than the written Word depended on a psychological judgment.[64] One could read a thing many times over and yet fail to understand it and apply it to himself. But when another person spoke the same thing with a living voice, then the hearer could know that he was the one being addressed.[65] As this was true of language in general, so it was particularly true of the Gospel. God had so constructed man that the Gospel and the Law could reach him most effectively through the medium of the living voice.[66] Christ Himself did not write anything; but He spoke and preached continually, to make it clear that the basic form of the Word of God was always the oral Word of proclamation.

Because of this emphasis on the oral Word, Luther also assigned great importance to the ministry of the Word of God. This helps to explain an apparent inconsistency in Luther's thought. On the one hand, he minimized the importance of the clergy through his doctrine of the universal priesthood and his attack upon the Roman hierarchy; on the other hand, he could speak of the ministry as the highest

[63] Werner Elert, *Morphologie des Luthertums* (2 vols.; Munich, 1931 to 1932), I, 60.

[64] Peter Meinhold's *Luthers Sprachphilosophie* (Berlin, 1958) is an unusually incisive study of this aspect of Luther's thought.

[65] "Christ did not write anything, but He spoke it all. The apostles wrote only a little, but they spoke a lot." *Works on the Psalms* (1519—21), W, V, 537.

[66] "There are many people nowadays who say: 'Oh, I have read and learned it all, and I know it very well. I do not need (to listen).' They may even come out and say: 'What do we need with any more clergy or preachers? I can read it just as well at home.' Then they go their way and don't read it at home either. Or even if they do read it, it is not as fruitful or powerful as it is through a public preacher whom God has ordained to say and preach this." Sermon of July 21, 1532, W, XXXVI, 220.

estate in the church, even as an order, and could use extravagant language about it.[67] He could speak both ways because his principal objection to the hierarchy was directed at its neglect of the preached Word, and the principal ground for his exaltation of the ministry was the preached Word. The ministry of the "Word of God" did not consist in distributing Bibles but in telling about the deeds of God. If the bishops were willing to carry on this ministry of the preached Word, they would get all the glory and honor on which they now insisted so vainly.[68] For in the ministry of preaching God had entrusted to the voices of men a privilege which He could well have reserved for the more eloquent voices of the angels.[69] Indeed, when a minister was privileged to preach the Word of God, he was doing the same work for which Christ was ordained; for, as Luther loved to emphasize, the ministry of Jesus was a ministry of the oral Word.[70]

The oral Word in Jesus' ministry was what the ministry of the oral Word continued to proclaim: the Word of God in the Law and the Gospel. Luther's doctrine of Law and Gospel was at once less consistent and more complex than most of his later interpreters have made it.[71] But for our purposes here it is important as a definition of both the form and the content of the Word of God. Both the Law and the Gospel were Word of God in the sense that they were not the word of man, but the Gospel was the Word of God also in the sense that by it God bestowed and sustained faith. In this latter sense the Law was not, strictly speaking, the Word of God. Even this distinction does not

[67] Cf. Wilhelm Maurer, *Pfarrerrecht und Bekenntnis* (Berlin, 1957).

[68] Cf. the comments of Ernst Benz, *Bischofsamt und apostolische Sukzession im deutschen Protestantismus* (Stuttgart, 1953), pp. 11—16.

[69] See p. 105.

[70] Elert, *Morphologie*, I, 165.

[71] Paul Althaus' *Gebot und Gesetz* (Gütersloh, 1952) is a brief but compact analysis.

do justice to the subtlety and profundity of Luther's position on the Word of God as Law and Gospel; for he did not simply mean to say that some words of God were Law and others were Gospel, but that the same word of God could be both Law and Gospel. The best example of this was his interpretation of the First Commandment.[72] He could say that this was the most threatening statement ever to come from God, because this Word denounced all idolatry and pretense.[73] But he could also say that the Gospel and justification by faith were really versions of the First Commandment, according to which the deity of God must always be uppermost.[74] To the believer the threats of God were a consolation, because he knew that God spoke His Word of threatening in order to console, as He crucified Christ in order to make Him alive. And to the wicked the consolations of God were a threat, because by this Word God made the wicked even more smug and thus destroyed him or let him destroy himself. The same Word of God was thus both Law and Gospel.

Luther contended against Rome that the proclamation of this Word of God in Law and Gospel was the primary responsibility of the church.[75] There were many other things the church had to do, still more that it was permitted to do;[76] but defining and limiting them all was the proclamation of the oral Word. For by this proclamation the church obeyed the command of its Lord to go and preach, and

[72] Aarne Siirala, in *Gottes Gebot bei Martin Luther* (Helsinki, 1956), has summarized this material, especially on pp. 53—104.

[73] Hayo Gerdes, *Luthers Streit mit den Schwärmern um das rechte Verständnis des Gesetzes Mose* (Göttingen, 1955), pp. 105—116.

[74] Franz Lau, *Erstes Gebot und Ehre Gottes als Mitte von Luthers Theologie*, in *Theologische Literaturzeitung*, LXXIII (1948), 719—730.

[75] Cf. p. 219, note 1.

[76] Jaroslav Pelikan, "Luther and the Liturgy," in *More About Luther*, pp. 10—13.

through the same proclamation it heard about the redemptive deeds of God to which it owed its very existence as the church. Addressing himself to his students in the theological lecture halls at Wittenberg, Luther continually urged them to remember that the basis of the church's life was the Word of God, whose basic form was the oral Word of preaching.[77]

Only in the light of the foregoing is it possible to understand what Luther meant in those places where he spoke of the Bible as the "Word of God." [78] Without the foregoing Luther's doctrine of the Word would become a caricature, according to which he meant the Bible wherever he used the phrase "Word of God." This would distort his whole understanding of revelation, his view of faith, his doctrine of the Holy Spirit, and most of the rest of his theology. Most of the time Luther, like the Scriptures themselves, did not mean the Scriptures when he spoke about the "Word of God." But sometimes he did, and a consideration of the Word of God as Scripture therefore belongs in any study of this component in Luther's work as an expositor.

The Scriptures were the "Word of God" in a derivative sense for Luther — derivative from the historical sense of Word as deed and from the basic sense of Word as proclamation. As the record of the deeds of God, which were the Word of God, the Scriptures participated in the nature of that which they recorded.[79] As the written deposit of the preaching of the apostles, they could properly be termed

[77] Ebeling, *Evangelienauslegung*, pp. 294–295.

[78] Ragnar Bring, *Luthers Anschauung von der Bibel* (Berlin, 1951).

[79] H. Noltensmeier's *Reformatorische Einheit* (Graz-Köln, 1953) is a comparative study of Luther and Calvin. There is additional material in Rupert E. Davies, *The Problem of Authority in the Continental Reformers* (London, 1946).

the "Word of God" also.[80] When they were so termed in Luther, this was sometimes set in opposition to the word and the traditions of men, which he accused of obscuring the Word of God in the church; [81] or in opposition to the visions and private revelations of the left-wing Reformers, which he accused of attempting to reinstate the word of man in place of the Word of God.[82] When either of these sides challenged him to support his opposition to their teachings, he held up the Bible as the Word of God, before which the word of man being purveyed by them had to be silent. But even when he made this equation complete and direct, when he simply identified the Bible as the "Word of God," the Word as deed and the Word as proclamation were still included in the definition of what he meant by "Word." [83] For the Word as deed always circumscribed the Word as proclamation. The proclamation was entitled to be called the "Word of God" only if it recited these deeds which were the "Word of God." And to do this task of reciting and thus to be the "Word of God" the oral proclamation had to rely on the "Word of God" as Scripture.[84]

The written Word thus had a twofold function in relation to the oral Word. First, its function was to sustain the oral proclamation of the Word of God. Studying conditions in the church of his time, Luther was convinced that the low state of preaching was responsible for the general decline of the church; [85] but he was also convinced that ignorance

[80] Cf. Peter Brunner's comments in *The Unity of the Church* (Rock Island, 1957), pp. 14—15.

[81] See pp. 77—78.

[82] See p. 103, note 76.

[83] Cf. H. Beintker, *Luthers Offenbarungsverständnis und die gegenwärtige Theologie*, in *Zeitschrift für systematische Theologie*, XXIV (1955), 241—265.

[84] Otto Scheel's *Luthers Stellung zur Heiligen Schrift* (Tübingen, 1902) is an outdated but still helpful study.

[85] Cf. the Introduction to *Luther's Works*, 51.

and neglect of the Scriptures had been responsible for the low state of preaching.[86] That was why he translated the Scriptures into German, and that was also why he devoted the major part of his professional career as a theologian to the exposition of the Scriptures. For he was sure that the preaching of the church could not be relied on to sustain itself but had to refresh itself from the record of the deeds of God in the Bible. To continue to be the Word of God the oral Word had need of the written Word. In fact, Luther suggested that this was why the written Word had been set down in the first place.[87] When the oral Word began to flag in the primitive church, the apostles were inspired to put down on paper what they had been preaching — in order that it might be preached once more! [88]

The second function of the written Word in relation to the oral Word was to preserve the proclamation from error.[89] This, too, Luther saw at work in the original composition of the New Testament. Specifically, he followed the tradition according to which the Gospel of St. John had been composed because the proclamation of the church was being distorted by Cerinthus.[90] The distortion made it clear that the church could not rely on the oral Word alone to keep its teaching and message pure but had to fix the content of the Word of God by writing it down. Ever since then, Luther said, the church had used the written Word of God in the Bible as a weapon against false teachers.[91] But he knew enough church history to point out that the false teachers had also treated the Bible as the "Word of God"

[86] Ebeling, *Evangelienauslegung*, pp. 30–37.

[87] See the passages cited on p. 63, notes 61–62.

[88] Elert, *Morphologie*, I, 165.

[89] See p. 85.

[90] *Sermons on the Gospel of St. John: Chapters 1–4* (1537–39), W, XLVI, 542; *Luther's Works*, 22, 7.

[91] *On the Councils and the Church* (1539), W, L, 509–653.

and had cited it as such.[92] In the face of this phenomenon Luther fell back upon his more basic definition of the Word of God as deed and as proclamation, pointing out that the false teachers interpreted the Bible in a way that contradicted the deed of God in Christ and the witness to that deed in the oral Word of God. Therefore they misinterpreted the Bible even though they called it the "Word of God." [93] For the "Word of God" in the Bible was the same "Word of God" which God had spoken in the Exodus and in Christ, and the same "Word of God" which the church was always obliged to proclaim.

Ultimately, then, there was only one "Word of God," which came in various forms. In its written form it was the Bible. But that raised the question of whether there was any other written or oral form of the Word of God, and specifically of whether any authority was to be ascribed to the tradition of the Christian centuries. Because this question was (and still is) inextricably bound up with the doctrine of the Word of God, an investigation of tradition as the second component of Luther's exegesis must likewise form part of this inquiry.

[92] Cf. Ernst Schäfer, *Luther als Kirchenhistoriker* (Gütersloh, 1897), pp. 268–288.

[93] Gerdes, op. cit., pp. 103–105.

CHAPTER FOUR

Scripture and Tradition

AT the Leipzig Debate in 1519 Luther had to admit that, in the name of the Scriptures as he interpreted them, he was setting the authority of the Scriptures against and above the authority of the tradition of the church.[1] Within less than five years Luther was defending the tradition of the church against those who, in the name of the Scriptures as they interpreted them, wanted to set aside the liturgical and ecclesiastical forms developed in that tradition.[2] And before Luther's death there had arisen men and movements in Western Christendom who, in the name of the Scriptures as they interpreted them, rejected the Trinitarian and Christological dogmas upon which the doctrinal systems of Christendom had been founded for more than a millennium.[3] All this in the name of the Scriptures! When Luther saw the results, he found himself closer in some ways to the Roman Catholicism that had excommunicated him than he was to the Protestantism that claimed to be carrying out in consistent practice a conception of Biblical authority which he had stated in theory.[4]

This situation is of primary importance in the interpretation and evaluation of the Reformation and of its place in the history of Christendom. It raises the perennial ques-

[1] See p. 114, note 19.

[2] See p. 119, note 41.

[3] It should be remembered that Servetus and the early Socinians were Biblicists as well as rationalistic in their theological orientation; cf. Earl M. Wilbur, *Socinianism and Its Antecedents* (Cambridge, 1945).

[4] See p. 120, note 45.

tion whether, like the sorcerer's apprentice, Luther had summoned spirits he could not control — spirits that his successors
were unable to exorcise even by fasting and prayer.[5] This
is a serious question, and one which every heir of the Reformation must answer before he can honestly take possession
of the Reformation heritage.[6] Our concern here is with
the different, though not unrelated, question of tradition
as a component in Luther's exegesis.[7] How could Luther
consistently assign prime or sole authority to the Word of
God in the Scriptures and yet retain all he did retain of
the church's tradition? What was the role of that tradition
in the exposition of the Scriptures according to Luther's
principles of interpretation? And did he remain consistently
loyal to those principles in the concrete performance of his
task as a Biblical expositor?

To put the question into proper historical perspective
it is necessary to see it in the context of the system of
authority developed by the ancient catholic church during
its struggle against Judaism, paganism, and heresy.[8] The
church emerged from that tripartite struggle with a tripartite
system of authority: a canon of Scripture, whose precise
limits still awaited delineation but whose contents included
the Old Testament and an equivalent collection of early
Christian writings; a tradition and a confession of faith, whose
text fluctuated from one section of the church to another,
but whose foundation remained the same; and a monarchical
episcopate charged with the perpetuation and transmission

[5] Karl August Meissinger's *Luther. Die deutsche Tragödie 1521*
(Munich, 1953) is a sensitive but overdrawn presentation of this question.

[6] Jaroslav Pelikan, *The Riddle of Roman Catholicism* (Nashville, 1959),
pp. 45—57.

[7] Jan Koopmans, *Das altkirchliche Dogma in der Reformation* (Munich,
1955).

[8] E. Flesseman van Leer's *Tradition and Scripture in the Early Church*
(Assen, 1954) is a summary and critique of the previous attempts to summarize this development.

of the catholic and apostolic faith. This system was subject to development in any of several directions, but the isolation of any one of the three elements and its elevation as the sole authority in the church would have been a difficult matter. Instead, the historical development of the system has preferred subordination to co-ordination as a way of arranging the three. Thus within Eastern Orthodoxy the Scriptures and the bishops have retained a high measure of authority and dignity in the church, but both belong to the ongoing living magisterium of the church tradition.[9] There was said to be a difference of degree, but not of kind, between the authority of the Gospel of St. John and that of the Council of Chalcedon; and the possibility of a conflict between the two was ruled out *a priori*.

The Western Church of the Middle Ages followed another fork of the same road.[10] Here it was not the tradition but the episcopacy that gradually came to assume the role of arbiter. Technically this position did not achieve dogmatic status until the Vatican Council of 1870, whose pronouncements on papal infallibility made it official; [11] but the council had much of the drift, if not all the weight, of the development on its side. In the century before Luther conflict over that development was a major issue for both theology and churchmanship, as papalists and conciliarists contended over the final seat of authority in the church.[12] In their opposition to the idea of papal authority some of the conciliarists went so far as to assert that while there

[9] Albert C. Outler, *The Christian Tradition and the Unity We Seek* (New York, 1957) is a provocative exposition of the problem of tradition.

[10] B. C. Butler's *The Church and Infallibility* (New York, 1954) is a recent Roman Catholic defense of papal infallibility.

[11] Geddes MacGregor's *The Vatican Revolution* (Boston, 1957) is a recent Protestant criticism of papal infallibility.

[12] Hubert Jedin's *Geschichte des Konzils von Trient*, I (Freiburg, 1949), traces the development of this conflict in the century before Luther.

were other authorities in the church than the Scriptures, these other authorities shone by a reflected light and derived their authority from that of the Bible.[13] As Kropatschek has shown, therefore, it was not a novelty for the Reformers to put the stress they did upon the supremacy of Scripture in theology.[14] They were continuing a trend present throughout the medieval church, one which had been articulated by some of the outstanding scholastic doctors. But the elevation of Scriptural authority by the scholastics of the twelfth and thirteenth centuries and by the conciliarists and nominalists of the fourteenth and fifteenth centuries did not eventuate in anything like the radical break with traditional authority which we see in the sixteenth century.

The place of the Lutheran Reformation in this development was somewhat ambiguous. In one way it may be said to represent a fundamental criticism of the development going back to Irenaeus, a criticism in the name of the authority of the Bible as the Word of God.[15] Yet if it is taken alone, this interpretation of the Reformation is inadequate; for it would also be correct to see in the work of the Reformers a fundamental criticism of late medieval perversions, voiced in the name of ancient and traditional catholicity.[16] And the Reformation was both of these at the same time! Perhaps no document from the first generation

[13] George Tavard's *Holy Writ or Holy Church* (New York, 1959) is the best available examination of the relation between Scripture and church in the systems of the late Middle Ages and the Reformation era.

[14] H. Kropatschek's *Das Schriftprinzip der lutherischen Kirche,* I, *Die Vorgeschichte. Das Erbe des Mittelalters* (Leipzig, 1904), was one of the first studies on either the Roman Catholic or the Protestant side to recognize the continuity between the Reformers and the Middle Ages on this score.

[15] See pp. 77—78.

[16] In his searching essay on *Die Anfänge von Luthers Theologie. Eine Frage an die lutherische Kirche,* in *Theologische Literaturzeitung,* LXXVII (1952), 1—12, Prof. Wilhelm Maurer has emphasized this defense of catholicity as the *raison d'être* of the Reformation.

of the Reformation made this dual character of its criticism more explicit than the Apology of the Augsburg Confession, which simultaneously defended and criticized the tradition of the church, sometimes setting the Word of God in opposition to the fathers, sometimes seeming almost to equate the Word of God with the teaching of the fathers.[17] The same dual character was present in Chemnitz' detailed refutation of the canons and decrees of the Council of Trent, in Flacius' *Catalogus testium veritatis,* and, two generations later, in Johann Gerhard's *Confessio catholica* of 1634.[18] All these documents illustrated the problem of an apparent ambiguity in Luther's attitude toward the relation between tradition and Scripture: he claimed to be defending Scripture against the fathers, and he claimed to be defending the fathers against their perverters.

Part of the solution to this problem lay in Luther's specific grounds for rejecting Roman Catholic traditionalism. He contended that the tradition provided a less reliable guide to the meaning of the Christian faith than the Scriptures did.[19] One of the grounds for this contention was his discovery that moralism had been a prominent feature in the theological tradition of the church. He criticized the traditional conception of the saint as a person without human emotions or weaknesses.[20] The fathers had often interpreted the narratives in the Scriptures on the basis of this conception, and they had therefore misunderstood the meaning of sainthood as a gift of grace. "As many as there were,"

[17] Jaroslav Pelikan, "Some Word Studies in the Apology," in *Concordia Theological Monthly,* XXIV (1953), 580—596.

[18] Jaroslav Pelikan, "Tradition in Confessional Lutheranism," in *Lutheran World,* III (1956), 214—222.

[19] For a concrete instance of this cf. Gerhard Ebeling, *Luther's Auslegung des 14. (15.) Psalms in der ersten Psalmenvorlesung im Vergleich mit der exegetischen Tradition,* in *Zeitschrift für Theologie und Kirche,* L (1953), 280—339.

[20] *Lectures on the Minor Prophets* (1524—26), W, XIII, 242.

he said of the church fathers, "all of them failed either to observe or thoroughly and correctly to understand the kingdom of grace through Christ." [21] Luther was willing to accuse even his favorite among them, St. Augustine, of sometimes having failed to grasp the full implications of the Biblical doctrine of grace and thus of falling into a moralistic distortion of the Gospel. [22]

Because of his own personal history Luther came to the conclusion that one source of this moralism was the stress of many fathers on asceticism and celibacy. The fathers who had formulated the theological tradition were the same fathers who had helped to establish clerical celibacy as the rule in the church. St. Athanasius transported the monastic ideal from the East to the West during one of his exiles; St. Augustine set down the principles upon which the Western sisterhoods were founded. Luther maintained that the conception of the Christian life involved in these efforts was bound to distort the theological judgment of the fathers. Thus he criticized Jerome for his stress on chastity in the exegesis of the Book of Jonah. [23] The elevation of the unmarried life to a higher position than the married life seemed to him to imply a depreciation of God's good gift in marriage. Luther recalled from his own experience that the celibate life often produced a pride that one had transcended the physical life with its appetites and was living spiritually. [24] Luther knew also that the fathers had contributed to the rise of this moralistic pride in the church. Because the

[21] Ibid., pp. 242–243.

[22] Cf. Adolf Hamel, *Der junge Luther und Augustin* (2 vols.; Gütersloh, 1934—35) for a detailed study of Luther's early Augustinianism.

[23] *Lectures on the Minor Prophets* (1524—26), W, XIII, 242.

[24] Hence his bitter polemic against the monk, who "makes a god who sits on high and thinks: 'Whoever observes the rules of St. Francis, I will save.'" *Commentary on Psalm 118* (1530), W, XXXI, 175; *Luther's Works*, 14, 99.

Scriptures so consistently repudiated the notion of sainthood as perfection — Luther's favorite passage here, all his life, was the seventh chapter of Romans, source of his doctrine that the Christian was both saint and sinner [25] — Luther pitted the authority of the Scriptures against the authority of the tradition of the fathers, even the best fathers. For he found that even the best fathers had been men and had often substituted trust in moral works for trust in the grace of God.

Similarly, Luther maintained that the tradition was full of concessions to philosophy. The same authority that sought to subordinate theology to the authority of the fathers also sought to subject it to the domination of Aristotle, he declared against Latomus.[26] While he was not as conscious as modern historical scholarship has been of the problem of Greek influence on the early church,[27] Luther did realize that the conflict between early Christian theology and classical philosophy had in some ways been a draw, in which theology was ostensibly victorious but in which philosophy had also scored some points. He became especially vehement on this point when the concept "tradition" was widened to include not merely the early church but the more recent theologians as well. Luther's vendetta against Aristotle was in reality a feud against these theologians, who had, in his judgment, perverted the interpretation of the Scriptures by their concessions to Aristotle.[28] He was angry enough with them for having done so, but he stormed most violently

[25] Rudolf Hermann's *Luthers These "Gerecht und Sünder zugleich"* (Gütersloh, 1930) is the most profound presentation of this motif, which was central to Luther's exegesis, piety, and theology.

[26] *Against Latomus* (1521), W, VIII, 98–99; *Luther's Works*, 32, 216–217.

[27] See p. 23, note 53.

[28] Jaroslav Pelikan, *From Luther to Kierkegaard* (Saint Louis, 1950), pp. 10–13.

against the idea that the example of these theologians should have binding force because they were part of the tradition. He exclaimed that the Scriptures were clear in teaching the primacy of divine grace, and that they did not need the illumination of philosophy to make them clearer.[29] On these counts, as on others, Luther broke with the authority of tradition in theology, maintaining that the authority of the Scriptures was enough and that traditionalism only muddied their clarity with its moralism and its philosophizing.

But the authority of the church fathers and of the tradition was not an isolated authority in medieval theology; it was, as we have seen, one aspect of the general system of authority. When Luther rejected the principle of Roman traditionalism, therefore, his opponents were able to charge him with rejecting the content of the tradition as well. They equated their particular traditions with the tradition; whoever attacked one seemed to be attacking the other as well. Hence their constant cry, "Fathers, fathers!"[30] Some of this was undoubtedly a polemical device on their part. If they could succeed in tarring Luther's cause with the brush of some ancient heresy, they would be able to dismiss it from any serious consideration.[31] Thus some of Luther's opponents professed to find Manichaean heresy in Luther's doctrine of the bondage of the human will before God.[32] Both in their private writings and in Art. I and Art. XIX of the Augsburg Confession Luther and his supporters had to defend themselves against this charge.[33] There was even an effort to

[29] *Lectures on Genesis* (1535–45), W, 43, 94.

[30] *Commentary on Psalm 45* (1532), W, XL-II, 564; *Luther's Works,* 12, 265.

[31] Hence Luther had to pay attention to ancient heresy on this account as well; cf. p. 70, note 92.

[32] Hugo Lämmer, *Die vortridentinisch-katholische Theologie* (Berlin, 1858), p. 161.

[33] See *Luther's Works,* 13, 96, note 34.

show that Luther was a crypto-Arian in his doctrine of the Trinity.[34] That charge was all the more ridiculous because of the truly central place of this doctrine in his theology.[35]

These various efforts to identify Luther's theology with heretical movements from the Christian past were an attempt to give historical content to the suspicion that his view of Scripture and tradition represented a threat to the Christian tradition as such, not merely to certain particular traditions. Behind this suspicion was the idea that by themselves the Scriptures were insufficient to establish the articles of faith.[36] The heretics of past and present had all claimed to espouse the authority of the Scriptures in opposition to one or another post-Scriptural tradition. To Luther's critics, and to the church generally, such an opposition was intrinsically fallacious. The fallacy was compounded by the historical fact that those who began with such an opposition between Scripture and tradition frequently ended by rejecting not only parts of the tradition but elements of the Scriptures as well — at least of the Scriptures as the church traditionally understood them. Nestorius had objected to the title θεοτόκος for the Blessed Virgin Mary partly on the grounds that the Scriptures did not apply it to her, although some theologians did.[37] Again and again in the history of Christian thought some alert theologian has discovered that the word "trinity" did not appear in the Bible.[38] On the basis of its experience with heretics over the centuries the church had concluded that it was wiser not to operate with the nude Scriptures

34 Because of comments like that on the *homoousios* in *Against Latomus* (1521), W, VIII, 117; *Luther's Works*, 32, 244.

35 See p. 52, note 16.

36 *Commentary on 1 Peter* (1523), W, XII, 360.

37 J. N. D. Kelly, *Early Christian Doctrines* (New York, 1958), pp. 310 to 317.

38 See Luther's defense of the use of non-Biblical terms in theology, *On the Councils and the Church* (1539), W, L, 572—573.

but to invoke the authority of the Scriptures plus the tradition against heresy.

Thus it was not merely polemical fancy when Luther's opponents claimed that his elevation of Scriptural over traditional authority would open the floodgates of heresy, which were now being held shut by the weight of tradition.[39] They truly believed that the authority of the Scriptures alone could not combat heresy; for heresy and orthodoxy both quoted the Scriptures, and who was to decide between them on the basis of the Scriptures themselves? Allegorical exegesis had been made possible — and necessary — by the tradition of the church, with which the exposition of the Scriptures had to square, or else.[40] Despite increasingly precise rules of procedure the ways of allegory led to unpredictable exegetical results. Hence the way to measure the correctness or incorrectness of those results was not to check the soundness of the exegetical procedures that produced them but to compare the results with the ecclesiastical tradition. Once the tradition was removed as an arbiter over theology, the way seemed to be open for an endless variety of opinions, all claiming to be derived from the Scriptures. Such was the spectacle conjured up by Luther's rejection of Roman Catholic traditionalism in the name of the authority of Scripture.

To this Luther replied that traditionalism was not merely a disparagement of the authority of Scripture; it was also a disfigurement of the tradition itself. As he said against Emser, "I cannot stand it that they slander and blaspheme Scripture and the holy fathers this way. They accuse Scripture of being dark . . . and they give the fathers credit for being the light that illumines Scripture, although all the

[39] Gordon Rupp, "Luther and the Puritans," in Gerhard Belgum (ed.), *Luther Today* (Decorah, 1957), pp. 107—164.

[40] Gerhard Ebeling, *Evangelische Evangelienauslegung* (Munich, 1942).

fathers confess their own darkness and illumine Scripture only with Scripture." [41] Or, as he said a year earlier, "We are like people who look at road signs and never get on the road. The beloved fathers wanted to lead us into Scripture with their writings, but we use them to lead ourselves out of it." [42] Luther understood the writings of the church fathers as an exposition of the Scriptures, while his opponents seemed to be making them an extension of the Scriptures.

In opposing traditionalism, therefore, Luther claimed to be opposing, not the tradition itself, or even the proper use of the tradition in theology, but the abuse of the tradition. He took the position of defending the tradition against its abusers; not they, but he, should be classified on the side of tradition. He repeatedly found instances in the writings of the fathers to back up this interpretation. They had not wanted to elevate their interpretations to the status of articles of faith.[43] They felt able to use Scripture rather loosely for illustrative purposes because they did not expect or want the church to canonize their interpretations.[44] From Gregory, Jerome, Ambrose, and especially from Augustine, Luther was able to prove that such canonization ascribed to the fathers an authority which they had been willing to ascribe only to the Scriptures. Hence he concluded that he was being loyal to the fathers when, like them, he put the authority of the Scriptures over all human opinions, including theirs and his. He professed loyalty to their fundamental intentions when he examined their teachings in the light of their com-

[41] *An Answer to the Super-Christian Book of the Goat Emser* (1521), W, VII, 639.

[42] *To the Christian Nobility* (1520), W, VI, 461.

[43] *Lectures on Genesis* (1535—45), W, XLII, 91; *Luther's Works*, 1, 121.

[44] See the passages cited on p. 112 below for a discussion of how, in Luther's judgment, the fathers had used the Scriptures loosely for illustrative purposes.

mon authority in the Scriptures and when he rejected what did not conform to that authority. This he regarded, not as disloyalty to the fathers but as the highest kind of reverence for them, because it was reverence for the Word of God.

From this interpretation of the place and purpose of the fathers Luther's followers developed an interest in the writings of the fathers that prompted them to study the patristic literature as it had not been studied for a long time.[45] Lutheran and Roman theologians vied with one another in their loyalty to the fathers. The Magdeburg *Centuries* and Caesar Baronius both provided interpretations of the tradition calculated to prove the soundness of their own theological viewpoint.[46] Regardless now of the accuracy of the interpretations put upon the tradition by either side, this conflict did refute the view that Luther's Reformation was simply a revolt against tradition. For example, Chemnitz' critique of the Council of Trent was based on a breadth and depth of patristic scholarship difficult to match.[47] He went through the patristic evidence with care and discrimination, sorting out the relevant from the irrelevant and demonstrating that Trent had done violence to the tradition, while the Reformation had been faithful to the best in the tradition by being faithful to the Scriptures. At its best the tradition was the voice of the church obediently listening to the Word of God and then responding to that Word as the Spirit gave it utterance. The fathers wanted to be understood as expositors of Scripture, and it was unfair to them to read them as substitutes for it.

The very form of the issue, however, raises a problem that does not admit of easy solution: What did Luther re-

---

[45] Cf. Johannes Quasten, *Patrology*, I (Westminster, 1950), p. 4.

[46] Jaroslav Pelikan, *The Riddle of Roman Catholicism*, p. 47.

[47] See the comments of Wilhelm Pauck, *The Heritage of the Reformation*, p. 109.

gard as the line between Scripture and tradition? On what basis did he find it possible to set Scripture against tradition and above it? In some ways this problem is prior to the one we have been discussing. Only when Scripture and tradition have been distinguished from each other can they be adequately compared, even though, on the other hand, the comparison may produce criteria that are helpful in making the distinction. As we have seen, the development of the concept of authority in the ancient church had eventually made the Scriptures only a part — though, to be sure, the supreme part — of an entire system of apostolic authority embracing the creedal tradition and the monarchical episcopate as well. From this the foundation of Luther's distinction between Scripture and tradition becomes apparent. Though he differed from the preceding centuries in the relative status he assigned to the two, he generally accepted the distinction as they had made it. Now it was one thing to distinguish between Scripture and tradition as different parts of a single system of authority; it was a vastly different thing to distinguish between them as two separate systems of authority.

The separation between Scripture and tradition in Luther involved the blending of historical and theological criteria that were not easy to hold together consistently. Of Luther's concept of the canon as an aspect of this separation we shall have more to say in a moment. On the historical side Luther sometimes made the separation on sheer chronological grounds. According to his knowledge of early Christian literature, there was a sizable gap in time between the writers of the New Testament and the earliest church fathers. Luther regarded Tertullian, who died in 230, as the earliest writer in the church after the apostles.[48] As Schaefer and Koehler have pointed out, he apparently did not know the

[48] *This Is My Body: These Words Still Stand* (1527), W, XXIII, 217.

writers who later acquired the title "apostolic fathers." [49]
He was, therefore, able to invoke the historical and chronological argument in a form no longer available to theologians
of the twentieth century. For even the most conservative
theologian today is compelled to admit that there is a longer
span of time between the first document and the last document in the New Testament than there is between the last
document in the New Testament and the first document in
post-Biblical literature — if indeed the two do not overlap
altogether. As Luther dated the documents, there was about
a century between the writings of John and those of Tertullian. He was thus able to think of the apostolic era as
something rather precisely circumscribed in a literary way
and thus quite clearly distinguishable from postapostolic
tradition.

Mingled with this historical-chronological argument, and
sometimes even in conflict with it, was the argument from
theological content. To the blurring of the distinction between Scripture and tradition Luther could reply with
"Whence?" [50] Where did the fathers get what they had,
except from the Scriptures? The distinction between them
was one between the brook and the spring, as Luther often
quoted from St. Bernard. [51] Thus the two sets of writings
could be handily classified as they reflected either the original creativity that betrayed apostolic authorship or the derivative dependence that betrayed postapostolic authorship.
Yet Luther could also point out that though the apostles may
have been a source for the fathers, they themselves drew
on the Old Testament as their source. [52] "The apostles," he
said, "were full of the Holy Spirit and were sure that they

[49] Cf. Schäfer, op. cit., pp. 253–255.
[50] *On the Councils and the Church* (1539), W, L, 547.
[51] Ibid., pp. 519–520.
[52] Bornkamm, *Luther und das Alte Testament*, pp. 151–184.

had been sent by Christ and were preaching the right Gospel. Still they subjected themselves and did not want people to believe them unless they thoroughly validated from Scripture that it was the way they said it." [53] Luther assigned a primary place to the Old Testament as Scripture, preferring the term "proclamation" (or κήρυγμα) for the New Testament.[54] This point did seriously qualify his argument for the distinction between the New Testament Scriptures and tradition on the grounds of originality. Indeed, it could conceivably be maintained from these and similar statements that Luther operated with three levels of written authority: the Scriptures of the Old Testament; the written form of the proclamation of the New Testament, which drew on the Old; and the written form of the Christian tradition, which drew on both the Old and the New Testament. But such a schematization would be a violent oversimplification of the complexity in Luther's approach to the problem, since a radically different scheme could also find support in his writings.

The argument from theological content involved also a comparison of the teachings in Scripture and in tradition. Luther had observed that because of the press of controversy the church fathers had tended to emphasize one doctrinal point and to ignore others. In the Scriptures, on the other hand, he found the whole of Christian teaching presented without any such overemphasis.[55] Similarly, he challenged his opponents to show him one church father who had not erred. If there was none such, the tradition of the fathers did not belong on the same level as the teaching of the

[53] *Commentary on 1 Peter* (1523), W, XII, 278.

[54] "Preface" to *Church Postil* (1522), W, X-I-1, 17.

[55] "In short, you may put them all together, both fathers and councils, and you cannot cull the whole doctrine of Christian faith out of them, though you keep on culling forever. If the Holy Scriptures had not made and preserved the church, it would not have remained long because of the councils and fathers." *On the Councils and the Church* (1539), W, L, 546—547.

Scriptures.[56] The various parts of the Scriptures, Old and New Testament, presented a harmonious whole, without any necessity for artificial or tortured harmonizations. The fathers had frequently contradicted themselves and one another, making necessary the elaborate and admirable work of harmonization in Luther's old theological textbook, the *Sentences* of Peter Lombard.[57] These and similar arguments were the ones Luther used in distinguishing between tradition and Scripture.

A related problem arises in Luther's view of the canon. How could Luther repudiate the binding authority of the very church fathers and ancient councils on whom he depended, at least in part, for the validation of the New Testament canon? Here the same combination of historical and theological appeared that was present in his distinction between Scripture and tradition. At times he proceeded on the assumption that for the New Testament "canonical" was synonymous with "apostolic," and that the demonstration of the apostolic origin of a writing gave it automatic entree to the New Testament canon.[58] Thus the status of the Epistle to the Hebrews was problematical partly on the grounds that its apostolicity was in doubt.[59] But it is well known that Luther also substituted a theological for a historical definition of what constituted apostolicity in a writing.[60] The urging of Christ was the characteristic mark of true apostolicity in a book, regardless of authorship. Sober scholarship has exploded — it is to be hoped, once and for all — the irresponsible conclusions which certain Biblical

[56] *Commentary on Psalm 37* (1521), W, VIII, 237.

[57] *On the Councils and the Church* (1539), W, L, 543.

[58] Otto Ritschl, *Dogmengeschichte des Protestantismus*, I (Leipzig, 1908), 61 ff.

[59] Cf. Luther's preface to Hebrews (1522), W, *Deutsche Bibel*, VII, 344.

[60] Bornkamm, *Luther und das Alte Testament*, pp. 164—165.

critics had drawn from this for their work.[61] But Luther's attitude toward the Epistle of James did illustrate his unwillingness to determine the apostolicity of anything — be it an epistle or an episcopate — on simply chronological grounds.

Many of the examinations of Luther's attitude toward the canon have failed to measure adequately what might be called his critical but pragmatic realism.[62] Luther's attitude toward the canon was a critical one. He did not accept a book as eternally binding upon him and the church simply on the grounds that it had been accepted as binding for a long time. Both his Roman Catholic and his extreme Protestant opponents chided him for this viewpoint.[63] At the same time his attitude toward the canon was a pragmatic one. He did not pretend that the church could undertake the construction of the canon anew, or that it could function with a canon open at both ends. Never, even at the height of his criticism of James, did he drop it from his editions of the Bible, any more than he dropped the Old Testament Apocrypha. From his own experience he could testify that often a Christian found one or another book of the canon difficult or useless to him at a particular time, only to discover later on that it was just what he needed in a time of trouble or temptation.[64] Had such a person been permitted to re-edit the canon on the basis of his passing mood, he would have been deprived of the patience and comfort of the Scriptures when he needed them most. Within the received canon Luther made sharp distinctions, to the point of constructing

[61] M. Reu, *Luther and the Scriptures* (Columbus, 1944), pp. 38—48.

[62] Ebeling, *Evangelische Evangelienauslegung*, pp. 402 ff.

[63] See the comments of Hartmann Grisar, S. J., *Martin Luther: His Life and Work*, translated by Frank J. Eble (Westminster, Md., 1950), pp. 263 and 264.

[64] Paul Althaus, *Gehorsam und Freiheit in Luthers Stellung zur Bibel*, in *Theologische Aufsätze* (Gütersloh, 1929), pp. 140 ff.

a private miniature canon.[65] But he was realistic enough in his theology to know that one had to operate with the canon as given by tradition. That realism provided the framework within which he could say and do the things he did in relation to the canon without involving himself in a hopeless set of contradictions.

Luther could not have been the exegete he was without the help of the church's tradition. The tradition gave him a footing on which he could and did move and shift, but which he never lost. But this was so because he believed that under this footing was the foundation of the Scriptures themselves, which he, as an expositor of the Scriptures and also as a son of the church, was to receive gratefully. Was this "dogmatic exegesis"? Yes, because Luther knew that he could not jump out of his own historical skin into some mythical "undogmatic Gospel" which he was to recover. No, because Luther knew the difference between gratitude and idolatry in the reception of the church's heritage. In this sense he advanced the audacious claim that by his exposition of the Scriptures he was a most loyal defender of the tradition, and that the idolatrous traditionalism of his opponents could mean the eventual destruction both of Scripture and of tradition.

[65] Cf. *Luther's Works*, 21, p. xv.

CHAPTER FIVE

The History of the People of God

ONE of the most obvious ways in which Luther diverged from the tradition of the church in his exegesis was his abandonment of allegorical interpretation.[1] "Beware of allegories"[2] was the motto of many of his lectures to his students. Gerhard Ebeling has documented in great detail the story of Luther's break with allegory, and there is no point in recounting the story here.[3] Yet it is important to see that a third component of Luther's exegesis, alongside his doctrine of the Word and his view of tradition, was his desire to read the Scriptures as history. Over and over he criticized both the fathers and the more recent expositors for their inability or refusal to recognize that the writers of the Scriptures intended to present history, not allegory, in their narratives.[4]

At the same time the history which Luther read in the Biblical narratives was not just any history; it was a special and particular history, the history of the church as the people of God. This qualifies and revises the interpretation of Luther's exegesis one often meets in secondary works, according to which Luther substituted a literalistic historical

[1] In an earlier form this chapter appeared as *Die Kirche nach Luthers Genesisvorlesung* in Vilmos Vajta (ed.), *Lutherforschung heute* (Berlin, 1958), pp. 102—110.

[2] *Lectures on Isaiah* (1527—30), W, XXXI-II, 243.

[3] Gerhard Ebeling, *Evangelische Evangelienauslegung* (Munich, 1942), pp. 44—89.

[4] "This is toying with ill-timed allegories (for Moses is relating history); it is not interpreting Scripture." *Lectures on Genesis* (1535—45), W, XLII, 15—16; *Luther's Works*, 1, 19.

exegesis for the earlier "spiritual" exegesis of the fathers.[5] The principle that Biblical history was always church history enabled Luther to attach the label "historical" to an exegesis of the Scriptures which seems to modern eyes allegorical or at least typological. Instead of developing this principle theoretically on the basis of Luther's own statements, as we have the principles expounded in the preceding two chapters, this chapter will analyze the principles on the basis of Luther's *Lectures on Genesis*.[6] It will examine the exegetical techniques and methods he employed to define and defend his doctrine of the church against several sets of opponents. Thus it will also prepare for the discussion in chapter six of the interrelations between commentary and controversy in Luther's exegesis.

Ever since the pioneering work of Erich Seeberg and particularly of Peter Meinhold any scholar who has undertaken an investigation of Luther's *Genesis* has found almost irresistible the temptation to engage in source analysis.[7] Such

[5] "It would appear," writes C. S. Lewis, "that all allegories whatever are likely to seem Catholic to the general reader, and this phenomenon is worth investigation. In part, no doubt, it is to be explained by the fact that the visible and tangible aspects of Catholicism are medieval, and therefore steeped in literary suggestion. But is this all? Do Protestant allegorists continue as in a dream to use imagery so likely to mislead their readers without noticing the danger or without better motive than laziness for incurring it? By no means. The truth is not that allegory is Catholic, but that Catholicism is allegorical. Allegory consists in giving an imagined body to the immaterial; but if, in each case, Catholicism claims already to have given it a material body, then the allegorist's symbol will naturally resemble that material body." *The Allegory of Love. A Study in Mediaeval Tradition* (Oxford, 1951), p. 322.

[6] Because of the many quotations from the *Lectures on Genesis* (1535 to 1545), W, XLII—XLIV, I have not repeated the title in each note but have given only the reference to the Weimar edition.

[7] Erich Seeberg, *Studien zu Luthers Genesisvorlesung* (Gütersloh, 1932); Peter Meinhold, *Die Genesisvorlesung Luthers und ihre Herausgeber* (Stuttgart, 1936).

a temptation becomes especially strong when the issue at hand is the doctrine of the church, for the oft-discussed and sometimes exaggerated differences between Luther's view of the church and Melanchthon's would provide the scholar with a convenient set of criteria for assigning various segments of the commentary to one or another redactorial hand. Any study of the commentary will bear out the importance of the caveat issued by Seeberg and Meinhold; but in the *Lectures on Genesis,* as in the Book of Genesis itself, it is far easier to develop a general hypothesis regarding multiple sources than it is indisputably to ascribe any specific section to its proper source. In other words, it is necessary to be as cautious in adopting Meinhold's results *in toto* as in accepting the commentary *in toto* at its face value. This problem is discussed further in the introduction to the first volume of this set.

For Luther the Book of Genesis was a book for the church. The command and the promise attendant upon Abram's departure from Ur of the Chaldeans were a condensation of the whole history of the church; Jacob's exile showed the fate of the church in all ages; and the genealogy of Abraham was the history of the first church.[8] Thus, as we shall see in detail, Luther was able to find the history of the church in every part of Genesis. Yet he was reluctant to embark upon an allegorical method to find it there. Genesis was the history of the people of God. The allegory of the church as the ark was harmless, and he had no objection to it; the same was true of the allegory of the church as the woman, though obviously his heart was not in it.[9] But he rejected Lyra's allegory of the sword in Paradise as a symbol of the church, as well as Augustine's allegory of the moon as a sym-

---

[8] W, XLII, 451; XLIII, 567; XLII, 427.
[9] W, XLII, 310; XLII, 98–99.

bol of the church.[10] Still the church was everywhere, for
God was not without His people.[11]

In expounding the Book of Genesis, Luther knew that
he was dealing with Hebrew Scripture. Despite his ability
to separate his view of the Old Testament from his view of
the Jews,[12] therefore, one of his continuing exegetical concerns in Genesis was with the title "people of God" and with
the question of how that title might legitimately be applied
to the Christian Church rather than to the Jewish nation.
The Jews continually said: "We are Israel!"[13] But Luther
insisted: "We are that people, as Moses said of his Jews."[14]
He did not question that God had chosen the Jews to be
peculiarly His, as the story of Cain and Abel showed; Jacob's
paternal blessing indicated that in spite of sinners and hypocrites the church was gathered in Israel.[15] But Luther was
always careful to expound the passages citing Israel's status
in such a way as to make room, *ex post facto,* for Israel's
rejection and for the creation of the new Israel; the prerogative of the Jews was that God manifested Himself to
them in His Word.[16] Thus Luther could give them all due
honor as the people of God and at the same time lay claim
to that title for the church. And he maintained that this had
been the intention behind the establishment of the people
of God all along. Commenting on the name Shiloh, he found
God saying through the prophets: "My people is the one
that believes and that worships Me in the way in which
I have revealed Myself to you. . . . Where that faith and
worship are extinguished, there is no people of God any

10 W, XLII, 172; XLII, 31.
11 W, XLIII, 123.
12 Bornkamm, *Luther und das Alte Testament,* pp. 1 ff.
13 W, XLIII, 536.
14 W, XLIII, 183.
15 W, XLII, 181; XLIV, 793—794.
16 W, XLII, 443.

longer." [17] Even in the Old Testament, therefore, the true
Israel was spiritual.[18]

In expounding the promises of Genesis, Luther took pains
to demonstrate that the blessing promised and the posterity
described were spiritual and not physical. The promise that
Abraham's descendants would be as numerous as the dust
of the earth proved that "the Jews are no longer the people
of God"; the prophecy and promise of the Exodus, given to
Abraham, proved the same thing.[19] The oath to Jacob and
the change of his name could, by a figure of speech, be applied to all the spiritual descendants of Jacob, the true Israel
in the church.[20] To support all this, Luther relied in part
on Rom. 9 and other New Testament discussions which made
a distinction between two Israels.[21] But he also argued from
the texts of the promises themselves. These had not been
fulfilled in the case of the Jewish nation, but they had been
fulfilled in the case of the Christian Church. As he did elsewhere in his writings,[22] he found it possible to argue for or
against a specific interpretation by using post-Biblical history
or even conditions in his own time as the minor premise of
a hypothetical syllogism: "If the promises applied to the
physical race of Israel, Israel would not be desolate today.
But Israel is desolate. Therefore it is clear that the promises
could not have applied to the physical race." [23] But like
his parallel doctrine of the Antichrist, whose minor premise
came from history, this exegesis failed to make quite clear
where the limits of such an exegetical argument from history
might lie.

[17] W, XLIV, 782.
[18] W, XLIV, 192.
[19] W, XLII, 520; XLII, 575.
[20] W, XLIV, 114.
[21] W, XLIV, 192.
[22] See pp. 117—118.
[23] W, XLII, 655—656.

As Luther's exegesis of the promises in Genesis was calculated to make possible the rise of a new Israel, so also
his exegesis of the curses in Genesis was aimed at finding
parallels between the apostasy of Israel and that of the
person being cursed. "Esau has the birthright. But he de-
spises it, and by despising it he loses it. Finally he is
despised, rejected, and despoiled. Therefore his boasting
amounts to nothing." [24] The story of Noah and Ham reminded Luther that "because they refused to listen to the
prophets during the entire period of the monarchy, God . . .
rejected His people, choosing instead the filth and refuse
of the world." [25] Even the curse of Adam meant that the
Jewish church was laid waste when it wandered off into disobedience and paganism.[26] Thus the promises of God given
to Israel were conditional. Israel's failure to live up to the
conditions had brought about Israel's rejection. The true
Israel was that people which did live up to the conditions.
Now the church had become a church of Jews and Gentiles.
Indeed, the shameful story of Tamar showed that Jews and
Gentiles were brothers, with no discrimination between them
in the one church.[27] When Jacob's Gentile neighbors sacrificed with him, that was another indication of the composite
nature of the church.[28] Already in the blessing of Noah "the
church of both Gentiles and Jews was depicted." [29] But it
was only in the New Testament that this process was com-
pleted, as Luther pointed out in a pregnant typology: Babel,
which preceded the calling of the old Israel, had been un-
done by Pentecost, where the body of Christ was formed.[30]

[24] W, XLIII, 428.
[25] W, XLIII, 381.
[26] W, XLII, 154.
[27] W, XLIV, 312.
[28] W, XLIV, 184.
[29] W, XLII, 388.
[30] W, XLII, 413.

In short, the Jews were right in claiming that only Abraham's posterity could be the people of God. But Luther's exegesis came to the conclusion that in promises and in curses, as well as in certain prefigurative incidents and statements, the Book of Genesis provided a key to the true identity of Abraham's posterity, and that therefore "we are God's people and the true church," the descendants of Abraham.[31]

Yet Luther's exegetical struggle with the Jews over the title "people of God" did not involve existential alternatives for him and his audience. A much more serious struggle was that with Roman Catholicism, and in it Luther used different exegetical procedures. In fact, while he argued against Jews on the grounds that they were so desolate, he laid claim to the titles "church" and "people of God" for the Protestant party on the grounds that, like the patriarchs, the true church suffered tribulation, while the false church of the papists was flourishing. The whole battle, he said on the basis of the story of Joseph, was over the claim to those titles.[32] As he carried on that battle with Roman Catholicism, it seems possible to distinguish at least three exegetical principles which Luther employed to find the church in Genesis. One of the principles was: to identify the conflicts in Genesis as representative of the continuing conflict between the true church and the false church. As Rachel's theft of the idols showed, this conflict had never ceased.[33] On the basis of a suggestion in Augustine's *City of God* Luther saw the beginning of the conflict in the story of Cain and Abel, though the temptation of Adam already reminded him of the rise of heresy in the church, and the fall of Eve prefigured the rejection of the Word.[34] There had always been "the hate between Cain

---

[31] W, XLII, 575.

[32] W, XLIV, 496.

[33] W, XLIV, 23.

[34] Augustine, *The City of God*, Book XV, ch. 7, *NPNF*-I, II, 288. W, XLII, 187; XLII, 229; XLII, 109; XLII, 118.

and Abel, Ishmael and Isaac, Esau and Jacob, the church of God and the church of the devil." [35] More even than the story of Cain and Abel, the conflict between Esau and Jacob showed that the false church had glory and power, while the true church was despised and humiliated. Esau was a bishop, a king and a pope in the church; incidentally, both Nimrod and Laban also earned the title "pope." [36] Esau's church, urged on by his wives, persecuted the true church.[37] It was in connection with the church of Esau that Luther described and defined the dual nature of the church more succinctly than he did anywhere else in the *Lectures on Genesis:* "The church is of two kinds: the one has the numbers, the other has the merit; the one has the appearance, the other has the reality; the one is a church in name, the other is a church in fact." [38] Scattered through the commentary were several excursuses on the contrast between the true church and the false church.[39] Most of them provide considerable opportunity for literary analysis, giving the impression of having been interpolated at the places where they seemed to be most appropriate. However that may be, the application of the fraternal conflicts in these narratives to the relation between the Roman Catholic and the Protestant parties must have been a favorite device in Luther's lectures. It enabled him to refute the claims that Roman Catholicism made on the basis of outward appearance, history, tradition, and similar criteria. Throughout the Genesis account the judgment of God consistently favored the oppressed party, the true church — Abel, Abraham, Isaac,

[35] W, XLIII, 384.

[36] W, XLIII, 418; XLIII, 499; XLII, 401; XLIII, 681.

[37] W, XLIII, 495—496.

[38] W, XLIII, 428. This terminology is Augustinian; cf. Fritz Hofmann, *Der Kirchenbegriff des hl. Augustinus* (Munich, 1933), p. 244.

[39] For example, W, XLIII, 597 ff.

Jacob — while Rome was the church of Cain.[40] That judgment, Luther warned, would one day be visited upon Rome too. In it "God will declare that He favors the suffering and hungry church but damns the hypocritical and bloody church."[41] To make his point Luther interpreted Abel's sacrifice eschatologically: God was pleased with it and showed His pleasure then and there, but the church had to wait for His judgment.

Referring the conflict of the churches to the judgment of God as illustrated in Genesis also enabled Luther to show from Genesis that externals did not guarantee the presence of the church. Noah was alone, yet the church was with him; for "size does not make the church."[42] Especially effective here was the story of Ishmael and Isaac. Ishmael was the first-born, but Isaac was the child of promise: "the people of God are not those who have the physical succession but those who have the promise and who believe it."[43] This showed that the church had nothing by right, but only by grace.[44] To be the church, it was not enough to claim apostolic succession or Peter's throne; what was necessary was the call and the promise of God.[45] This insight into the nature of the church was what Luther called "the principal article of our faith and our highest wisdom."[46] Esau was also the first born, but Jacob received the promise; in fact, the birthright was already his by promise when Esau "sold" it to him. In the same way the Reformation party was the church, despite outward appearances.[47] Luther went so far

[40] W, XLII, 192.
[41] W, XLII, 189.
[42] W, XLII, 332 ff.
[43] W, XLIII, 157 ff.
[44] W, XLIII, 166.
[45] W, XLIII, 387.
[46] W, XLIII, 182.
[47] W, XLIII, 425.

as to say that not even the external promise was sufficient to guarantee the church's presence, and he cited the case of Esau's descendants to prove it.[48] As the judgment of God finally settled the conflict between the two churches, so the freedom of God determined when and where the true church was to arise. Luther found this documented in the call of Abram. The true church was with Shem and his followers. Nevertheless, "God, so to speak, overlooks all of these and . . . chooses an idolater, a stranger from God, to be a patriarch."[49] Luther emphasized this freedom of God in opposition to the Roman Catholic claims of legitimacy and of guaranteed rights to the title "church." As will be pointed out, his exegesis was equally insistent on the obverse side of this emphasis: the availability of God to the church in the means of grace.

Thus the patriarchal church could find its consolation in that which made it the church, even when it was in the minority. Joseph was plunged into exile; but he could be assured of God's voice and presence, just as Christians could be assured through Baptism, absolution, and the Lord's Supper.[50] Luther was particularly moved to look for such consolation and assurance because he saw parallels between the way he was defying Rome and the way the patriarchs remained obedient to God even when they were outnumbered. The members of the established church mocked Noah and asked: "Are you the only one who is wise? Are you the only one who is pleasing to God? Are all the rest of us in the wrong, and will we all be damned? Are you the only one who is infallible and who will not be damned?"[51] Luther compressed a great deal of self-searching into a few words

[48] W, XLIV, 211.
[49] W, XLII, 37—38.
[50] W, XLIV, 272.
[51] W, XLII, 300.

when he admitted that he could not have endured this mockery from the church.[52] Similar self-searching lay behind his description of Abraham's loneliness. Like Luther, Abraham forsook the religion of his youth.[53] What Noah's critics said to Noah, Abraham said to himself: "Are you the only one who is holy? Are you the only one about whom God cares?"[54] His exegesis of the history of the people of God in the Genesis record taught Luther "how very difficult it is . . . single-handedly to set oneself against the consensus of all the other churches." [55] But this history also taught him to look away from the outward appearances, away from numbers and size and power, to that which actually constituted the church. Since it was the freedom and the condescension of God that constituted the church, one man could be the church, if God so pleased; this could be Noah or Abraham, or even Luther.

At the same time Luther did not minimize externals in such a way as to forget the necessity of external forms in the church. There are some statements in the commentary that sound as though he did. He talked about "degeneration from the simplicity of antiquity"; about "the very bare, pure, and simple religion" given to Adam in the garden; about sacrifices as an ordinance for the sake of ignorant people — all statements that sound like echoes of Renaissance or even Enlightenment rationalism.[56] But to evaluate such statements, it is necessary to note that they were only half of a fundamental exegetical principle: to expound the priestly sections of the Pentateuch in such a way as simultaneously to condemn ritualism and to exalt the significance of rituals. For example, shortly after the statement just quoted regarding the reli-

[52] W, XLII, 323–324.
[53] W, XLII, 440.
[54] W, XLII, 471.
[55] W, XLII, 301.
[56] W, XLIII, 333; XLII, 80 ff.; XLIV, 173.

gion of Adam, Luther added that when Adam was forbidden to eat from the tree, this was the establishment of outward forms of worship for the church to come.[57] An even more striking instance of this method came in the interpretation of the story of Ishmael. Earlier Luther had pointed out that Abraham's worship was very simple: "no stone, no building, no honor paid to gold and silver." [58] In the same way the Ishmael story taught him that "the chief worship of God does not lie in building churches or in multiplying ceremonies; for all these things are childish and silly." [59] Yet he added that God used these very things to invite men to Himself. And a little later — if the integrity of the material has been preserved at this point, it might even have been in the same lecture — he declared that in Ishmael's house some of the children and other members of the household were converted to genuine piety as a result of the ceremonies.[60] For he realized that "outward spiritual matters cannot be administered without outward ceremonies." [61] Because there was a church in Sodom, there had to be cultus and ceremonies.[62] The exposition of passages in Genesis on sacrifice and worship gave Luther an opportunity he did not have very often in his polemical writings: to combine a prophetic warning against externalism and ceremonialism with a priestly stress on the need for externals and ceremonies — both at the same time. This illustrates our earlier observation regarding the relation between polemical and exegetical theology — a relation to which we shall return in the next chapters.

57 W, XLII, 105.
58 W, XLII, 500.
59 W, XLIII, 368.
60 W, XLIII, 372.
61 W, XLIII, 521.
62 W, XLIII, 54.

. These passages on sacrifice also enabled Luther to show the priority of the Word of God in the church. In interpreting Jacob's construction of the altar at Shechem he pointed out that the altar "was not erected for pomp or show, nor for the sacrifices of the Mass, but for the preaching of the Word." [63]   In fact, it was axiomatic that wherever altars were mentioned, their purpose was "not for sacrifice but for the preaching of the Word." [64]   It was yet another attack upon Roman Catholicism when Luther pointed out in connection with the Deluge that "the church is a daughter, born of the Word, not the mother of the Word." [65]   For that matter, the whole story of Noah was an illustration of how the church needed to obey the Word.[66] Likewise, the willingness of Isaac and Rebecca to send Jacob to Laban indicated that the church was present in Haran because the Word was there, and vice versa.[67] When Abraham was to begin a new church, he had to have a new Word of God.[68] The antiquity of the church, going back to Adam in the garden, was validated by the preaching of the Word, when there was no written Word because there was neither paper nor ink.[69] Conversely, a neglect of the Word would bring heresy upon the church, as it brought death upon Lot's wife.[70] Luther's exegesis of the Book of Genesis thus provided him with ample proof for his contention that the Word of God (mediated, as we shall see, through the ministry) was always constitutive of the church. He read the conflicts in Genesis as particular instances of the general conflict between the

63 W, XLIV, 138–139.
64 W, XLIII, 483.
65 W, XLII, 334.
66 W, XLII, 341–342.
67 W, XLIII, 573.
68 W, XLII, 230.
69 W, XLII, 80.
70 W, XLIII, 90.

true church and the false church. His exegesis showed him that the freedom and sovereignty of God manifested in Genesis would ultimately vindicate the cause of the true church against the false church. In his interpretation of the worship of the patriarchal church Luther found the right balance between the priestly and the prophetic. These three themes, which ran throughout the history of the people of God in the Book of Genesis, gave Luther the exegetical weapons he needed against Roman Catholicism.

Since the beginning of his theological career Luther had been searching for exegetical support in his attack upon Roman Catholicism. The results of that search were evident, for example, in the exegetical discussions at Leipzig, which we shall analyze in chapter six. A later conflict over the doctrine of the church came from another source, from the "fanatics" on the left wing of the Reformation. They, too, claimed to be the people of God.[71] Luther saw them turning against him from some of the very same arguments he had been using against Roman Catholicism.[72] Here in the *Genesis* he met those arguments with two fundamental exegetical principles. Both of them, at least in their beginnings, antedated the conflict with the left wing, as did most of Luther's other positions in this controversy.[73] One of these exegetical principles was to interpret the theophanies in Genesis as appearances of the ministry of the Word of God. The other principle was to interpret the promises and signs in Genesis as proof that God had always worked through both Word and Sacrament to call the church into being.

[71] W, XLIII, 643.

[72] For example, the argument from martyrdom and from their minority status as proof of the righteousness of their cause. Cf. *Instruction to the Clergy to Preach Against Usury* (1540), W, LI, 400—401.

[73] That is the thesis of Regin Prenter's *Spiritus Creator*.

One of the most remarkable exegetical feats in the whole *Lectures on Genesis* was the consistency with which Luther's exegesis related the manifestations and revelations of God to the ministry.[74] Like the scene at Mamre, all these theophanies were intended to magnify the dignity of the ministry.[75] Luther's opponents on the left wing were interpreting the visions and dreams of the Scriptures in support of their own claims to immediate divine revelation.[76] Therefore it was not enough for him merely to find Christ as "the Son of God who was to become incarnate" in some of the theophanies; [77] he had to find the ministry in them. If possible, this was the ministry of men; in a few cases, where that was manifestly impossible, it was the ministry of angels. Luther received help in this tour de force from an unexpected quarter, his literal interpretation of the accounts about the longevity of the patriarchs. Thus he could contemplate a true golden age, when all these holy men lived together and preached.[78] And wherever Genesis said that God spoke, Luther was able, by his computation of Old Testament chronology, to find a patriarch still alive to do the speaking in God's name.[79]

In the case of "Adam, where are you?" this was obviously impossible; but Luther was pleased with the suggestion that

[74] Therefore I cannot accept Meinhold's contention that this "emphasis upon the ministry" as such is evidence of an "alien theology," *Genesisvorlesung*, p. 373; for this is a general exegetical device in Luther, as, for example, in the *Commentary on Psalm 110* (1535), W, XLI, 124; *Luther's Works*, 13, 265.

[75] W, XLIII, 41.

[76] W, XLIV, 487.

[77] W, XLIV, 96.

[78] W, XLII, 245–246.

[79] He had been engaged in the computation of Old Testament chronology in preparation for his *Computation of the Years of the World* (1541), W, LIII, 22–184.

even here God did not speak directly but through an angel.[80] God asked Cain what he had done with Abel, but He did so through the mouth of Adam.[81] God told Noah to enter the ark, but He did so through the ministry, perhaps through Methuselah.[82] The call to Abraham was "not immediately from God"; God used "certain holy men, inspired by the Holy Spirit." [83] God spoke to Abraham through a human ministry, as described by Paul.[84] It took an external word, not merely a theophany, to persuade Abraham not to sacrifice Isaac; otherwise he could not have been certain.[85] God spoke to Hagar in the wilderness of Beersheba by the ministry of an angel, but He told Christians to hearken to the ministry of men.[86] When Genesis said that Rebecca consulted the Lord, this meant that she consulted a patriarch, most likely Shem.[87] And when it said that the Lord spoke to her, Luther added the gloss: "*scilicet,* through Shem." [88] Possibly as a result of further chronological computation Luther suggested that it might have been Eber rather than Shem. But whoever it was, a spoken Word of God from a minister was what emboldened Rebecca to trick Isaac into conferring the blessing upon Jacob.[89] She would never have had the courage to do this on her own initiative, but she was full of faith and of the Spirit, and therefore obeyed that spoken Word.[90] God's command to Jacob to go up to Bethel may well have

[80] W, XLII, 129.
[81] W, XLII, 204.
[82] W, XLII, 320—321.
[83] W, XLII, 439.
[84] W, XLII, 518.
[85] W, XLIII, 227.
[86] XLIII, 182.
[87] W, XLII, 425; XLIII, 394.
[88] W, XLIII, 396.
[89] W, XLIII, 505.
[90] W, XLIII, 509.

been through a minister, possible through Isaac or even through Deborah.[91] When Joseph explained Pharaoh's dream to him, this, too, was the ministry of the Word of God.[92] Sometimes there were obstacles in the way of such "historical" exegesis, but Luther retained the emphasis on the people of God and the ministry throughout his interpretation. We have already noted the case of the voice of the Lord in the garden, where Luther suggested that an angel was the agency. He used the same device in one of the theophanies to Jacob.[93] The history of Joseph was an indication to him that even when God chose to manifest Himself in a dream, He sent along a true prophet to expound the dream orally.[94] Thus even the Biblical accounts of revelations in dreams could be interpreted in such a way as to support the dignity of the ministry.

Believing as he did that "the church is holy because the ministry is pure," [95] Luther used every possible exegetical device to interpret the immediate revelations of Genesis in a manner consistent with the way God had always revealed Himself to His people. In the hostility of the "fanatics" toward the ministry he claimed to see an instance of their general antipathy toward the means of divine self-disclosure.[96] The Book of Genesis suggested that they did not understand the church because this antipathy drove them to spurn the human instruments that God used; in this respect the heretics were all alike.[97] Luther, therefore, made it an exegetical principle to show that as there could be no Spirit without

[91] W, XLIV, 166—167; XLIV, 190.
[92] W, XIV, 421.
[93] W, XLIII, 442.
[94] W, XLIV, 249.
[95] W, XLIV, 25.
[96] W, XLIII, 599—600.
[97] W, XLIII, 70; XLII, 625 ff.

the Word, so there could be no Word and no church without the Sacraments. Early in the *Lectures on Genesis,* discussing the sacrifices of Cain and Abel, he summarized this point. There was no sacrifice "without the preaching of the Word. God is not worshiped with a mute work; there must be the sound of a word. . . . But God always establishes some outward and visible sign of His grace alongside the Word. . . . an outward sign and work or Sacrament. . . . Thus the church has never been without outward signs." [98] God added these signs to give the church a means of assurance that it was pleasing to Him; and when He added them, the church came into being.[99] Hence the church of the patriarchs had both Word and Sacraments.[100]

In support of this contention Luther looked for the various signs that attended God's words and promises to the patriarchs. The tree of the knowledge of good and evil, like the elements in the Christian Sacraments, had no power in itself; but God, "so to speak, clothed a creature" with His Word to give it power.[101] Thus Luther's exegesis of this story was free of all animism. God made clothes for Adam and Eve as a memorial and sign of their terrible fall.[102] But after the Fall they also had sacrifices and signs of grace to console and assure them, as the church had the Word, Baptism, and the Eucharist.[103] The rainbow proved that God always attached a sign to His promises.[104] Luther interpreted passages on circumcision not only to strengthen his exegetical case against the Anabaptists but also to reflect upon the outward

[98] W, XLII, 184.
[99] W, XLII, 242–243.
[100] W, XLII, 401.
[101] W, XLII, 170.
[102] W, XLII, 165.
[103] W, XLII, 184 ff.
[104] W, XLII, 363.

signs which God joined to His promise and covenant.[105] Even
the Hebrew custom of swearing to a person with a hand on
his thigh became, in Luther's exegesis, a way of inculcating
the coming incarnation of Christ, "not only by a Word but
also by an outward action and sign." [106] God revealed Himself in physical forms; in the New Testament church these
were the Sacraments.[107] And this did not stop with the coming of Christ. As a matter of fact, one of the principal ad-
vantages the New Testament people of God enjoyed over
the Old Testament people were their Sacraments.[108] Luther
interpreted this as the way God had gathered a church for
Himself in every age of history, though men had despised
the foolish means of grace He had chosen.[109]

Both these exegetical principles, the stress on the ministry and the emphasis on the signs always attached to the
Word even in the Old Testament, were Luther's way of
finding the history of the people of God throughout the
Scriptures. Research into Luther's exegesis has sometimes
been content to recite his strictures upon allegorical exegesis.
This has created the impression that he broke altogether with
the tradition of "spiritual" interpretation of the Bible. A more
accurate formula to designate what he envisioned and accomplished as an expositor is the term "the history of the
people of God." He saw the Scriptures as history, in contra-
distinction to an extreme allegorism which tended to rush
past the historical sense with undue haste. But in contra-
distinction both to literal exegesis and to historical exegesis,
as these are practiced by opposing schools of Biblical interpretation in modern Protestantism, Luther made the doctrine

[105] W, XLII, 622; XLII, 609 ff.
[106] W, XLIII, 307.
[107] W, XLIII, 462.
[108] W, XLII, 636—637.
[109] W, XLII, 651—652.

of the church a basic component of what he meant by "literal"
and by "historical." He was forced to clarify what he meant
because of the theological controversies which his reformatory work evoked. For that very reason, however, it becomes
necessary to consider a fourth component in his exegesis —
the role of polemics. To this we turn in chapter six.

CHAPTER SIX

Commentary and Controversy

As the preceding chapter has already made clear, a fourth component of Luther's exegesis was theological controversy. He divided his time and attention as a theologian between the two basic tasks of expounding the Scriptures and waging controversy. It is, of course, true that finally these were not two separate tasks at all. Luther's commentaries on the Bible constantly argued with his opponents living and dead, as chapter five has shown. On the other hand, Luther's polemical works fairly bristled with Biblical citations and Biblical exposition. This mutual influence of commentary and controversy was so basic to Luther's expository work that it deserves to be classified as a component of his exegesis alongside the other three components described in earlier chapters.

The theological controversies in which Luther engaged dealt with issues and opinions that came out of his exegesis. He often charged that his opponents had permitted controversy to blind them to the true meaning of the Scriptures, and his opponents often made the same charge against him.[1] If these charges were true, it was not the first time in the history of theology that this had happened, nor yet the last. Nevertheless, it is also possible that something quite different was happening in Luther's theological controversies, in addition to the overemphasis that may have been present. Possibly it was only in controversy that Luther found the true

[1] See p. 121, note 54.

meaning of the Scriptures at one or another crucial place.[2] As a debater, lecturer, and preacher accustomed to think on his feet, Luther seems frequently to have developed insights ad lib which had escaped him during the calm reflection of his study. Thus the problem of the mutual influence of commentary and controversy in Luther is a complex one. He was not merely defending his view of the exegesis of the Scriptures in a controversy; he was shaping it. He was not merely using the Scriptures to support his previous exegesis; he was re-examining his exegesis in the light of further study of the Scriptures.

To deal with this problem of commentary and controversy, this chapter will take up two of the controversies in which Luther was involved: that with John Eck as an illustration of how he dealt with the Scriptures in his polemics against Roman Catholicism; and that with Ulrich Zwingli as an example of how he used the Scriptures in his battle against various forms of Protestantism. In each case we have selected two passages of Scripture prominent in the controversy, one that Luther regarded as irrelevant to the issue and one that he regarded as decisive in its importance. We shall examine his reasons for eliminating the one and his procedure in interpreting the other. Thus we shall see how in Luther the expositor commentary and controversy interacted.

Luther's controversy at Leipzig with John Eck made clear to everyone, including Luther himself, just how far he had been alienated from what passed for normative Western Catholic theology.[3] A central element in that clarification was his realization of the difference in the use which the two sides made of the Scriptures. At Leipzig, Luther con-

[2] See pp. 36—38.
[3] Cf. *The Leipzig Debate* (1519), W, II, 158—161; *Luther's Works,* 31, 313—325.

cluded that though Eck was "a man variously and richly
learned in human knowledge and scholastic opinions, he was
a miserable debater on the Sacred Scriptures." [4] Eck, on the
other hand, demanded that Luther interpret the Sacred Scriptures "in accordance, not with his own ideas but with those
of the saints." [5] Thus two methods of Biblical exegesis met
head-on: one subjected itself to tradition and ecclesiastical
authority; the other struck at the meaning of the text, even
though that meaning might have eluded many great saints
in the past.

The contrast between the two methods of exegesis was
apparent in the dispute over the applicability of John 5:19
to the question of papal primacy: "The Son can do nothing
of His own accord, but only what He sees the Father doing."
Eck introduced the text into the debate on the primacy of
the pope near the beginning of his first protestation against
Luther on July 4, 1519. He used it to prove his general
contention that through Christ God had established an ordered hierarchy in the universe, and that the hierarchy in
the organization of the church was a specific instance of this
hierarchical structure in the very nature of things. [6] Luther
replied that "according to the opinion of all the theologians,"
this text spoke neither of the church militant nor of the
church triumphant but of the equality of the Son with the
Father; he therefore debarred it as irrelevant to the point
in question. [7] Eck's response was that "the holy and inestim-
ably praiseworthy father, Bernard of Clairvaux," had used
this text to demonstrate the existence in the universe of
an ordered hierarchy, to which the hierarchy in the church

[4] *Luther's Resolutions* (1519), W, II, 393.
[5] *Leipzig Disputation* (1519), W, II, 304.
[6] Ibid., p. 255.
[7] Ibid., p. 257.

was an analogy.[8] Despite his reverence for Bernard,[9] Luther had to say that here the medieval doctor was using a passage for illustration rather than for proof; for the text did not establish this teaching.[10] Eck took this as an insult to the holy fathers and continued to maintain that from the relation of the Son to the Father, as taught by this text, it was possible to argue to the point Bernard was making.[11]

Two features of this dispute were particularly important for a consideration of Luther's exegesis. One was Luther's insistence that in a theological controversy, where proof rather than mere illustration was needed, only the precise meaning of a Scriptural text was to be used. He did not mean that it was altogether illegitimate to use Scriptural passages for the illustration of a point analogous to their meaning. His sermons and commentaries abounded with instances of just such use, some of them skillful, others humorous. But he put such use of the Scriptures into the same category as allegory. It was legitimate for illumination, not for support. "In a controversy," he said, "one must take the correct and proper meaning of Scripture, which can stand up in battle. Occasionally the fathers depart from this meaning in order to embellish their speech. There is nothing wrong with this."[12] Eck believed that no passage of Scriptures could conceivably conflict with the catholic faith as it was already known and possessed.[13] Therefore

---

[8] Ibid., p. 260.

[9] Indicated by passages like *Commentary on Psalm 117* (1530), W, XXXI, 256; *Luther's Works*, 14, 38.

[10] *Leipzig Disputation* (1519), W, II, 264.

[11] Ibid., pp. 267–268, p. 282.

[12] Ibid., p. 264.

[13] As Hofmann says of Augustine's exegesis, op. cit., p. 298: "It is one of the chief principles of Augustinian exegesis that Scripture cannot conflict with the faith of the church and that it must therefore be expounded accordingly under all circumstances."

every passage was, in a sense, illustrative of this catholic faith, which was an *a priori* of Biblical interpretation. Arguments from analogy, like arguments from allegory, were a legitimate way of supporting a doctrinal position, provided that this doctrinal position was part of the catholic faith. Any passage was a possible proof, and no passage was a necessary proof. In Luther and Eck we see opposed to each other a fundamentally inductive and a fundamentally deductive method of Biblical exegesis.

Closely allied with this feature of the dispute was a second: Luther's insistence that the Scriptures, not the fathers, should decide a theological controversy. To Luther's charge that John 5:19 was irrelevant Eck replied by referring to St. Bernard: the passage was applicable here just because St. Bernard had applied it here, and Luther's position was a calumny of the fathers. Nowhere in the dispute over the relevance of the passage did Eck embark upon any exegesis of it. He assumed that he understood the meaning of the passage, and that Bernard's exegesis had caught its meaning. What was at stake now was the question whether someone could come along to dispute the traditional interpretation of a passage on whatever grounds. Not only was the catholic faith an *a priori* principle of Biblical exegesis for Eck; so was the assumption of a consensus among the fathers on the meaning of the Scriptures. On the other hand, Luther was not only disputing the relevance of this passage for the issue of papal primacy. He was daring to dispute the correctness of the patristic consensus as an authoritative guide to the exegesis of the passage at all. On both these counts Luther the expositor and Eck the expositor stood in the sharpest contrast.

But the principal exegetical issue at Leipzig was the interpretation of Matt. 16:18: "You are Peter, and on this rock I will build My church, and the gates of hell shall not prevail against it." [14] Luther recognized that this passage was Eck's principal Biblical support in the argument.[15] The exegesis of these words, like that of John 5:19, provided the occasion for a conflict between the two men over the authority of the fathers in the interpretation of the Scriptures. Having just been challenged on the relevance of the passage from John, Eck took pains to introduce the passage from Matthew in the context of a quotation from St. Jerome.[16] Later on he backed up his exegesis of the word "rock" by reference to other authorities — the *glossa ordinaria*, Augustine, Jerome, Ambrose, Chrysostom, Cyprian, Leo, Bede, Bernard, Anacletus, Marcellus, Julius, and the Pope Pelagius.[17] It was, he said, Hussite poison "to claim that you understand Holy Scripture better than the popes, the councils, the doctors, and the universities." [18] For Luther was willing to say that "though Augustine and all the fathers were to take the 'rock' to mean Peter, I should withstand them all alone by the authority of the apostle, that is, by divine right, as he writes (1 Cor. 3:11): 'No other foundation can anyone lay than that which is laid, which is Jesus Christ.' " [19] Later on he made the point that the variety in the fathers' interpretation of the passage also militated against using them as the authority.[20]

The chief question between Eck and Luther in the inter-

[14] Cf. Karl Adam, *Cyprians Kommentar zu Mt. 16, 18 in dogmengeschichtlicher Beleuchtung*, in *Theologische Quartalschrift*, XCIV (1912), 99 ff., 203 ff.; Oscar Cullmann, *Peter*, tr. by Floyd V. Filson (Philadelphia, 1953), pp. 155—238; Charles Journet, *The Primacy of Peter from the Protestant and the Catholic Point of View*, tr. by John Chapin (Westminster, Md., 1954).

[15] *Leipzig Disputation* (1519), W, II, 286.

[16] Ibid., p. 262.

[17] Ibid., pp. 274—275, p. 293.

[18] Ibid., p. 282.

[19] Ibid., p. 278.

[20] Ibid., p. 297.

pretation of Matt. 16:18 was the meaning of the word "rock" in the passage, and much of the argument about the fathers was an argument about their exegesis of that word. By his lengthy parade of patristic sources Eck sought to throw dust in his hearers' eyes and to give the impression that the fathers had unanimously interpreted the word to mean Peter. Luther caught him in this subterfuge and demonstrated from both patristic and liturgical sources that this was not the case.[21] Eck's efforts to show that Augustine was at least not against him in the interpretation of "rock" did little to strengthen his point, and the argument over patristic support ended in a draw.[22] Rejecting the application of the term to the person of Peter, repudiating even more completely the notion that it could be applied to the successors of Peter, Luther came to the conclusion that the word "rock" meant "faith." He argued that the term *My* church" made the word "rock" universal rather than particular, since nothing less than the universal church of Christ was to be built upon the rock. And since the Christian faith was the one universal element among the particular churches, as Jerome had said, faith had to be the rock upon which Christ had built His church.[23] A few years later Luther was to say that the rock was Christ Himself.[24] But in any event it certainly was not the pope. Whatever present-day exegetes may say about Luther's interpretation,[25] it does illustrate his exegetical method of paying more attention to an analysis of the sentence than to a compilation of other people's opinions about what the sentence might mean.

[21] Ibid., p. 286, p. 289.

[22] Cf. *Against Catharinus* (1521), W, VII, 715.

[23] *Leipzig Disputation* (1519), W, II, 272.

[24] *Defense and Explanation of All the Articles* (1521), W, VII, 411 to 412; *Luther's Works*, 32, 68—69.

[25] Cullmann, *Peter*, p. 162.

Eck also tried his hand at such an analysis. In reply to Luther's argument that if Peter had been the rock, his denial would have undermined the church, Eck pointed out somewhat sarcastically that Luther had failed to observe his own rule about the superiority of grammar to Aristotelian philosophy.[26] For the verb in the sentence was in the future tense — "I *will* build" — indicating that the Lord was not building His church by the statement itself but was only promising to do so in the future. Since He was the Way, the Truth, and the Life, He must have kept this promise.[27] To this Luther replied that the words were indeed a promise, but that the Lord had kept the promise when He conferred the Holy Spirit and the authority of absolution not only upon Peter but upon all the apostles.[28]

From the readiness of Luther's response to this point it is clear that instead of ransacking the fathers for the meaning of a passage Luther did what the fathers themselves had done. He endeavored to throw the light of other Biblical material on a passage and to expound a particular passage in the light of the whole of Scripture.[29] In addition to analyzing the passage for its meaning, Luther summoned pertinent material from other parts of the Scriptures. In this case he drew on two incidents in the life of Peter which appeared to demonstrate his incapacity to serve as the rock upon which the church was built. The first was his denial: if Peter had been the rock, this would have meant that the church was felled, not by the gates of hell but by the voice of a maid.[30] The second was the conflict between Peter and Paul, in which Peter kept his faith but sinned against

---

[26] *Leipzig Disputation* (1519), W, II, 282; cf. also p. 267.
[27] Ibid., p. 293.
[28] Ibid., pp. 286—287.
[29] See p. 12, note 20.
[30] *Leipzig Disputation* (1519), W, II, 278.

the truth of the Gospel.[31] Eck's reply to both incidents was a distinction between Peter the man and his apostolic office,[32] a distinction which Luther also employed throughout his own exegesis.[33] According to this distinction, even a mortal sin would not have disqualified Peter or any of his successors as the rock upon which the church was built. The conflict between Peter and Paul, which suggested itself to Luther as a refutation of Eck's exegesis, continued to be of interest to him as his conflict with Rome went on.[34] At the same time it should be noted that Luther did not let the polemical situation divert him from the New Testament teaching that "Peter was the first in honor in the entire world," [35] an interpretation of Petrine primacy that remained with him throughout his career.

The debaters made use of historical material as well as of Biblical material to clarify the meaning of the text. Since the promise declared that the gates of hell would not prevail against the church founded upon the rock, the victory of Islam and of the heretical Hussites over sections of the church persuaded Eck that the text referred specifically to the church at Rome rather than to the church universal, as Luther maintained.[36] It was unthinkable that the promise in the text should have failed of fulfillment; [37] hence the exegetical task was to explain what it could have meant in the light of what had actually taken place in the course of that fulfillment. With this procedure as such Luther had

[31] Ibid., p. 286.

[32] Ibid., pp. 293—294.

[33] Cf., for example, *Commentary on Psalm 90* (1534—35), W, XL-III, 491—492; *Luther's Works*, 13, 80.

[34] Cf. Ebeling, *Evangelienauslegung*, pp. 256 ff.

[35] *Leipzig Disputation* (1519), W, II, 278.

[36] Ibid., p. 262.

[37] Ibid., p. 293.

no quarrel, since he shared its presuppositions.[38] But the introduction of post-Biblical history as a resource for exegesis made such argumentation fair for both sides, and Luther took advantage of the situation. History showed, he said, that the Church of Rome had not been the only one to preserve the faith of the fathers intact. In fact, history testified that at times Rome had even been a party to heresy, as in the days of Arianism.[39] Neither Luther nor Eck made clear just how far such argumentation could legitimately go in exegesis. There was a difference between using post-Biblical or extra-Biblical history for the illumination of what the text meant and calling upon that history for the substantiation or even the determination of what the text meant. Eck could do this more consistently than Luther, because he regarded the history of the church since the first century as revelatory in a sense that Luther did not. Luther never clarified completely why it was legitimate to argue this way from history and yet illegitimate to argue from the fathers.[40]

At Leipzig, Luther came to see the difference between Biblical exegesis and traditionalism. For traditionalism, as exemplified by Eck, the church fathers determined the meaning of the text; for Luther's exegesis, on the other hand, what the fathers said illumined but did not determine what the text meant. A more subtle difference, and in its way an even more important one, was in the very handling of the text. Eck's brief sally into grammatical exegesis proved to be a failure for his position, and he retreated to tradition. Luther's method was to call upon the resources of the Bible and of tradition to help him, not in the substantiation of

[38] *Defense and Explanation of All the Articles* (1521), W, VII, 411; *Luther's Works*, 32, 69.

[39] *Leipzig Disputation* (1519), W, II, 266.

[40] One illustration of this exegetical method is Luther's doctrine of the Antichrist; cf. p. 93 above.

a traditional position but in the clarification of the text. His years of lecturing on the Scriptures stood him in good stead when he began to debate on exegetical issues, but only in controversy did he clarify for himself and for others what he meant by Biblical exposition.

It was in another theological controversy that Luther was to clarify his exegetical procedure still more precisely. That was the controversy with fellow reformers over the Lord's Supper. Against Eck he had maintained that it was his right as a student of the Scriptures to interpret the Scriptures as they read, even if this should involve the rejection of ancient and hallowed interpretations. Yet here he found himself defending what he repeatedly called "the old interpretation" [41] against the exegetical novelties of other Protestants. His opponents were quick to sense the incongruity of the two positions, and they charged him with softness toward Roman Catholicism.[42] This charge Luther repudiated, and he countered with a weird rumor that their theories were being well received by some papal circles as support for the sacrificial interpretation of the Mass.[43] But he did declare that if their way of interpreting Scripture was representative of what went on in Zurich, Basel, and Strassburg, he would prefer that they were Roman Catholics.[44] He would rather hold with the Roman Catholics that only the blood was present than with his fellow Prot-

[41] See Ebeling, *Evangelienauslegung,* pp. 91—273, on Luther's relation to the exegetical tradition.

[42] Throughout this chapter and Part Two of this volume I am heavily dependent on the researches of Walther Koehler, *Zwingli und Luther. Ihr Streit über das Abendmahl nach seinen politischen und religiösen Beziehungen* (2 vols.; Gütersloh, 1924—53). Although it pays less attention to the exegetical issues than one would wish, Koehler's work lays the basis for the kind of exegetical-historical study set forth in the present volume.

[43] *This Is My Body* (1527), W, XXIII, 271.

[44] *Confession on the Lord's Supper* (1528), W, XXVI, 313.

estants that only wine was present.[45] Years later he admitted that his pastoral experience and the spectacle of the left-wing extremists had made him mollify his earlier eagerness to abolish the elevation and other aspects of the Roman Mass.[46] Therefore he felt obliged to defend the eucharistic teaching of the medieval church against these "fanatics." [47]

In addition to defending the medieval church against Carlstadt and Zwingli, Luther also defended his interpretation of the church fathers against them. Just as at Leipzig, both sides claimed to have the fathers on their side, though in this case it was not so urgent a matter for either side to document the claim. Oecolampad had written a book seeking to provide documentation for the claim that the fathers supported a spiritualistic interpretation of the presence of Christ's body and blood in the Sacrament.[48] The book created something of a stir in the circle of Luther's associates, among whom Melanchthon was perhaps the most exercised.[49] Luther was not overly concerned about the question, and he kept his critical attitude toward the fathers. "We are not concerned here," he said, "whether Tertullian and other teachers teach correctly or incorrectly. For we want to build our faith, not upon men but upon the Word of God, the only rock." [50] Still he wanted to rescue the fathers from what he regarded as the distorted interpretations that had been foisted upon them. Therefore he devoted a careful and lengthy discussion to the words of Tertullian and to Oecolampad's interpretation of them, coming to the con-

[45] Ibid., p. 462.

[46] *Brief Confession on the Holy Sacrament* (1544), W, LIV, 162—163.

[47] Ibid., p. 145.

[48] Ernst Staehelin, *Das theologische Lebenswerk Johannes Oekolampads* (Leipzig, 1939), pp. 607—618.

[49] Cf. Helmut Gollwitzer, *Coena Domini* (Munich, n. d. [1938]), pp. 65—96.

[50] *This Is My Body* (1527), W, XXIII, 219.

clusion that "Tertullian confessed Christ's true body under the form of the bread in the Lord's Supper." [51]

Although he went into their patristic and Biblical arguments with great care, Luther had little hope of convincing his opponents that they were wrong and he was right. For he felt sure that exegesis was only a screen for the rationalism which underlay their view of the Sacrament. He was happy that they sometimes admitted this to be their real motive.[52] He complained that usually they refused to acknowledge their rationalism and tried instead to use exegesis in support of their view.[53] No one would believe, Luther argued, that they had come to their position through an exegesis of the passages in the New Testament dealing with Christ's ascension.[54] Because he maintained that they rejected the real presence on rationalistic grounds, he accused them of employing various exegetical artifices to evade the real presence as he found it taught in the Scriptures. "Their lie would not be so coarse nor their shame so great," he said, "if they interpreted the same word in different passages in a dissimilar and different way, or different words in the same passage; but that they interpret the same word in the same passage in the same speech in a different and contradictory way" was a demonstration to him of their insincerity.[55] Still Luther took it as his duty to accept the challenge of their exegesis, for his own sake and for the sake of his people, to find out for sure whether his exegesis was the right one. As at Leipzig, he did this by ruling out of the discussion those passages which he found irrelevant to the

[51] Ibid., pp. 217–229.
[52] Ibid., p. 161.
[53] Ibid., pp. 123–125.
[54] *Confession on the Lord's Supper* (1528), W, XXIV, 316.
[55] Ibid., p. 264.

point in question and by minutely examining the crucial passage which was relevant.

The passage quoted most often against Luther was John 6:63: "It is the spirit that gives life, the flesh is of no avail." Oecolampad called this passage his "iron wall." [56] Luther thought it was paper rather than iron, though he granted that it might have the color of iron.[57] In order to demonstrate the irrelevance of this passage to the question of the real presence, Luther subjected it to a careful analysis. It is useful for a consideration of the relation between commentary and controversy in Luther to compare this analysis with the explanation of the same words which he delivered as part of his sermonic exposition of the sixth, seventh, and eighth chapters of John in 1530 to 1532.[58] The accents were different in the two presentations; but the method of extracting the meaning of the text was remarkably similar, as was the argumentation against other interpretations. We shall return to this comparison later.[59]

Underlying Luther's interpretation was his insistence that the sixth chapter of John was not talking directly about the Lord's Supper at all but about that spiritual eating and drinking of the Lord's body and blood which should indeed be present in the reception of the Lord's Supper, though not only there — in short, about faith. "To the very end of the chapter," so Luther maintained in his polemics, this was the theme of Christ's words.[60] There were times when Luther did apply at least some parts of the chapter to the Sacrament; but from the time of the sacramentarian con-

[56] *This Is My Body* (1527), W, XXIII, 167; cf. *Brief Confession on the Holy Sacrament* (1544), W, LIV, 152.

[57] *This Is My Body* (1527), W, XXIII, 167.

[58] These are contained in *Luther's Works*, 23.

[59] See p. 174.

[60] *Confession on the Lord's Supper* (1528), W, XXVI, 372.

troversy on he continually maintained that the sentence "The flesh is of no avail" did not talk about the Sacrament at all. Still the chapter did talk about eating and drinking, and except for this verse it commended such eating and drinking as essential to the life in God. Hence Luther had to provide a fuller explanation of what he took this verse to mean within a chapter devoted to a discussion of spiritual eating and drinking.

There were two elements in the sentence upon which Luther fastened in his explanation: the word "flesh" and the article. For the interpretation of what the text meant by "flesh" he set down this general axiom: "Where the two words 'flesh' and 'spirit' are set against each other in Scripture, there flesh cannot mean the body of Christ, but it always means the old flesh which is born of the flesh." [61] He later explained that he was referring to passages in which the two words were set in opposition to each other, not to passages like 1 Tim. 3:16, where the two belonged together.[62] The distinction between flesh and spirit had passed through a checkered history.[63] The passages making the distinction had been a favorite support for various Christian Platonists. Even though the words may not originally have been used with a Platonic audience in mind, they certainly acquired Platonic overtones from which it was very difficult to rescue them. But as Luther drew on the Old Testament to de-Platonize the word "spirit," so he also distinguished two uses for the word "flesh" in the New Testament: one referring to the body as God's good creature in which the Son of God had become incarnate, the other

[61] *This Is My Body* (1527), W, XXIII, 193—195.

[62] *Confession on the Lord's Supper* (1528), W, XXVI, 432.

[63] Heinrich Karpp's *Probleme altchristlicher Anthropologie* (Gütersloh, 1950) traces this history through Tertullian, Clement of Alexandria, Lactantius, Arnobius, and Origen.

referring to that phase of human existence which set itself in opposition to God.[64]

A failure to distinguish between these two uses led either to a contempt for physical existence as beneath the dignity of man's immortal soul or to a minimization of the ravages of sin or (as in the case of some elements in medieval theology) to both. The sixth chapter of John's Gospel used the word "flesh" in both senses, and Luther criticized Zwingli for failing to see the shift from the one to the other. To this failure Luther traced Zwingli's inability to interpret either use correctly, as well as his application of the word "flesh" here to the meaning of the word "body" in the words of institution. Luther's exegesis of the Biblical dichotomy between the flesh and the spirit led him to a different conclusion regarding both "body" and "flesh."

The question of the precise meaning of "flesh" in John 6:63 hung in part on the meaning of the definite article attached to it. Luther laid down the axiom here that "as often as Christ speaks of His flesh or body in Scripture, He appends the word 'My' and says, 'My flesh,' 'My body.' " [65] Zwingli's reply was that the word "My" did not have to be appended to "flesh" to make it mean Christ's flesh any more than it was to "spirit" to make it mean His Spirit.[66] Luther countered that there was a fundamental difference between the two terms; for whereas the Spirit of Christ was not His alone but was common to all believers, His flesh was only His. If it were His flesh that was being spoken of here, the personal pronoun "My" would have had to be attached.[67]

---

[64] Cf. Erdmann Schott, *Fleisch und Geist nach Luthers Lehre unter besonderer Berücksichtigung des Begriffes "totus homo"* (Leipzig, 1928).

[65] *This Is My Body* (1527), W, XXIII, 169; see also *Sermons on the Gospel of St. John: Chapters 6–8* (1530–32), W, XXXIII, 183; *Luther's Works*, 23, 119.

[66] Cf. Ebeling, *Evangelienauslegung*, pp. 311–344.

[67] *Confession on the Lord's Supper* (1528), W, XXVI, 376–377.

Therefore Luther contended that the phrase "the flesh" here could not refer to the flesh of Christ but had to refer to "flesh" in the second sense mentioned above, namely, whatever it was in human existence that stood in opposition to God and to His Spirit. It was, according to Luther, a misapplication and distortion of these words to apply them to the Lord's Supper at all.

Zwingli tried to turn the tables here and to charge Luther with distorting the text. Luther had translated the sentence without the definite article: "Flesh is of no avail," whereas the Greek original had the article.[68] This gave Luther the opportunity to lampoon Zwingli's knowledge of Greek and to urge Zwingli to study it five more years in order to make his point.[69] He saw in Zwingli the weakness of the autodidact, and at Marburg he was to complain of his pedantry again.[70] But, over and above this, Zwingli's charge compelled Luther to expatiate on the meaning of the definite article in Greek and in German.[71] He pointed out that the German word *das* could be either the definite article or a demonstrative pronoun, depending on how it was pronounced.[72] In this passage, he said, not the demonstrative pronoun but the article was intended. Hence the Latin translation was not at a loss to render these words, despite the absence of the article in Latin grammar, whereas it would have had to supply a demonstrative or a personal pronoun if that had been the meaning.[73] By his general contention that the theme of the sixth chapter of John was spiritual eating and drinking rather than the Sacrament, but

[68] Luther's German translation read: *fleisch ist kein nütze.*
[69] *Confession on the Lord's Supper* (1528), W, XXVI, 360.
[70] Ibid., p. 405.
[71] Ibid., pp. 356 ff.
[72] Cf. Meissinger, *Der katholische Luther,* p. 57, note 4, and p. 274.
[73] *Confession on the Lord's Supper* (1528), W, XXVI, 356.

especially by his analysis of the text of the controverted verse itself, Luther attempted to demonstrate that the verse was irrelevant. And from the circumstance that Zwingli's last book did not use the passage Luther concluded that he had disqualified this exegesis of the passage so conclusively that they did not dare use it again.[74]

But the passage "The flesh is of no avail" was only a side issue in the exegetical debate. The pivotal exegetical question was: What was the meaning of the words "This is My body"? Over the exegesis of these words the true clash came, and in the exegesis of these words Luther showed his underlying hermeneutical presuppositions. More clearly than his purely exegetical works, his polemical works from the controversy with Zwingli defined the hermeneutical principles from which he worked.

The fundamental hermeneutical principle which Luther believed he was defending was this: A text of the Scriptures had to be taken as it stood unless there were compelling reasons for taking it otherwise. "Whoever takes it upon himself to interpret the words in Scripture otherwise than they read has the obligation to prove this from the text of the same passage or from an article of the faith." [75] It was forbidden both by grammarians and by theologians to introduce a contrary exegesis without some such compelling reasons.[76] Apparently Luther allowed for three such possible reasons: the statement of the text itself that it was not to be taken literally; the powerful indication by another passage to this same effect; [77] the clash between a literal inter-

---

[74] *Brief Confession on the Holy Sacrament* (1544), W, LIV, 152.

[75] *This Is My Body* (1527), W, XXIII, 93.

[76] *Confession on the Lord's Supper* (1528), W, XXVI, 278–279.

[77] ". . . *odder werde aus andern orten der schrifft mit gewalt beweiset*," ibid., p. 279.

pretation and "a clear article of the faith."[78] Even in the case of these reasons, however, the evidence would have to be compelling. For example, the argument against the real presence on the basis of the doctrine of the ascension (surely "a clear article of the faith") was invalid for Luther; and he argued at length that there was no conflict between the doctrine of the ascension, correctly understood, and the doctrine of the real presence as he found it taught in the words of institution.

Clearly, this axiom involved a problem whose detailed implications Luther did not work out. Just how compelling would the evidence of another passage have to be before it would require that the passage at hand be taken in another sense than the literal one? On what grounds was the exegete to decide which passage interpreted which? Nor did the introduction of the concept "article of faith" help the problem a great deal.[79] It seemed to imply the existence somewhere of a set of such articles, present in the exegesis of the Scriptures and yet somehow present before it. Luther's attitude toward the authority of the Apostles' Creed belonged to the general problem of what he meant by "articles of faith."[80] In opposition to traditionalism he had been able to proceed as though every article of faith were ultimately subject to exegetical re-examination, though he himself did not necessarily subject it to such re-examination. In opposition to a rejection of the tradition, however, he proceeded as though there existed a given body of articles of faith.

One of the devices Luther employed to get around the difficulty was a distinction between the clear and the obscure

[78] *Confession on the Lord's Supper* (1528), W, XXVI, 403; cf. also *Against the Heavenly Prophets* (1525), W, XVIII, 147.

[79] See the comments in Ebeling, *Evangelienauslegung*, pp. 342–343.

[80] Still useful on this problem is Ferdinand Kattenbusch, *Luthers Stellung zu den ökumenischen Symbolen* (Giessen, 1883); for a brief summary cf. Elert, *Morphologie*, I, 176–185.

passages of Scripture. He contrasted his opponents with
the fathers. "The holy teachers had the practice in the exposition of Scripture to take distinct and clear statements
and use these to make clear the obscure and uncertain
ones"; [81] Luther's opponents, like most heretics, tore an obscure word out of its context and used it to obscure what
had been a clear text.[82] For Luther "an uncertain text is
no better than no text at all." [83] Hence he insisted that clear
texts explain obscure ones. The application of this principle
to certain problems of exegesis was obvious; indeed, it had
a precedent in the explanations of the parables supplied by
the Gospels themselves. But it did not specify the procedure
which the exegete was to follow in classifying the passages
of Scriptures according to their relative clarity or obscurity.
Luther claimed that the words "This is My body" were
altogether clear. So clear were they that whether the reader
were Christian or pagan, Jew or Turk, he would recognize
that what was spoken of here was the true body of Christ
in the bread.[84] The introduction of this argument was not
without its difficulties either. Luther did not indicate the
relation between this definition of verbal clarity and his
contention that one should consult articles of the faith in
determining whether a passage was to be taken literally.
Nor did he relate it to his oft-repeated axiom that the meaning of the Scriptures had to be experienced before it could
be correctly understood.[85]

Luther set this discussion of verbal clarity in opposition
to Zwingli's hermeneutical principles, notably his concept of

[81] *This Is My Body* (1527), W, XXIII, 225.
[82] Cf. *Commentary on Psalm 37* (1521), W, VIII, 237.
[83] *Confession on the Lord's Supper* (1528), W, XXVI, 263.
[84] Ibid., p. 406.
[85] Hans Michael Müller, *Erfahrung und Glaube bei Luther* (Leipzig, 1929), esp. pp. 162—176; also Walther von Loewenich, *Glaube und Erfah- rung bei Luther* (Erlangen, 1928), a brief but suggestive presentation.

alloeosis. Zwingli claimed to derive this principle from the Chalcedonian doctrine of the two natures. Briefly stated in his own words, the principle was this: "a substitution or exchange of the two natures that are in the one Person, by which one is named and the other is meant, or that is named which they both are and yet only one of them is meant." [86] Thus he maintained that Luke 24:26, "Was it not necessary that the Christ should suffer?" referred only to the human nature, since the divine nature could not suffer. [87] Zwingli may have introduced the discussion of this principle only in order to prove the presence of figurative language in the Scriptures, but Luther pounced upon it as proof of Zwingli's rationalistic spirit.

Luther's reaction to *alloeosis* was instantaneous, and it was violent. It was "the devil's mask," he said in response to this exegesis of Luke 24:26; and "that old witch, Dame Reason, was the grandmother of *alloeosis*." [88] "We damn and curse *alloeosis*," he said, "all the way to hell as the devil's own inspiration." [89] It was "blasphemous exegesis." [90] He accused it of distorting the doctrine of the real presence and of introducing a rationalistic principle into the interpretation of Scripture, because it sought to be the mistress of the Scriptures rather than their servant. [91] To Luther *alloeosis* finally meant a division of the Person of Christ Himself, and it left no Christ at all, but a mere man. [92] Thus it represented nothing less than a threat to what Luther took to be the heart of the Christian Gospel.

[86] On the introduction of the doctrine of two natures into the eucharistic discussion cf. Köhler, *Zwingli und Luther*, I, 306—307.

[87] Ibid., pp. 477—480; 660—661.

[88] *Confession on the Lord's Supper* (1528), W, XXVI, 319—321.

[89] Ibid., p. 323.

[90] Ibid., p. 420.

[91] Ibid., p. 346.

[92] Ibid., p. 342.

Viewing the logical consequences of *alloeosis* this way, Luther made very little allowance for the failure of its proponents to draw these consequences. "It does not help," he said, "for them to boast that they correctly teach and praise Christ in other points. For whoever intentionally denies, blasphemes, and defames Christ in one point or article cannot correctly teach or honor Him in another place." [93] He was willing to make all sorts of concessions in other theological controversies, as his negotiations with Bucer and especially with the Bohemian Brethren demonstrated.[94] But in this controversy he was immobile, and he maintained to the end that the inevitable outcome of this sort of exegesis was a denial of the Christian faith itself. In this controversy, more than in any other, Luther took the position that the Holy Spirit would not let Himself be separated or divided up; it was all or nothing at all.[95]

Luther also attacked the method of determining the exegesis of a specific text on the basis of generalities. He wanted to make the issue as narrow as possible: not the question whether "body" could mean "sign of body" anywhere in Scripture, but whether it meant that in this specific passage.[96] If need be, he was prepared to argue the more general issue as well, and he sometimes did. But finally the question came down to the meaning of this particular passage. He charged that if his opponents were not such frivolous despisers of Scripture, one clear passage of Scripture would be enough for them, as it was for him, to make

[93] *This Is My Body* (1527), W, XXIII, 253.

[94] Jaroslav Pelikan, "Luther's Endorsement of the *Confessio Bohemica,*" in *Concordia Theological Monthly,* XX (1949), 829–843; Ernst Bizer, *Studien zur Geschichte des Abendmahlstreites im 16. Jahrhundert* (Gütersloh, 1940), pp. 11–130, on the Wittenberg Concord.

[95] *Brief Confession on the Holy Sacrament* (1544), W, LIV, 158.

[96] *This Is My Body* (1527), W, XXIII, 97.

the whole world too narrow.[97] He claimed to see another instance of their frivolity in the tendency to argue from the possible rather than from the necessary meaning of a passage. The two, the possible and the necessary, were as far apart as heaven and earth; for on the basis of possibility one could prove almost anything.[98] Only what must be, not what might be, the meaning of the text could be decisive.[99] Luther would permit neither general Scriptural usage nor possible interpretations to determine the exegesis of the passage "This is My body."

In this way Luther came down to his exegesis of this controverted passage itself; this will occupy us at length in chapter seven. And as in the final analysis it was his exegesis of the words themselves that compelled the elimination of John 6:63 from the discussion, so it was his exegesis of these words that necessitated the literal rather than the figurative interpretation of the passage. Had it not been for the controversy, Luther might never have had to clarify either his exegesis of the passage or the hermeneutical principles that produced this exegesis. But in the controversy it became necessary for him to do both. Over against the exegesis of Zwingli, Carlstadt, and Oecolampad he proceeded to apply his hermeneutical axioms that the literal sense of the text was to stand, and that obscure texts were to be explained in the light of clear ones.

"This is My body" was a clear text for Luther, and he insisted that it was to be taken as it stood. He accused his opponents of seeking to evade the text by their contention that "is" meant "signifies." He replied with the statement that the text was talking about things as they were, not about things as they seemed to be. From the Biblical sen-

97 Ibid., p. 105.
98 Ibid., p. 169.
99 Ibid., p. 213.

tences "The Rock was Christ" (1 Cor. 10:4) and "I am the vine" (John 15:1) his opponents sought to show that the verb "to be" in the Scriptures could mean "to signify"; for obviously Christ was neither a rock nor a vine.[100] Luther met this argument with the observation that Christ was indeed both a rock and a vine, though not a natural rock or a natural vine.[101] The figure of speech in these sentences was not in the verb "is." According to Luther's exegesis, if one were to say that "Christ is a flower," the word "flower" would "become a new word and acquire a new meaning. . . . For Christ does not *mean* a flower. He *is* a flower — but another flower than the natural one." [102] In this respect Scripture followed the example of sacred history itself.[103] It was God's way to let the image precede and to follow it with that for which the image stood. The symbol came first, then the thing symbolized. Thus the Old Testament provided the symbols, and the New Testament provided the realities. Zwingli's exegesis seemed to be reversing this order, as though the symbol followed the things symbolized.

At first this argumentation seemed to drive Luther from Zwingli's exegesis to that of Oecolampad, who had found the symbolic character of the words, not in "is" but in "My body." [104] Was Luther saying now that though the word "is" was not symbolic, the word "body" was? No, he was saying that according to the relation between symbol and symbolized, "all the tropes in Scripture indicate the precise new reality, not the symbol of that reality." [105] So Luther took the word "body" in "This is My body" to mean the true

---

[100] Cf. *This Is My Body* (1527), W, XXIII, 101 ff.; *Confession on the Lord's Supper* (1528), W, XXVI, 269 ff.

[101] *This Is My Body* (1527), W, XXIII, 103.

[102] *Confession on the Lord's Supper* (1528), W, XXVI, 271—272.

[103] Ibid., pp. 382—383.

[104] Ebeling, *Evangelienauslegung*, pp. 340—343.

[105] *Confession on the Lord's Supper* (1528), W, XXVI, 380.

body of Christ, not a symbol of His true body. Yet Luther resisted the implication drawn by his opponents that then Christians would bite their Lord with their teeth. For he paraphrased the Bible's figure of speech to say: "The word 'body,' according to its old interpretation, means the natural body of Christ. But according to its new interpretation it must mean another, new body of Christ, of which His natural body is a symbol." [106] Therefore Luther would take neither "is" nor "body" in the words of institution symbolically. On the contrary, what Zwingli called symbol Luther called reality, and what Zwingli called reality Luther called symbol. The "natural" or, as we would say, "historical" body of Jesus of Nazareth was, according to Luther, the symbol of that body which was given in the Lord's Supper. We shall consider this interpretation of the connection between the historical body and the sacramental body further in chapter seven.

Luther's controversy with Eck compelled him to clarify his ideas about the authority of the Scriptures in comparison with both church and tradition. His controversy with Zwingli not only revealed to him how close he was to the theological tradition of the West, but it also evoked from him his most detailed statement of hermeneutical principles. Thus what we have sought to isolate as four components of Luther's exegesis — the Scriptures as the Word of God, the tradition of the church, the history of the people of God, and the defense of doctrine — were all at work in both of these controversies, as they were in the Biblical commentaries that continued to come from Luther's study and his classroom during the years of controversy. Commentary and controversy depended on each other and drew on each other in the development of Luther's theology.

[106] Ibid., pp. 381–382.

This mutual influence of commentary and controversy is evident throughout that development, but nowhere does it stand out as clearly as it does in the development of Luther's doctrine of the Lord's Supper. As we said in the introduction to this volume, the doctrine of the Lord's Supper was one of the issues over which Luther contended on both fronts of his theological warfare; it was likewise a continuing issue in his preaching and lecturing, as some of the references in chapter five have indicated.[107] To show the interaction not only of commentary and controversy but of all four components in Luther's exegesis of the Scriptures, we shall now examine how he handled some of the traditional themes in the doctrine of the Lord's Supper. In the treatment of each theme we shall begin with the Biblical text in which the theme is sounded, and then we shall compare Luther's statement of the theme with its form in other parts of the tradition. We shall also examine his use of what we have called "the history of the people of God" as a device for interpreting the text. Thus we shall set forth a case study of Luther the expositor and see his exegesis in practice.

[107] See pp. 105–107.

PART TWO

The Practice of Luther's Exegesis: A Case Study

CHAPTER SEVEN

"This Is My Body" (Matt. 26:26)

IN chapter six we have examined some of the exegetical and hermeneutical issues at stake in the controversy over the Lord's Supper between Luther and Zwingli. Decisive among these issues was the meaning of "This is My body" in the words of institution. What did "body" mean in these words, and how was its meaning related to other patterns of Biblical speech? Luther's exegesis of this text, as he developed it in both his polemical and his constructive writings, was an effort to distinguish the sacramental meaning of "body of Christ" from the other connotations attached to the phrase in the Scriptures. Yet at the same time his exegesis recognized that the usage of the Scriptures did suggest affinities and analogies between the sacramental and the nonsacramental meanings of the phrase.[1]

To interpret any exegesis, one must examine not only the Biblical answers which an exegete has set forth and defended but also the theological questions which have driven him to his exegesis. This is doubly true when the exegesis under study is one that was formulated while the exegete was engaged in theological controversy, for here it is essential to go beyond the questions raised by the exegete himself and by his text to the questions and problems that were raised for him by his opponent. To a considerable extent such questions and problems dominate practically any theology, and they dominated Luther's theology more than most.

---

[1] See p. 112, note 12.

It was Luther's method of authorship to answer an opponent's treatise point by point rather than to present an answer of his own, built around the structure of his own thought. Hence the point of view of his opponent determined Luther's own discussion to a considerable — and sometimes to a lamentable — extent.[2]

During the controversy about the exegesis of the words "This is My body," for example, Luther's opponents brought up many objections to his interpretation of the text. Some of these objections were material, but others represented a diversionary tactic. At times Luther recognized this difference and labeled certain objections as the tricks that they were.[3] One such tactic of diversion was the introduction into the debate of speculation about the location of Christ's physical body since His ascension. The text could not mean that the body of Christ was present in the bread, Luther's opponents objected, because that would conflict with the texts which said that Christ had ascended into heaven and was seated at the right hand of God.[4] Underlying this objection was an exegesis of Biblical phrases like "heaven" and "the right hand of God" which pictured them as a specific location where Christ was sitting and waiting for the Last Judgment.[5] Luther ridiculed this exegesis with the sarcasm for which he had such a gift, accusing Zwingli of painting a child-

---

[2] Heinrich Bornkamm, *Probleme der Lutherbiographie*, in Vilmos Vajta (ed.), *Lutherforschung heute* (Berlin, 1958), pp. 22—23, makes some telling comments on this characteristic of Luther's authorship.

[3] See p. 121, notes 52—55.

[4] Cf. Walther Köhler, *Zwingli und Luther*, 2 vols. (Leipzig, 1924—53), I, 497—498.

[5] It was in response to this that Luther stated his own view of what the omnipresence of God meant: "God is smaller than anything small, bigger than anything big, shorter than anything short, longer than anything long, broader than anything broad, slimmer than anything slim, and so on. He is an inexpressible being, above and beyond all that one can name or think." *Confession on the Lord's Supper* (1528), W, XXVI, 339—340, as translated in Wilhelm Pauck, *The Heritage of the Reformation*, p. 18.

ish picture of Christ in a make-believe heaven with a cape
and a golden crown.[6] Christ was not at God's right hand
as though in a swallow's nest for people to stare at Him! [7]

But Luther did not let it go at that. After answering
Zwingli's objections to his interpretation on the basis of the
ascension of the body of Christ, he went ahead to expound
his own exegesis of texts dealing with the ascension of Christ.[8]
Here he sought to show, not only that his interpretation of
"This is My body" was not inconsistent with the orthodox
and Biblical doctrine of the ascension of Christ, but that
a sound exegesis of New Testament texts about the relation
between the two natures in Christ actually produced corollaries that made the real presence more plausible. Specifically, Luther set forth his semiexegetical and semispeculative
doctrine of the "ubiquity" of the body of Christ. The basis
of this doctrine was a distinction — taken over, as Luther
freely admitted, from the scholastic philosophers — between
three modes of presence: the ordinary "local" mode; the
"definitive" mode characteristic of the angels; and the "reple-
tive" mode characteristic of God.[9] A little later in the same
treatise he applied this scholastic distinction to the presence
of the body of Christ, and in the course of applying it he
also revised it a little. Christ's body likewise had three modes
of being present somewhere: the comprehensible and physical; the incomprehensible and spiritual; and the heavenly.[10]

The temptation involved in the construction of these

[6] *This Is My Body* (1527), W, XXIII, 131.

[7] Cf. Luther's sermon on John 17:11 (September 26, 1528), W,
XXVIII, 141.

[8] This has been carefully summarized by Paul Wilhelm Gennrich, *Die
Christologie Luthers im Abendmahlstreit* (Berlin, 1929).

[9] "The sophists [scholastics] speak correctly when they say that there
are three ways of being in a place." *Confession on the Lord's Supper*
(1528), W, XXVI, 327.

[10] Ibid., pp. 327–332.

various distinctions was to make the exegesis of the key text, "This is My body," dependent on a general theory regarding the presence of the body of Christ as such, which general theory was, in turn, dependent on an even more general theory regarding the presence of anything in anything. This temptation was, in a way, the one to which Zwingli had succumbed when he had interpreted the text on the basis of what was implied by his doctrine of the ascension. At times Luther found the temptation very attractive. In one passage he wrote: "If Christ had not said or instituted the words 'This is My body' in the Lord's Supper, it still follows necessarily from the words 'Christ is sitting at the right hand of God' that His body and blood can be there as well as in all other places. No transubstantiation or transformation of the bread into His body is necessary; for it can be there anyway, just as the right hand of God does not have to be transformed into everything, even though it is there and in everything. How this happens, however, is not for us to know. We should believe it, because the Scriptures and the articles of the Creed support it so powerfully." [11] In the same vein the Formula of Concord was able to say, after presenting the doctrine that the body of Christ participated in His omnipresence: "Therefore He is also able — and it is quite easy for Him — to impart the presence of His true body and blood in the holy Lord's Supper." [12]

From such formulations as these it might well appear that the text "This is My body" was speaking only about a special instance of the general omnipresence of Christ. A proper exegesis of the text would then be contingent on assent to the elaborate exegetical and philosophical argu-

[11] *This Is My Body* (1527), W, XXIII, 145.

[12] Formula of Concord, Epitome, Article VIII, 12, *Die Bekenntnisschriften der evangelisch-lutherischen Kirche*, 3d ed. (Göttingen, 1956), p. 808.

mentation that Luther presented in his doctrine of the "ubiquity" of the body of Christ. It might even seem that Luther's exegesis was impossible without the acceptance of a particular theory of physics current in the late Middle Ages, with its unique interpretation of space, mass, volume, motion, and the like.[13] Nevertheless, it was only seldom that Luther based his exegesis of "This is My body" on an *a priori* doctrine of the omnipresence of the body of Christ, and this doctrine did not represent the main body of his exegetical case for the assertion that the true body of Christ was present in the bread of the Blessed Sacrament.

If Luther had made such argumentation the basis of his exegesis of "This is My body," he would have fallen into the same rationalism that he claimed to discern in his opponents on both sides.[14] What saved him from such rationalism in this and in other aspects of his teaching was his exegetical method. His exegesis sought to derive the teachings of the Scriptures from the particular statements of the Scriptures rather than from the *a priori* principles of a theological system. Not even to his own theological speculation, therefore, would Luther consciously accord the status of an *a priori* principle that would dictate his exegesis, even though it cannot be denied that in his exegetical practice he sometimes operated with such *a priori* principles. Hence he was unwilling to have his doctrine of the ubiquity of the body of Christ, which was compounded of exegetical and speculative elements, lay down the terms for his exegesis of "This is My body."

Just a few paragraphs after he had elaborated the three modes of presence that were possible in general and the three modes of presence that might be predicated of the body of Christ in particular, Luther's exegesis broke the

[13] Cf. Elert, *Morphologie*, I, 363—433.
[14] See p. 121.

bonds of his own speculative categories. And in the process he also showed that any effort to make his terms "in, with, and under" a plausible paraphrase of "This is My body" was rationalistic. "Our reason," he said, "is accustomed to understand the little word 'in' only physically and tangibly, as straw is in the sack or bread is in the basket. When it [the reason] hears, therefore, that God is in this or in that, it always thinks of the straw sack or of the breadbasket. But faith perceives that in this matter 'in' is equivalent to 'over, outside of, under, through, throughout, and everywhere.'" [15] In other passages he multiplied these prepositions still further, simply to make clear that the meaning of "This is My body" could not be deduced from any theory of presence, regardless of how many distinct modes of presence such a theory might be inclined to posit, but had to come from an exegesis of the Biblical text itself.

For the presence of the body of Christ was a matter of faith. In the defense of his sacramental teaching Luther came closer than he did anywhere else to saying that faith consisted in affirming that a proposition was true contrary to reason.[16] Still he was finally concerned also here to see faith as a confidence in the faithfulness of God, born of His promises in Christ.[17] Faith did not cause the presence. Luther understood the text to teach the objective presence of the "body," and he taught that unworthy communicants, too, received the true body and blood.[18] But the believer ap-

[15] *Confession on the Lord's Supper* (1528), W, XXVI, 341.

[16] Jaroslav Pelikan, "The Origins of the Object-Subject Antithesis in Lutheran Dogmatics," in *Concordia Theological Monthly*, XXI (1950), 94—104.

[17] Jaroslav Pelikan, "The Relation of Faith and Knowledge in the Lutheran Confessions," ibid., pp. 321—331.

[18] "Not only the worthy receive this broken bread, but also Judas and the unworthy; for the breaking of the bread takes place in the presence of both the good and the bad. Now it is impossible that they receive it spiritually, for they have neither the Spirit nor faith. Moreover, Christ has no

proached the Sacrament in faith — not faith in the ubiquity of the body of Christ but faith in the promising God. Behind that distinction was an even more fundamental distinction: "There is a distinction between His presence and your grasping. He is free and unrestricted everywhere that He is. Although He is present everywhere, He does not permit Himself to be grasped and seized everywhere. . . . Why is this so? Because it is one thing when God is present and another thing when He is present *for you.* But He is present for you when He adds His Word to it and binds Himself to it and declares: 'Here you shall find Me.'" [19] It was not to the general omnipresence of the body of Christ that the exegete was to look when he came to interpret the meaning of the text "This is My body," but to the Word and the promise of God declared in the text. The center of Luther's case for the real presence was thus shifted from speculation to exegesis. Luther maintained that the body of Christ was present everywhere by virtue of the communication to Christ's human nature of the property of omnipresence, but the basis of the doctrine of the real presence was to be an exegesis of the precise meaning of "body" in the words of institution themselves.

Luther felt obliged to defend that meaning against the doctrines of Zwingli, Carlstadt, and Oecolampad. As we have seen, this defense brought him to the conclusion that the medieval exegesis of "This is My body "was sounder than the glosses of these Protestants. He therefore defended the doctrine of the medieval church, even the actions of Pope Nicholas II (d. 1061), who had forced Berengar (d. 1088) to affirm that in the Blessed Sacrament he ground and crushed

more than one body. If, then, the unworthy receive and share it [the body of Christ], it must be physical and not spiritual; for there is no other receiving than the physical or the spiritual." *Confession on the Lord's Supper* (1528), W, XXVI, 491.

[19] *This Is My Body* (1527), W, XXIII, 151.

the true body of Christ with his teeth.[20] He exclaimed: "Would to God that all the popes had acted in as Christian a way about everything as this pope acted toward Berengar about this confession! For the meaning of this statement is that whoever eats and bites this bread eats and bites that which is the real and true body of Christ, and not plain ordinary bread; for this bread is the body of Christ." [21] Luther had his objections to the medieval exegesis of "This is My body" also, but he was in agreement with its rejection of a purely symbolic interpretation of "body" in the words of institution.

Luther's criticism of the medieval exegesis of "This is My body" was not as severe as was his criticism of Protestant interpretations. The reasons for this difference were mainly theological, but partly chronological. By the time Luther had made his break with the medieval exegesis he was already becoming embroiled in polemics against the Protestant interpretation. Thus there was only a short period in his theological career when he was directing his criticism primarily against Roman Catholic theories without having to dissociate himself at the same time from other Protestant theories.[22] But for theological and not chronological reasons Luther recognized that despite the rationalistic theory of transubstantiation, despite the denial of the chalice to the laity, and even despite the unbloody sacrifice of the Mass, Rome still held to a literal interpretation of "This is My body." [23]

Nevertheless, Luther did realize the dangerous tendencies in the medieval exegesis of "This is My body." Although the

[20] A. J. Macdonald, *Berengar and the Reform of Sacramental Doctrine* (London, 1930), pp. 130–131.

[21] *Confession on the Lord's Supper* (1528), W, XXVI, 443.

[22] See p. 156, note 62.

[23] Elert, *Morphologie*, I, 271.

chief object of his criticism was the idea of the Mass as an atoning sacrifice,[24] there were also times when he blamed this idea of the sacrifice on the theory of transubstantiation. Part of his critique of the Roman Catholic exegesis was directed, therefore, at what seemed to be an almost fetishistic interpretation of the power of the stuff in the Sacrament.[25] In the theology of some late medieval theologians, but even more in the piety of the common people, the transubstantiated bread, which was now, in literal prose, the body of Jesus Christ, was said to have the power to effect miracles, to heal the sick, to give safety to the building where it was housed, and, conversely, to poison and kill those who profaned it.[26] That power was thought to be resident in the elements, and Luther's attack upon the medieval exegesis of "This is My body" was aimed at the theory of transubstantiation. He condemned also the processions and other practices which the theory had spawned through the piety of the tabernacle.[27]

Exegetically, Luther accused transubstantiation of confusing the meaning of "body" as used in the text "This is My body" with the meaning of "flesh" in the Scriptures. In taking this stand Luther put himself into the difficult position of maintaining, against both Roman Catholic and Protestant exegesis, that the lengthy discourse on "flesh" in the sixth chapter of John's Gospel did not deal specifically with the Lord's Supper.[28] The Protestant theologians were using this chapter to show that the real presence would be useless, since "the flesh is of no avail." In his rejoinder to them, sum-

[24] See pp. 237 ff.

[25] See p. 165, note 26.

[26] See p. 172, note 45.

[27] *A Treatise on Prayer and the Processions* (1519), W, II, 177–179.

[28] In a sermon dated June 4, 1523, Luther was already criticizing the eucharistic interpretation of John 6:55 ff., W, XII, 580–584.

marized in chapter six above, Luther made the point that wherever in Scripture "flesh" and "spirit" were set into antithesis, the word "flesh" could not refer to the flesh of Christ but had to mean that flesh which was born of the flesh.[29] When the text said that "the flesh is of no avail," therefore, this could not mean that the real presence of the body of Christ did not benefit the communicant; for the word "flesh" here was not the same as "body." But several times in the discourse Jesus spoke of "My flesh" and even of "eating My flesh." Opposed as he was to the eucharistic exegesis of the entire chapter, Luther held that here, too, "flesh" and "body" were not identical, and that Christ was speaking of a spiritual eating of His flesh, namely, of faith.[30]

There are not many exegetes today who would accept such an exegesis of the Fourth Gospel, but many who would admire Luther's insight into the distinctiveness of New Testament speech.[31] For both patristic and medieval theology had sometimes tended to identify "flesh" and "body," and thus, among other things, to circulate the notion that the body was more sinful than the soul.[32] Luther knew from his own religious experience that it was the pride of his soul, not the desire of his body, that raised the highest barriers between himself and God.[33] And he knew from his exegesis of the Scriptures that this had been the experience of all

[29] *This Is My Body* (1527), W, XXIII, 193–195; he explained this further in the *Confession on the Lord's Supper* (1528), W, XXVI, 375.

[30] *Confession on the Lord's Supper* (1528), W, XXVI, 372.

[31] See, for example, Helmut Gollwitzer, *Zur Auslegung von Joh. 6 bei Luther und Zwingli*, in Werner Schmauch (ed.), *In Memoriam Ernst Lohmeyer* (Stuttgart, 1951), pp. 143–168.

[32] Cf. Karpp, *Probleme*, pp. 195–198.

[33] As he said at table early in 1533, "I often made my confession to Staupitz, not about women but about the real problems." W, *Tischreden*, I, No. 518, p. 240.

the saints.[34] "Flesh" in Biblical terminology, therefore, meant whatever was opposed to God and whatever alienated a man from God, be it sex or money or learning or even and especially religion. "Spirit," on the other hand, meant that which God had renewed and vivified; and it included the physical life of the believer, just as it anticipated the resurrection of the body.[35]

Applied to the text "This is My body," this interpretation meant that the gift of the Lord's Supper was, as the literal sense of the words declared, the true body of Christ. And Luther took this to be the meaning also of the medieval doctrine. Speaking in defense of the medieval doctrine and of his own doctrine against Protestant attacks, he wrote in 1544: "When you receive the bread from the altar, you are not tearing an arm from the body of the Lord or biting off His nose or finger. But you receive the entire body of the Lord; the next one who follows you also receives the same entire body; so does the third; and so do thousands upon thousands over and over again." [36] Hence Luther set his exegesis of "This is My body" against the identification of "body" and "flesh." Not the *flesh* of Christ in a cannibalistic sense — or, as a peculiar term in sixteenth-century polemical theology styled it, "Capernaitic" sense [37] — but the *body* of Christ was meant by the text "This is My body."

Luther's opposition to transubstantiation as an exegesis of "This is My body" was shared by a large group of Protestant thinkers, but the reasons for their opposition were quite different from his. Lumping Luther's exegesis with transub-

[34] That is the theme of the *Commentary on Psalm 51* (1532), W, XL-II, 315—470; *Luther's Works*, 12, 303—410.

[35] " 'Flesh' means man through and through, as he lives in this life." *Commentary on 1 Peter* (1523), W, XII, 373.

[36] *Brief Confession on the Holy Sacrament* (1544), W, LIV, 145.

[37] Cf. *Oxford English Dictionary*, II (Oxford, 1933), 91—92. The term is an allusion to the question cited in John 6:52.

stantiation, these men sought to spiritualize the term "body" in "This is My body" and to posit a "spiritual" presence of the body of Christ. The precise meaning of "spiritual" in their usage was not always easy to determine, and they were not consistent with themselves or with one another in their usage.[38] But the connotations of the term included the notion of a symbolic presence, the idea of a presence in memory, and similar attempts to eliminate the "materialistic" exegesis of the text. When the text spoke of "body," according to this interpretation, it did not mean Christ's true body, but a sign of His body.[39]

Luther thought that he could perceive a non-Christian idealism at work behind such "spiritual" exegesis. What animated this exegesis, he believed, was a revulsion at the material and physical as such, not merely the objection that his exegesis of "This is My body" was materialistic. Luther was as opposed to such idealism as he was to materialism. In his own exegesis, which has sometimes been characterized as Biblical realism, the material was generally regarded as God's good creature, to be appreciated and used without being worshiped.[40] That same Biblical realism became evident in his picture of Christ. His exegesis of texts from the Gospels fairly reveled in the most material proofs of the reality of the incarnation — the swaddling clothes of the Holy Infant, His hunger and sleep, His perspiration, and the hair on His body.[41] It has not always been easy for the orthodox doctrine of the Person of Christ to avoid idealism in its pic-

[38] See the discussion of this by Abel Burckhardt, *Das Geistproblem bei Huldrych Zwingli* (Leipzig, 1932).

[39] See p. 130.

[40] Heinrich Bornkamm, *Luther's World of Thought*, tr. by Martin H. Bertram (Saint Louis, 1958), pp. 176—194.

[41] See the quotations compiled by Gennrich, op. cit.

ture of Christ, but Luther's exegesis kept creature and Creator together in the paradox of the incarnation.[42]

In the idealistic effort to spiritualize the exegesis of "This is My body" Luther, therefore, saw a threat, not only to the reality of the presence of the body of Christ but to the reality of the incarnation itself. Consistently carried out, so he maintained, this method of Biblical exegesis would undermine the reality of everything the New Testament said about what Christ was and did. Taking on the role of the devil's advocate, Luther showed the implications of this exegesis by "spiritualizing" away the whole New Testamant portrait of Christ in the flesh, since "the flesh is of no avail." Finally he had his opponents exclaim: "Stop, for God's sake! You will fanaticize yourself to death! On this basis you could fanaticize Christ out of the garden, off the cross, and out of all His suffering. You could prove that none of these took place physically; for He had to be physically present in all of these, and yet His flesh is of no avail where He is physically present." [43] The same objections that they were voicing to the exegesis of "This is My body" could thus eliminate the Biblical picture of Christ altogether, leaving not only a spiritual presence rather than a real presence, but a spiritual Christ rather than a real Christ. And such a Christ, Luther said, would be of no avail.

Although he was concerned, therefore, to avoid the identification of "body" and "flesh" in the exegesis of "This is My body," he was even more concerned not to let a false idealism separate the term "body" in this text from the Biblical term "flesh" so radically as to make the presence merely spiritual rather than real. For as an expositor of St. Paul, Luther knew that the primary connotation of "flesh" in his epistles was the pejorative connotation: the "flesh" was the

[42] Ebeling, *Evangelienauslegung,* pp. 359—369.
[43] *This Is My Body* (1527), W, XXIII, 175.

enemy of God. But Luther was also an able expositor of
St. John; recent research has shown that he entered into the
thought world of the Johannine literature much more deeply
than has usually been assumed.[44] And there he found the
word "flesh" used not only in a pejorative sense but also in
a generic sense, to denote humanity. Luther saw that when
"flesh" was used in this sense in the New Testament, "flesh"
and "body" could be very close together in their meaning.
Therefore the exegesis of "This is My body" could not be
completely dissociated from that realism about material
things which the Bible expressed in this generic use of the
word "flesh." [45]

What was "spiritual" about the Lord's Supper, according
to Luther's exegesis, was not the food but the eating. "The
object is not always spiritual," Luther formulated in a Latin
axiom, "but the use of the object ought to be spiritual." [46]
This meant, he said: "Eating, drinking, or using is not spiritual when that which one eats or drinks or uses is spirit or
a spiritual being, because then the flesh of Christ could not
be spiritually eaten or drunk. For regardless of where it may
be — in a spiritual or in a physical being, visible or invisible —
it is real, natural, physical flesh, which one can grasp, feel,
see, and hear, which was born of a woman and died on the
cross. But it is called 'spiritual' because it comes from the
Spirit and because it is necessarily intended for our spiritual
reception." [47] Luther refused to concede to Zwingli a monop-
oly on the "spiritual" exegesis of "This is My body," but he

[44] See p. 36, note 17.

[45] "In Scriptural parlance 'flesh' denotes a complete human being."
Sermons on the Gospel of St. John: Chapters 1–4 (1537–40), W, XLVI,
631; *Luther's Works*, 22, 110.

[46] *Obiectum non est semper spirituale, sed usus debet esse spiritualis.*
This Is My Body (1527), W, XXIII, 185. The axiom is presumably a quotation, but I do not know its source.

[47] *This Is My Body* (1527), W, XXIII, 183–185.

also refused to equate the word "spiritual" with "invisible" in his exegesis of passages dealing with the Lord's Supper or with the church.[48] The Lord's Supper was a spiritual act, not because "body" in the text "This is My body" connoted a nonphysical or nonmaterial entity, but because the text meant that this real body was to be received in a way that came from, and led to, the Holy Spirit.

Perhaps the most convincing Protestant alternative to Luther's exegesis of "This is My body" was the effort to make the word "body" in that text refer to the Pauline metaphor of the church as the "body of Christ." What helped to make it so plausible and convincing was, among other things, the alternation between the use of the term "body" for the Sacrament and the use of it for the church in the most extended discussion of the Lord's Supper anywhere in the New Testament, the tenth and eleventh chapters of 1 Corinthians. It is not always clear whether by the "body" of Christ in a particular verse St. Paul meant the church or the Eucharist or both. The most crucial such passage in the debates of the sixteenth century was 1 Cor. 10:16-17; "The cup of blessing which we bless, is it not a participation in the blood of Christ? The bread which we break, is it not a participation in the body of Christ? Because there is one loaf, we who are many are one body, for we all partake of the same loaf." [49] Was "participation" or "communion" or even "communication" the correct translation here? The answer is still not easy to give in the light of the entire context, and we shall return to it in a later chapter.[50] But it is easy to see how an exegesis like Zwingli's was inclined to conclude that the term "body" in "This is My body" referred to the

[48] Ernst Rietschel, *Das Problem der sichtbar-unsichtbaren Kirche bei Luther* (Leipzig, 1932).

[49] Elert, *Morphologie*, I, 151–153.

[50] See pp. 191 ff.

church as the body of Christ, not to a presence of Christ's real body.

Luther's refutation of this exegesis was based on several arguments. He took the word "participation" in this passage to mean "communication" or "distribution," [51] and he argued that the use of the term "body of Christ" as a metaphor for the church would make no sense whatever in this context. "If body here is really a figure of speech," he argued, "then it must mean the spiritual body of Christ, which is the church. But then the content of the text would be: The bread which we break is a spiritual distribution of Christendom, which would mean: Wherever this bread is being broken, there Christendom is being distributed. And even more abominable abominations would follow from this." [52] If the word meant "distribution" or "communication," then, by Luther's exegesis, that which was communicated had to be a thing rather than a person or group of persons.

A little later in this treatise Luther put forth another argument against such an exegesis of the term "body" in "This is My body," and even to one who is quite familiar with Luther the argument is rather unexpected. The argument was that when the apostle wrote, "We who are many are one body," he was referring merely to the unity of Christians in general and was not employing the metaphor of the "body of Christ" that he used elsewhere in this and in other epistles: "We know that St. Paul does not say here: We are one body of Christ, but merely: We are one body, that is, one group, one community, just as every city is a special body in relation to every other city." [53] The consequence of

[51] "Therefore 'participation' in this passage must mean simply physical communication or distribution [*schlecht leibliche gemeinschafft odder austeilunge*]." *Confession on the Lord's Supper* (1528), W, XXVI, 488.

[52] Ibid.

[53] Ibid., pp. 491—492.

this exegesis of Paul would be to make the idea of the church as the body of Christ a part of "natural theology" and to treat the unity of Christians with Christ and with one another as a special instance of the general corporateness of human existence. Interestingly, Luther had applied the term "body" to a secular community already in his treatise on the Sacrament of 1519: "The meaning or the effect of this Sacrament is the communion of all saints. . . . It comes from the fact that Christ is one spiritual body with all the saints, just as the population of a city is one community and one body, and every citizen is a member of every other citizen and of the entire city. Thus all the saints are members of Christ and of the church, which is a spiritual and eternal city of God. And whoever is received into this city is received into the community of the saints, incorporated into Christ's spiritual body, and made His member." [54] On this ground the term "body" in "This is My body" could not mean the church, for the designation of the church as the "body of Christ" would be an application to the church of what "body" meant in human society generally.

Luther's paramount objection to this exegesis, however, was his argument that such an interpretation of the text changed the sacramental action from the Lord's Supper into the church's supper. Throughout his exegesis of Biblical passages dealing with the means of grace Luther was intent upon what God was doing through these means rather than upon what people did. It was not the human act of washing but the divine act of baptizing that made Baptism a means of grace. [55] It was not human speaking but divine proclama-

---

[54] *Treatise on the Blessed Sacrament* (1519), W, II, 743.

[55] "Even today Baptism and the proclamation of the divine Word are not mine but God's. When we hear this Word, we must bear in mind that it is God Himself who is addressing us. When kings hear the Word and see the administration of the Sacraments, they should place their crowns and scepters at His feet and say: 'It is God who has His being here, who

tion that made the spoken Word of God a means of grace.[56] Thus also it was not the human act of assembling and eating in a corporate group but the divine bestowal of the gift of Christ's body and blood that made the Eucharist a means of grace. Although he undoubtedly misunderstood his opponent, Luther took Zwingli to be saying that the Sacrament was "simply a token of Christians among themselves, and not something toward God, an action by which they exercise and preserve their mutual love. . . . But we know that it is and is called the Lord's Supper, not the Christians' supper." [57] If the term "body" were taken to mean the church rather than the real presence of the body of Christ, then the theocentric emphasis of the Biblical message would give way to an anthropocentric outlook. Therefore Luther demanded that the sacramental meaning of the term "body" in "This is My body" be distinguished from its broader meaning in St. Paul's usage.

Yet it was part of Luther's genius as a Biblical theologian to hold emphases together without confusing them. This ability made itself evident also in his exegesis of "This is My body." For while he took the literal sense of the term "body" in this text to mean the body of Christ which suffered and died on the cross, he also recognized that the spiritual sense could mean the church. He would not concede that "My body" in the text could merely symbolize or represent the body of Christ, and that "My blood" could merely sym-

speaks here, and who is active here.' You will perhaps be tempted to interpose: 'Why, it is just a plain priest standing there and administering the Lord's Supper!' If that is your viewpoint, you are no Christian." *Sermons on the Gospel of St. John: Chapters 1—4* (1537—40), W, XLVII, 211; *Luther's Works,* 22, 505.

[56] "We have the authority: what we preach is as valid as though God Himself were saying it. When a Christian preaches, baptizes, or absolves, it is the same as though God Himself came down and said and did everything Himself." *Sermons on Genesis* (1527), W, XXIV, 282.

[57] *This Is My Body* (1527), W, XXIII, 269—271.

bolize or represent the blood of Christ. But even in his vehement *Confession* of 1528 he remained aware of the symbolic nature of the Eucharist: "Thus also the Sacrament of the Lord's Supper is intended to symbolize and represent something, namely, the unity of Christians in one spiritual body of Christ through one Spirit, one faith, one love, one cross, and the like." [58] Even his antithesis to an anthropocentric exegesis did not cause Luther to lose sight of the horizontal dimension altogether.

When one has said this, however, one must go on to say that the controversy did cause Luther to lay less stress upon the horizontal than he had in earlier years. Expositors of Luther have often paid attention only to his polemical writings on the Eucharist and not to his exegesis, as we have pointed out earlier; [59] therefore the notion of corporate fellowship in the Lord's Supper has had less prominence in Lutheran systematic theology than it deserved. To see the full scope of Luther's exegesis of the term "body of Christ," however, one must go back to his sacramental treatise of 1519. [60] In this treatise the metaphor of the church as the body of Christ played a very prominent role, along with the idea of fellowship in the Lord's Supper. "One must pay attention to this metaphor" of the body of Christ, Luther wrote, "if one wants to understand this Sacrament; for Scripture uses it on account of the simple people." [61] He accused late medieval theologians of failing to notice this metaphor in their undue preoccupation with the real presence. He went so far as to say: "Christ puts a lower estimate upon His own natural body than He does upon His spiritual body, which is the

[58] *Confession on the Lord's Supper* (1528), W, XXVI, 411.

[59] See p. 40.

[60] *Treatise on the Blessed Sacrament* (1519), W, II, 742—758; *Works of Martin Luther*, II (Philadelphia, 1943), 9—31.

[61] *Treatise on the Blessed Sacrament* (1519), W, II, 744.

communion of His saints. . . . Therefore be careful. It is more necessary that you pay attention to the spiritual body of Christ than that you pay attention to the natural body, and that you believe in the spiritual body than that you believe in the natural body." [62] Failure to give heed to Biblical terminology, Luther said, had led medieval theologians to the theory that the Sacrament was efficacious automatically.[63]

Yet Luther's break with medieval exegesis was not abrupt, and therefore he was able to speak of sacramental transformation in a manner quite medieval. But this manner of speaking, too, made it possible for him to emphasize the horizontal dimension in the Sacrament: "At the same time that the bread is being transformed into His true and natural body and the wine into His natural and true blood, we are truly transported and transformed into the spiritual body, that is, into the fellowship of Christ and all the saints." [64] The Eucharist as the church's rite was constituted by the sacramental presence of the body of Christ, explained here on the basis of the theory of transubstantiation and described in more cautious language later in Luther's career. Hence Luther's exegesis recognized an affinity or an analogy between this precise use of the term "body" in "This is My body" and the metaphorical use of the term "body" as a designation for the church. But even in his early exegesis the literal sense of "This is My body" was basic and constitutive; the spiritual sense of "My body" as the church, metaphorical and derivative. The implications of this subordination of the spiritual to the literal in Luther's exegesis of Biblical texts about the Eucharist will become clearer as we examine his interpretation of other passages.

[62] Ibid., p. 751.
[63] Ibid., p. 752.
[64] Ibid., p. 749.

CHAPTER EIGHT

"For the Forgiveness of Sins" (Matt. 26:28)

A PROMINENT feature in Luther's exegesis of the Biblical texts dealing with the Lord's Supper was the statement that the Sacrament had been instituted "for the forgiveness of sins," and that it was therefore a means of grace.[1] The technical theological term "means of grace" was less common in Luther's language than the Biblical term "forgiveness," but the idea was basic to his whole method of interpreting the Scriptures.[2] It was likewise a basic point of difference between his exegesis and that of his fellow reformers, and it continues to be regarded as one of the "Catholic elements" which he never managed to shed.[3] Still it was a mistake when his opponents lumped his exegesis with medieval doctrines without paying attention to the significant contrasts between his interpretation of the forgiveness conferred by the Sacrament and the eucharistic teachings of the scholastics. On what grounds did Luther interpret the text of the words of institution to say that "the forgiveness of sins" was conveyed by the Lord's Supper? And how did this interpretation differ from the exegesis of these same words in medieval theology and in the thought of other Protestants? That is the question with which this chapter will deal.

When Luther first set about the task of articulating his

[1] Koehler, *Dogmengeschichte*, pp. 203–220.

[2] The best discussion of Luther's view in English is that of Regin Prenter, *Spiritus Creator*, pp. 101–172, 254–266.

[3] Thus Adolf Harnack regards it, *Dogmengeschichte*, III, 880–895.

exegesis of the words "for the forgiveness of sins," the chief object of his polemics was the medieval sacramental system, which underlay earlier exegesis of these words. This exegesis followed the lead of St. Augustine in emphasizing the objective validity of the priesthood and the Sacraments as the guarantee of the Spirit's presence and activity in the church. Although St. Augustine had tempered this emphasis by his stress on the doctrine of predestination,[4] the main stream of medieval exegesis resolved the Biblical paradox between predestination and Sacraments in favor of the Sacraments. Augustine's exegesis of the texts from Romans on predestination had prevented his exegesis of "for the forgiveness of sins" from curtailing the freedom of God. But medieval thought laid such stress upon the Sacraments as means of this "forgiveness" that its assertion of divine freedom was seriously jeopardized. The main objection that Luther raised against this exegesis was that it had misinterpreted the Biblical doctrine of grace. He accused it of interpreting grace as something in man that merited God's favor, a disposition that was infused into man to change him.[5] Grace thus became a predicate of human life. In opposition to this interpretation Luther's exegesis of Romans made grace an attribute of God and of His relation to human life, and he defined it as the favor of God.[6] Even in the "forgiveness" of the Sacrament, therefore, God remained free and sovereign.

[4] Gotthard Nygren, in *Das Prädestinationsproblem in der Theologie Augustins* (Lund, 1956), pp. 228—267, discusses grace and predestination in Augustine.

[5] As Reinhold Seeberg put it, "Luther speaks of 'infused grace' or righteousness, but he is no longer thinking of a supernatural-natural quality that is poured into the soul, but of God's spiritual activity which sets the human soul into motion." *Dogmengeschichte*, IV-1, 126—127.

[6] "I take grace in the proper sense of the favor of God — not a quality of the soul, as is taught by our more recent writers." *Against Latomus* (1521), W, VIII, 106; *Luther's Works*, 32, 227.

When grace was made into a kind of supernatural stuff [7] which automatically conferred this "forgiveness of sins," it seemed to Luther that the free and sovereign Lord stood in danger of becoming the captive of His own Sacraments. For the piety of simple people as well as for the speculations of learned theology the "forgiveness" spoken of in the text seemed to be manipulable and subject to man's control. As in paganism the divine forces were susceptible to bribes and threats if one knew the right techniques and employed the right formulas, so in vulgar Christian sacramentalism God could be forced to yield His grace and to grant His forgiveness. When the priest at the altar commanded, the Son of God had to obey and come down from heaven to the altar. The legends that described the miraculous powers of the sacred host and the folk customs that surrounded the Lord's Supper all served to emphasize the belief that the eucharistic Lord, like the genie of the lamp, was there to do the bidding of the initiated.[8] It was as though God would not dare disengage Himself and His forgiveness from the ceremonies of the Mass, because the priest who performed these ceremonies was the one who knew God's secret.

Luther struck out against the priestcraft that had gained such control over the church and its worship. Therefore even his exegesis of the eucharistic texts championed the freedom of the church and, above all, the freedom of God. Although the Sacrament had been instituted "for the forgiveness of sins," as Luther was convinced that it had, this "forgiveness" was still an act of God's sovereign freedom, based on His own will and intention rather than on any human action, priestly or lay. Luther's exegesis of the New Testament was no less insistent upon the freedom and sov-

[7] Artur Michael Landgraf, *Dogmengeschichte der Frühscholastik*, III-1 (Regensburg, 1954), 145 ff., on *opus operatum*.

[8] See p. 172, note 45.

ereignty of God than was his exegesis of the Old Testament.[9] For to Luther the cross meant that God was not bound to any of the usual religious channels of self-disclosure through miracle or oracle but had done whatever He had pleased by selecting the cross as His point of action.[10] Although in one sense God could be said to have bound Himself by the words "for the forgiveness of sins," Luther never forgot that the Christ who spoke those words was a revelation of the sovereign freedom of God.

The revelation of the sovereign freedom of God made it imperative that theology distinguish between "forgiveness" and the channels of forgiveness. An identification of the two, which was the direction if not the intention of vulgar sacramentalism, could reverse the polarity of the words "for the forgiveness of sins" by making the priest rather than God the center of attention. Then grace would be, not something in God but something in the Sacraments and therefore in the believers. Taken this way, grace and forgiveness were deprived of their personal quality, and the relation between God and man in the Sacrament became, not the relation of grace and mercy spoken of in the words "for the forgiveness of sins" but a new version of the priestly barter between God and man that had filled so much of the history of religion. Luther observed that a theology which professed to defend man and his free will by obscuring the freedom of God would eventually lose both the free will of man and the freedom of God in a religion of works, magic, and superstition.[11]

Against Roman Catholicism, then, Luther proclaimed

---

[9] Bornkamm, *Luther und das Alte Testament*, pp. 165—169.

[10] "It follows that 'free will' is altogether a divine title, which cannot be applied to anyone except the divine Majesty. It can do and does do 'whatever He pleases in heaven and on earth,' as the psalm sings (Ps. 135:6)." *The Bondage of the Will* (1525), W, XVIII, 636.

[11] Ibid., p. 755.

the freedom of God to forgive as He pleased. Against Protestantism, on the other hand, Luther proclaimed that the Sacrament was intended "for the forgiveness of sins." Although he would not identify "forgiveness" and the channels of forgiveness, he would not separate them either. God in His freedom might confer His forgiveness wherever and whenever and however He pleased, but men were obliged to cling to the channels which He had selected and designated "for the forgiveness of sins." For Luther this obligation was a necessary corollary derived from the nature of divine revelation itself. When other Protestants joined him in many of his exegetical principles but then went on to deny that the external Word, Baptism, and the Lord's Supper were means "for the forgiveness of sins," Luther came to see this corollary more clearly. Thus a concentration upon revelation and upon its corollary was one of the most characteristic features of Luther's exegesis.

Luther's exegesis described this availability of God through the channels of forgiveness in the language of the fundamental distinction referred to in chapter seven between the presence of God and His presence "for you." [12] Even though God was present somewhere in His power, this did not necessarily mean that He was accessible there "for the forgiveness of sins." He was present, Luther wrote, in the rock, the fire, and the water. But one was not to smash himself against the rock or hurl himself into the fire and the water in order to find Him. Only where through His Word He had promised to be was He to be sought — and found. [13] This distinction between the presence of God and His presence "for you" was part of Luther's larger distinction, basic to his exegesis, between God as He was for Himself and God

[12] See p. 143, note 19.
[13] *Treatise on the Sacrament* (1526), W, XIX, 492.

as He was "toward us." [14] He accused all his various opponents of attempting to pry into the inner mystery of God's own being.[15] With this mystery, Luther declared in his exegesis, a man dare have nothing to do; for this God was a consuming fire and none of man's legitimate business. The exegesis of the Scriptures dealt with God as He was "toward us," for in the Scriptures He had appointed certain historical events and certain actions as the places where He had disclosed His secret will. Whoever speculated about His secret will apart from these events and actions, Luther discovered in his early development, could have no assurance of the forgiveness of sins.[16]

Luther discovered, too, that such assurance could not come from contemplation of the universe. Both experience and exegesis made it clear that such contemplation was inadequate. Exegesis did so by showing that the Bible did not content itself with the doctrine of creation, as though kinship with the rest of the creatures were a sufficient basis for trust in God for forgiveness. Christian theology needed a doctrine of forgiveness simply because creation was not enough.[17] Christian experience likewise led Luther to the conclusion that the world of creatures could not provide the specific assurance of God's forgiveness. For repeatedly in his exegetical writings he spoke about his own reflections on the world of creatures. A warm day in spring after a long, cold German winter or the wonder of the rebirth of the plants and flowers might indeed arouse one to hope that God

[14] On this distinction cf. John Dillenberger, *God Hidden and Revealed* (Philadelphia, 1953).

[15] "These are the limits of God's revelation of Himself, and we must not believe anything else." *Sermons on the Gospel of St. John: Chapters 1—4* (1537—40), W, XLVII, 33; *Luther's Works,* 22, 304.

[16] Pauck, op. cit., pp. 15—23.

[17] Ebeling, *Evangelienauslegung,* p. 255, notes 565—566.

would grant rebirth to men too.[18] But the same world of creatures was filled with evidence to the contrary, reeking of death and testifying to its own futility.[19] Therefore Luther's exegesis of Lev. 26:36 told him that Adam and Eve were terrified by the rustling of a leaf.[20] All the blades of grass could become tongues to accuse a man of his sin.[21] Although poets and mystics might speak of a sacramental universe, a forgiveness of sins that was diffused all over the universe without a particular locus could not explain the universe. But to a man who knew that Word and Sacrament were intended "for the forgiveness of sins" the birds and the trees could become veritable Sacraments, or at least very potent reminders of God's mercy and bounty.[22]

And therefore Luther's exegesis would not separate the "forgiveness" of which the text spoke from the Sacrament as a channel of that forgiveness, just as it would not identify the two. God was not identical with His revelation. If He were, He would be simply one thing in a world of things

---

[18] Cf. *Commentary on Psalm 147* (1531), W, XXI, 447–452; *Luther's Works*, 14, 125–131.

[19] "This simile of the flower indeed exalts the blessings of creation, for it reminds us that in our tragic life we are nevertheless cheered by a beautiful flower. But it is also a phase of life's misery that the petals of the flower so soon fall to the ground and wither and that it cannot preserve its color and distinctive fragrance." *Commentary on Psalm 90* (1534–35), W, XL-III, 530; *Luther's Works*, 13, 303.

[20] Cf., for example, *Lectures on Genesis* (1535–45), W, XLII, 127 to 128; *Luther's Works*, 1, 170–171.

[21] See the delightful quotations assembled by Roland H. Bainton in *Luther Today*, pp. 3–12.

[22] "Thus you must be ashamed of yourself when you look at the sun, which preaches this to you every day, ashamed even when you are in a field and you look at a little flower or at the leaf of a tree. For this is written all over the leaves and the grass. There is no bird so small, indeed, no fruit or berry or grain so tiny, that it does not show this to you and say: 'For whom do I bear my beautiful fruits and berries? For the vilest rogues and rascals on earth.'" *Commentary on the Sermon on the Mount* (1530–32), W, XXXII, 404; *Luther's Works*, 21, 126.

rather than the God of all things; and it was in his works on the Sacrament that Luther made this distinction most clearly.[23] But not all things led a man to the God of all things. This God had condescended to man in His Word and revelation. To know Him as the God of all things, therefore, the church looked for Him in certain particular things. This was the paradox which Luther's exegesis found in the Bible: to know the God of the universe, the church sought Him in the particular events of Christ's life and death; and to receive forgiveness, the church looked to the Word and the Sacraments, instituted "for the forgiveness of sins." In His freedom God had chosen these events and these actions as bearers of His will and forgiveness to the church.

The exegetical material reviewed so far should help to locate Luther's exegesis of the words "for the forgiveness of sins" more accurately in the history of the Christian interpretation of Biblical texts about the Sacrament. This interpretation has been characterized by fluctuation between rationalism and magic.[24] Almost every exegesis of these texts has inclined in either the one or the other direction. Protestant exegesis, carried to an extreme, has led to the first; Roman Catholic exegesis, carried to an extreme, has led to the second. Very often in the history of exegesis a reaction against the one tendency has gone to the opposite extreme, with the result that theologians and Christian believers have sometimes come to believe that the only alternatives to choose from were a magical and a rationalistic exegesis of texts like "for the forgiveness of sins."

Yet Luther realized that neither a magical nor a rationalistic exegesis was consistent with the Biblical picture of God. The error of the magical interpretation became evident to Luther as his exegesis brought him to a consideration of the

[23] See the quotation on p. 138, note 5.
[24] Jaroslav Pelikan, *The Riddle of Roman Catholicism,* p. 229.

concrete objects which had figured in the history of God's dealings with His people during the Old Testament. One such object was the brazen serpent spoken of in Numbers and referred to again in St. John.[25] God had chosen it as a means for saving Israel when its disobedience had brought upon it the punishment of the venomous serpents. At that selected time and for that selected purpose the brazen serpent was a means of forgiveness and deliverance. But long after the time had passed, Israel preserved the serpent and worshiped it. Thus a gift of God, instituted "for the forgiveness of sins," had been distorted into an object of idolatry and a device of magic. Magic began by identifying God with the means He employed, and it ended by worshiping the means and forgetting God. God's demand through Hezekiah that the people get rid of the serpent was a declaration of His freedom from the means He had chosen to use. Determined as it was by the description of God's actions in these texts, Luther's exegesis went a long way toward overcoming the magic which had appeared so often in the history of sacramental piety, including his own piety.

Sometimes Luther's attacks upon this magic sounded very rationalistic, as he ridiculed the notion that some sort of divine power resided in certain objects, for example, in baptismal water.[26] On the positive side, too, he could sometimes speak of the Sacrament as part of the larger world of signs that granted assurance of forgiveness.[27] This motif certainly had a place in his exegesis; but if it had been the whole of Luther's exegesis of phrases like "for the forgiveness of sins," the result would have been a shallow and rationalistic inter-

[25] *Sermons on the Gospel of St. John: Chapters 1–4* (1537–40), W, XLVII, 65–67; *Luther's Works*, 22, 338–340.

[26] *Lectures on Genesis* (1535–45), W, XLII, 170; *Luther's Works*, 1, 227–228.

[27] Ibid., W, XLII, 227–228; *Luther's Works*, 1, 309.

pretation which sacrificed all mystery to the oversimplifications of an artificial theory. Luther's exegesis of both the Old Testament and the New Testament was too profound to let him set forth any such theory.

In principle, therefore, though not always in practice,[28] Luther repudiated both the magical and the rationalistic exegesis of the words of institution. In saying that he stressed the phrase "for the forgiveness of sins" one must be careful to distinguish Luther's exegesis of this phrase from both these extremes. There are at least two ways by which Luther managed to extricate his own exegesis from the alternatives of rationalism and magic. One was an exegesis of what "This is My body" did and did not mean in the Lord's Supper; we have summarized it in chapter seven.[29] The other way — and the one with which the remainder of this chapter will deal — was to relate the Lord's Supper to the other means instituted "for the forgiveness of sins," the proclamation of the Word of God and the Sacrament of Baptism. In this way Luther's exegesis supplied the main outlines for what could have become a comprehensive doctrine of the means of grace, and his doctrine of the Lord's Supper belonged to this doctrine of the means of grace. Actually, as he worked it out in his study of the Scriptures and in controversy, the exegesis of "This is My body" and the exegesis of "for the forgiveness of sins" grew together. Therefore they should be studied together.

One of Luther's most important exegetical achievements was his recovery of the New Testament emphasis on the proclamation of the Word of God. It shaped his entire method of Biblical interpretation. Although chapter 12 will summarize Luther's exegesis of the Pauline statement, "you

[28] See, for example, p. 187, note 38.
[29] Cf. pp. 137 ff.

proclaim the Lord's death," [30] this exegesis is relevant to the present chapter as well. When Luther expounded the words "for the forgiveness of sins," he interpreted this "proclaiming" of the Lord's death as the means by which this "forgiveness of sins" was to be applied to people. The essential content of this "proclaiming" was to be divine judgment and divine forgiveness. As chapter three has pointed out, most efforts to define Luther's view of the Scriptures have missed the mark because of their failure to realize what he meant by this "proclaiming" of the Word of God and, therefore, what he took to be the connection between Scripture and the Word of God. [31] The Word of God in Luther was primarily the proclamation of the message of God as that message spoke to men about divine judgment and divine forgiveness.

To this exegesis of "proclaim" Luther's exegesis of "for the forgiveness of sins" was attached, for he taught that in the Lord's Supper both judgment and forgiveness were communicated. Chiefly it was forgiveness that was communicated, of course; and the text proved that this was the intent of the Sacrament, to be the conveyor of forgiveness. [32] Because Luther saw the Lord's Supper as more than a sign, he was not content to say only that reception of the Sacrament served as a dramatic reminder of that forgiveness which one knew by other means. On the contrary, the gift of the Lord's Supper was the very body and blood of the Lord which had been instrumental in effecting God's for-

[30] See pp. 219 ff.

[31] Cf. pp. 48 ff.

[32] "Dearly beloved, you must not look at yourself, how worthy or unworthy you may be, but at your need, how much you need the grace of Christ. If you see and feel your need, you are worthy and prepared enough. For He instituted it to give us, not poison nor His displeasure but comfort and salvation." *Exhortation to the Sacrament of the Body and Blood of Christ* (1530), W, XXX-II, 622.

giveness. Receiving this body and blood in true faith, there-fore, meant participating in the death of Christ and in its blessings; thus the Sacrament was intended "for the forgive-ness of sins." As the Gospel in the proclaimed Word con-veyed the forgiveness of God through preaching and hearing the story of Christ's death, so the Gospel in the sacramental Word conveyed the forgiveness of God through eating and drinking the tokens of Christ's death, His body broken and His blood shed.

But judgment, too, could work through the Lord's Supper, just as it could work through the proclaimed Word. Against other Protestants Luther defended the idea that also the unworthy recipients of the Sacrament received the true body and blood of the Lord, but received it to their judgment.[33] The proclamation of the cross was "for the forgiveness of sins" to the believer; but to the unbeliever it was for judg-ment, for it condemned him and his sin. Thus it was that the body of Christ in the Lord's Supper could be a source of consolation to the believer, who received it for his eternal benefit, and yet could be a source of condemnation for the nonbeliever, who received the true body of Christ and was judged by it.[34] Judgment and forgiveness were both opera-tive in the Lord's Supper, just as they were in the procla-mation of the Word of God. And therefore the Lord's Supper, like the proclamation of the Word of God, was truly a "means of grace" in Luther's exegesis. Later Lu-therans dulled the point of this exegesis by involving them-selves in debates over whether the Law was a means of grace.[35] According to Luther, the Word of God was a means of grace; and according to his customary usage, the Word

[33] See p. 142, note 18.
[34] Cf. the *Letter to a Good Friend* (1534), W, XXXVIII, 264—265.
[35] Lauri Haikola's *Usus legis* (Uppsala, 1958) is a careful discussion of this development.

of God was both the Law and the Gospel, although it was
intended to be the Gospel. So also the Lord's Supper was
intended "for the forgiveness of sins," as this text said; but
to those who spurned that forgiveness this same means
became the instrument of divine judgment.

Although there was a correlation between "proclaiming"
and the Lord's Supper in Luther's exegesis of "for the forgiveness of sins," there was also a close correlation between
the Lord's Supper and Baptism.[36] Baptism was the Sacrament of initiation; the Lord's Supper was the Sacrament of
continuation. Baptism was the point at which the Christian
life began; the Lord's Supper was the line of the Christian
life drawn from that point. Baptism was to faith as birth
was to physical life; the Lord's Supper was to faith as food
was to physical life. Baptism made men members of Christ;
the Lord's Supper kept them members of Christ. In these
and in dozens of other ways Luther's exegesis of the New
Testament drew an intimate connection between Baptism
and the Lord's Supper. It was characteristic of Luther's
method that he did not approach this exegesis from a pre-
conceived definition of "Sacrament" [37] but worked out his
several definitions of a Sacrament on the basis of texts dealing with Baptism, the Lord's Supper, and absolution, which
he often called a Sacrament too.[38]

As divine judgment and divine forgiveness were the
themes of the means of grace in the preached Word of God,
so the death and the resurrection of Christ were the themes
of the means of grace in Baptism. Baptism for Luther was
always Baptism into the death of Christ. Some of his most

[36] But see *Lectures on Genesis* (1535—45), W, XLII, 170; *Luther's Works*, 1, 228, note 73.

[37] Luther was well aware of the evolution through which the term "Sacrament" had passed, as he showed in *The Babylonian Captivity of the Church* (1520), W, VI, 550—553.

[38] Ebeling, *Evangelienauslegung*, pp. 371—373.

dramatic and effective sermons were those which contained his exegesis of the sixth chapter of Romans, describing the incorporation of the believer into the dying Lord through Baptism.[39] It was not mere chance that Luther should have included in his Small Catechism these words of St. Paul about Baptism from the sixth chapter of Romans.[40] This exegesis figured so prominently in Luther's doctrine of Baptism at least partly because of his interpretation of the atonement. As chapters nine and thirteen will show, Luther's exegesis had found many ways of speaking about the reconciliation between God and man.[41] One of the most prominent of these came from the Biblical texts picturing the crucifixion as the death of death. Luther interpreted these texts to mean that when Christ went to the cross, He took with Him the mortal nature of man and, with it, died to sin.[42] Therefore Romans could treat Baptism as Baptism into His death; for by it men appropriated the the death of their mortal nature, accomplished through His death. According to Luther's exegesis, the self of sin was thus technically dead from the time of Baptism, even though it acted as though it were alive. To be "baptized into the death of Christ" thus meant to regard as dead everything in human life that would seek to alienate man from God. Baptism was said to convey the benefits of the death of Christ because the Epistle to the Romans declared that it made men one with Him in His death.

But the Epistle to the Romans said also that Baptism made men one with Christ in His resurrection. Therefore

[39] Two such were delivered on July 4, 1535, W, XLI, 368—374; and on July 20, 1544, W, XLIX, 511—519.

[40] Cf. the various recensions of the Small Catechism, W, XXX-I, 312 to 315.

[41] See pp. 174 ff. and 237 ff.

[42] Gustaf Aulén, in *Christus Victor,* tr. by A. G. Hebert (London, 1931), has summarized — and overstated! — this interpretation.

Baptism was both a dying and a rising, both an immersion and an emergence. Here again Luther's exegesis enabled him to grasp the full import of Biblical language, for he made the resurrection of Christ an integral part of the atonement rather than merely a sign that God had accepted the sacrifice on the cross. In the resurrection, according to this exegesis, Christ had put behind Him the old humanity and had arisen as the Head of a new humanity, the church.[43] Luther interpreted Romans to say that this new humanity was available to men through Baptism, which united them to His death and therefore also to His resurrection. Baptism was intended "for the forgiveness of sins," according to Luther, because "forgiveness" was the word for that attitude of God toward men which was made possible by the death and resurrection of Christ.

This was also one of the ways Luther interpreted the "for the forgiveness of sins" in the words of institution. As chapter nine will point out at greater length, both the death of Christ and the resurrection of Christ had a role in Luther's exegesis of texts dealing with the Lord's Supper.[44] The Lord's Supper was "for the forgiveness of sins" because it strengthened unity and community with Christ's death, a unity and community created in Baptism. But Baptism was not limited to the death of Christ, and neither was the Lord's Supper; nor, for that matter, was the proclaimed Word. All of them communicated Good Friday, but all of them communicated Easter also. Because the texts drew a direct analogy between the Lord's Supper and Baptism in this regard, both were channels of this "forgiveness." Against Zwingli and against the Anabaptists Luther had to defend his exegesis

[43] This is the theme of Luther's *Exposition of 1 Corinthians 15* (1534), W, XXXVI, 478—696.

[44] See p. 184.

of "for the forgiveness of sins" as he had applied it to both Baptism and the Lord's Supper.

From the preceding it should be clear that Luther's exegesis found a profound meaning in the New Testament formula "for the forgiveness of sins." Because he recognized, with a clarity shared by few exegetes, the distinctiveness of Biblical speech, he saw that the New Testament formula did not simply identify this "forgiveness" with the Lord's Supper. Saying that the Lord's Supper was meant "for the forgiveness of sins" could not mean that a little piece of God had been trapped by man, or that a formula of incantation had been provided by means of which a Christian conjurer could force God to forgive. Luther realized that far from making the Lord's Supper a channel of forgiveness, such an exegesis cheapened forgiveness and secularized it, until the Christian meaning of forgiveness was lost. He declared that if the people of his day had really believed that the Sacrament was instituted "for the forgiveness of sins" and not merely for warding off floods, disease, and agricultural crises,[45] they would have been more devout and more regular in their use of this channel of forgiveness. The very identification of "forgiveness" with "channel of forgiveness" had managed to debase them both and to pervert the text "for the forgiveness of sins."

Still it would have done violence to Biblical exegesis to discard the concept of channels of forgiveness altogether, or to generalize it so completely that it was no more applicable to the Lord's Supper than it was to anything else in the church or the world that ennobled human life or uplifted the human spirit. For when forgiveness was separated from the channels of forgiveness, this, too, ended in a per-

[45] "When someone's pig is sick or when he has lost a groschen or when some other petty trouble strikes him, this is all to be averted with money through the Mass." *Proposal for Order* (1526), W, XIX, 441.

version of the text. What was needed was an exegesis of "for the forgiveness of sins" that avoided both identification and separation. This Luther found in his theocentric exegesis of these words, that is, in his refusal to let man stand at the center of such language about God. Because he was theocentric in his exegesis, he usually managed to speak about the Lord's Supper as a means "for the forgiveness of sins" without falling into the traps surrounding the history of this idea. For the same reason he could insist upon his exegesis of "This is My body" and nevertheless reject transubstantiation as an artificial theory.

The best English word for the role of the Lord's Supper as channel of forgiveness according to Luther's exegesis of "for the forgiveness of sins" would seem to be the word "communicate." This distinguishes between forgiveness and the channels of forgiveness; for if they were identical, it would not be necessary to communicate the forgiveness. And yet it does not separate them; for if they were separate, it would be impossible to communicate the forgiveness. And it says precisely what Luther's exegesis interpreted "for the forgiveness of sins" to be saying: that the Sacrament communicated the forgiveness of God for this life and for the next. How this exegesis dealt with the connection between this life and the next and with a text that appeared to make the connection a sacramental one will concern us in the next chapter.

CHAPTER NINE

"If Anyone Eats of This Bread, He Will Live Forever"
(John 6:51)

LUTHER's sermonic exposition of the sixth chapter of the Gospel of John, delivered between November 5, 1530, and May 13, 1531, was undertaken with the conviction that "this fine text has been tortured and manhandled for approximately six or seven years." [1] His method of exegesis was an effort to prove that not the eating and drinking in the Lord's Supper but the "spiritual" eating and drinking of faith was the theme of this chapter. As we have seen in chapter six, Luther's exegesis of this chapter was reinforced by his stand in the controversy with Zwingli. [2] Yet his exegesis of this very chapter could also paraphrase Christ as saying here: "If you touch My flesh, you are not touching simple flesh and blood; you are eating and drinking flesh and blood which makes you divine. It does not make you flesh and blood, but it has the nature and strength of God." [3] This was an exegesis which had led Christian theologians since the second century to speak of the Lord's Supper as a "medicine of immortality." How could Luther's method of exegesis reject the eucharistic interpretation of the sixth chapter of John and yet apply the words of John 6:51, "If anyone eats of this bread, he will live forever," to the Eucharist?

[1] *Sermons on the Gospel of St. John: Chapters 6–8* (1530–32), W, XXXIII, 260; *Luther's Works*, 23, 165.

[2] See pp. 109–134.

[3] *Sermons on the Gospel of St. John: Chapters 6–8* (1530–32), W, XXXIII, 188; *Luther's Works*, 23, 122.

Many of Luther's followers have found this exegesis of John 6:51 strange and even offensive, and that for several reasons.[4] For one thing, they have become accustomed to think of Christianity as something "purely spiritual," while Luther was thinking of its bearing upon the total life, including the life of the body. In addition, this exegesis has often been set forth by its proponents as well as by its critics in language that smacked of magic.[5] But as Luther freed the exegesis of passages like "This is My body" or "For the forgiveness of sins" from the legalism and magic with which it had often been freighted, so he gave to his exegesis of this passage a more profound and more evangelical meaning than it had often possessed in the tradition. Some of this is summarized in chapter four.

Luther's explanation of "If anyone eats of this bread, he will live forever" rested on an assumption regarding the physical nature of man. One of Luther's great exegetical insights was his discovery of the significance that the Scriptures attached to the body, in contrast to the exegetical tradition which had treated the body as part of man's lower nature.[6] This exegetical rediscovery of the body was important for Luther's interpretation of passages on marriage, on Christ as true man, and on the Lord's Supper. Because his exegesis recognized that the body was indispensable to the life of man in God, he concluded that it had its share in the Sacrament too. As he said in 1527: "The mouth, the

[4] Cf. Ernst Sommerlath, *Der Sinn des Abendmahls* (Leipzig, 1930), pp. 81—90.

[5] On the backgrounds of this exegesis cf. the essay by the Roman Catholic theologian Th. Schermann, *Zur Erklärung der Stelle Epistula ad Ephes. 20, 2 des Ignatius von Antiocheia* φάρμακον ἀθανασίας, in *Theologische Quartalschrift*, XCII (1910), 6—19.

[6] An interesting insight into this is presented by the study of Erdmann Schott, *Luthers Anthropologie und seine Lehre von der manducatio oralis in wechselseitiger Beleuchtung*, in *Zeitschrift für systematische Theologie*, IX (1931—32), 585—602.

throat, the body which eats the body of Christ is also to have its benefit from it, in that it will live eternally and arise on the Last Day to eternal blessedness. That is the mysterious power and benefit which, in the Lord's Supper, goes from the body of Christ into our body. For it must be beneficial and cannot be present without a purpose. Therefore it must give life and blessedness to our body." [7]

Such an exegesis of "If anyone eats of this bread, he will live forever" was based not only on a general understanding of what the Scriptures taught about the physical nature of man but also on a specific exegesis of their statements regarding the physical nature of Christ and its role in the way of salvation. Luther's exegesis could claim that the human body was able to participate in salvation because he maintained that this salvation had been accomplished through the physical body and blood of Christ and that it was this very body and blood which was God's gift in the Sacrament. Therefore this exegesis maintained that the Sacrament could be of benefit also to the body, because Christ had redeemed men not merely through His soul or His mind but through His physical nature. The task of exegesis was to discover that the ground of the Lord's Supper was the death of Christ, and that its function was to "proclaim the Lord's death." [8] This it did through the body of Christ broken for men. The Biblical portrait of the saving Christ was emphatically physical, and so was Luther's exegesis of it. [9] Luther was a "medieval" exegete in his stress on the broken and crucified body of the Lord. This did not mean that his exegesis was engrossed with the grim clinical details of the suffering and death of Christ on the cross. But it did

[7] *This Is My Body* (1527), W, XXIII, 259.

[8] See pp. 219 ff.

[9] A good illustration was Luther's sermon for April 17, 1538, W, XLVI, 256—265.

mean that in his exegesis of passages dealing with the sufferings of Christ Luther assigned great significance to the pains of body through which Christ passed while He hung on the cross.

When this exegesis of passages about the suffering and death of Christ was combined with Luther's exegesis of "This is My body," the result was that the crucified and broken body of Christ became the primary focus for all his eucharistic exegesis. As chapter seven has shown, the main connotation of the term "body of Christ" in Luther's exegesis was the connotation it acquired for him through the Passion story.[10] In part this was due to the setting of the original supper within the Passion story. But this cannot have been the decisive consideration; for the original supper was set within the context of the Hebrew Passover as well, and this was a motif which played a relatively minor role in Luther's exegesis.[11] Principally the stress on the broken body in Luther's exegesis came from the realization, born of his exegetical study, that in the New Testament the suffering and death of Christ provided the Lord's Supper not merely with its original historical setting but also with its basic meaning. Although Luther's exegesis formulated the meaning of the Sacrament in many ways and was more conscious of the nuances in New Testament texts than some subsequent exegesis has been, it found the basic meaning of the Sacrament, from which all these exegetical nuances were to be derived, in the body that was broken and the blood that was shed.

Since it was both the body and the blood, Luther even-

[10] See p. 149.

[11] It did occur occasionally, as when Luther used it to prove that the Mass was not a sacrifice of atonement on the grounds that Christ could not have sacrificed on the Passover, since He was not in the temple. *The Abuse of the Mass* (1521), W, VIII, 525.

tually urged the restoration of the chalice to the laity.[12] Luther's exegesis recognized that the symbolism of the broken wafer and the poured wine pointed to the centrality of Christ's death in the Lord's Supper; for it must be remembered that in making the Lord's Supper more than a sign Luther's exegesis did not make it less than a sign. According to Luther's exegesis, the Lord's Supper was a bridge to the series of events remembered in the words of Paul (1 Cor. 11:23): "The Lord Jesus on the night when He was betrayed." The Biblical picture of that night of betrayal and of the night of death which followed it was the presupposition for Luther's exegesis of texts about the Lord's Supper.

Although the Sacrament united the church to the Lord's action on the night when He was betrayed, this did not exhaust its significance in Luther's exegesis. He also expounded the text which said that on that very night and in the very process of instituting the Sacrament the Lord Himself had prophesied that one day He would drink a new cup with His disciples in the Father's kingdom.[13] If exegesis dealt only with past history in its interpretation of texts about the Lord's Supper, therefore, it would not be doing justice to these texts; for in them the past history pointed beyond itself to the coming of the Father's kingdom. Luther's exegesis interpreted also this coming kingdom as part of what the Lord's Supper gave. His exegesis was an eschatological exegesis in that it found the ultimate value of the Lord's Supper not only in the church's faith about the past, nor only in its love here in the present, but also in its hope for the future.

Luther pointed out in his exegesis that the church could

[12] In his treatise On Receiving Both Kinds in the Sacrament (1522), W, X, II-1, 11—41, Luther explained his hesitation about the restoration of the chalice to the laity and his decision to go through with it.

[13] Most familiar is his comment on this passage at the conclusion of The Babylonian Captivity of the Church (1520), W, VI, 572.

not dispense with its hope for the future, because what it now knew and possessed of its Lord could not exhaust everything He was ever to be for the church.[14] The faith of the church demanded hope, because the church knew its faith to be less than it should be and would be. The love of the church similarly produced longing, because the church knew from the love of God in Christ that its own love was, by contrast, cold and fragmentary. Luther's exegesis, especially that of his later years, was filled with the poignancy of this longing.[15] As he saw his own expectations for the church disappointed and his own predictions about the success of the Gospel unfulfilled, he came to deal more existentially than he had before with the texts which said that the church could not live without its hope for something better than even the best of here and now could supply.

As faith and love both pointed to hope in Luther's exegesis, so the Lord's Supper pointed to the future as well. Intimate as was the communion between Christ and the church in the Sacrament, it promised an intimacy even more profound and more permanent.[16] Similarly, the contemplation of God's great deeds in the cross of Christ, as this contemplation was nurtured in the piety of the Sacrament, only served to accentuate the contrast between what Christ had wanted to accomplish and what the reality of the Christian life manifested. United to the death of the Lord, the Christian came to see that though Christ had died for him, he had not yet died to sin. Receiving here the instruments of Christ's perfect obedience and death, the believer had to acknowledge how imperfect his own obedience was; and

[14] *Lectures on Genesis* (1535–45), W, XLII, 159–160; *Luther's Works*, 1, 214.

[15] "Our dear Lord Jesus Christ," he wrote in his preface to the Smalcald Articles (1537), W, L, 196, "do Thou Thyself convoke a council and rescue Thine own through Thy glorious coming."

[16] So in the *Summer Postil* (1544), W, LII, 211–212.

therefore he longed for an obedience more nearly like Christ's. Luther's exegesis continually sounded these themes and called upon Christians to examine themselves and then to desire what the Sacrament offered for the present as well as what the Sacrament guaranteed for the future.[17]

Past, present, and future — the rhythm of Luther's exegesis oscillated from one to the next. Memory of the night in which Christ was betrayed aroused hope for the future. But that hope for the future, in turn, fed on a further element of Christian memory, the resurrection of Christ.[18] The very expectation which caused believers to look away from the present to a future with God simultaneously caused them to look back at the event which promised such a future. For Luther's exegesis of the word "until He comes" made clear that in the Lord's Supper it was not possible to go directly from the memory of Christ's death to the hope of His coming without paying attention also to the significance of His resurrection, which was the link between His death and His coming. From such exegesis it followed that because the Sacrament proclaimed the Lord's death, but did so "until He comes," it also conveyed the meaning of His resurrection. As much as Luther's exegesis emphasized that the ground of the Lord's Supper was the death of Christ, he never forgot to view the death of Christ through the glasses of His resurrection. Death and resurrection belonged together in the language of the Bible.[19] They belonged together also in the exegesis of the Bible, including the exegesis of eucharistic texts. Luther's exegesis, therefore,

[17] Some of this exegesis is collected in Erwin Mühlhaupt (ed.), *D. Martin Luthers Evangelien-Auslegung*, V (Göttingen, 1950), 168—261.

[18] Cf. Richard R. Niebuhr, *Resurrection and Historical Reason* (New York, 1957), pp. 129—161.

[19] Wilhelm Traugott Hahn, *Das Mitsterben und Mitauferstehen mit Christus bei Paulus* (Gütersloh, 1937).

made the cross basic to the meaning of resurrection texts like "If anyone eats of this bread, he will live forever."

In Luther's exegesis, as chapter eight has tried to show, the concept of forgiveness was always connected to the cross and death of Christ.[20] This was true of his exegesis of the sixth chapter of Romans, which interpreted Baptism as an act of incorporation into the death of Christ. It was true also of his exegesis of the Biblical term "Word of God" as that which preached Jesus Christ and Him crucified. In Luther's exegesis the Word and the Sacraments were not general reminders about God and His will; they were means of grace, the grace of the Lord Jesus Christ granted and sealed in His death on the cross. Luther took the New Testament to say that through these means the Holy Spirit conveyed and conferred the benefits of Christ's death, granting an intimate participation in His death. There were three terms in which Luther often paraphrased New Testament statements about the benefits of such a participation in the death of the Lord: forgiveness of sins, life, and salvation.[21]

A great Swedish theologian of the past generation, Einar Billing, once said: "Never believe that you have a correct understanding of a thought of Luther before you have succeeded in reducing it to a simple corollary of the thought of the forgiveness of sins." [22] This is undoubtedly an over-simplification of Luther's complex thought and exegesis, but it does serve to point out the prominence of the forgiveness of sins in Luther's own religious development and in his exegesis of the Scriptures. The hunger for forgiveness had been his consuming passion in the monastery, and the discovery of forgiveness was the beginning of his career as

[20] See pp. 167 ff.

[21] So most familiarly in the Small Catechism (1529), W, XXX-I, 316 to 317.

[22] Einar Billing, *Our Calling*, tr. by Conrad Bergendoff (Rock Island, 1947), p. 7.

a Reformer. From this experience, which also shaped his exegesis of the Scriptures, Luther learned to find the forgiveness of sins at the center of any text that spoke of what man needed from God and obtained from Him. In his sacramental exegesis, therefore, the forgiveness of sins may probably be said to have occupied the dominant position. Many passages in Luther's writings give the impression that the forgiveness of sins exhausted the content of the Lord's Supper for him.[23] There is undoubtedly some validity to the criticism that Luther exaggerated this element in the Sacrament and tended to underestimate others, including some of those which this book seeks to recover in his exegetical work.[24] Nevertheless, his exegesis was right in assigning great importance to forgiveness; for the New Testament did say that the Lord's Supper conferred upon the church an intimate participation in the death of the Lord, and that therefore it was a means by which the forgiveness of sins became available to the believers.

But where there was forgiveness of sins, there also was life and salvation. This formula from Luther's Small Catechism applied also to his exegesis of passages on the Lord's Supper. "If anyone eats of this bread, he will live forever" could make sense only because "living forever" in this sense had been made possible through the Lord's death. A study of how Luther used the word "life" has revealed that here, as elsewhere in his exegesis, he penetrated to the special and subtle connotations of St. John's Gospel.[25] For Luther as an expositor of the Fourth Gospel "life" described the status for which man had originally been created and to which, in Christ, he had now been restored. It did not

[23] Cf. *Confession on the Lord's Supper* (1528), W, XXVI, 478—479.

[24] Yngve Brilioth's *Eucharistic Faith and Practice* (New York, 1934) is perhaps the best known statement of that criticism.

[25] See p. 36, note 17.

refer to a biological existence alone, nor merely to a mental or spiritual existence. It described the whole man as that whole man was completely dependent on God for his total existence. Where the death of Christ, conveyed through the means of grace, had granted the forgiveness of sins, there this "life" came as a result of this death.

And this, in turn, brought "salvation." Despite his opposition to any exegesis of "justification" that made it a gradual process of healing throughout life,[26] Luther nevertheless retained the idea of healing in his exegesis. He saw that health was the essential content of the Biblical word "salvation," and even in later years his exegesis applied the parable of the Good Samaritan to Christ in His healing ministry.[27] At times, as in his exegesis of Isaiah, Luther spoke of his amazement that the wounds of Christ should confer health, as the death of Christ conferred life.[28] Such exegesis sounded very "medieval," especially when it went on to describe the Lord's Supper as a way to regain health in God after the sickness of sin.[29] Like Baptism and like the proclaimed Word, the Lord's Supper conferred forgiveness of sins, life, and salvation — all by granting an intimate participation in the death of Christ.

Decisive though this idea of participation in Christ's death was for Luther's exegesis, he did not restrict the redemptive work of Christ to His death; and therefore the benefit of the Sacrament could not be confined to participation in the death of Christ either. One of the reasons why later exegetes have often had difficulty comprehending

[26] Ebeling, *Evangelienauslegung*, pp. 496–506, is a history of the exegesis of the Good Samaritan.

[27] A stirring example is his sermon of August 22, 1529, W, XXIX, 536 to 538.

[28] *Commentary on Isaiah 53* (1544), W, XL-III, 717–718.

[29] See *Commentary on Psalm 8* (1537), W, XLV, 230–231; *Luther's Works*, 12, 118–119.

the eucharistic interpretation of "If anyone eats of this bread he will live forever" was their failure to measure the full scope of Christ's redemptive work in Luther's exegesis.

For Luther, more perhaps than for any Western exegete in a thousand years, the redemptive work of Christ was coextensive with His entire life. Of special interest and importance was the revival in Luther's exegesis of the patristic picture of Christ as the Conqueror of sin, death, and the devil.[30] This picture was not the only image for the atonement in Luther's exegesis, but it was a significant metaphor. According to this metaphor, the reconciliation between God and man was not primarily a transaction between Christ and God, in which Christ represented the human race, but rather a conflict between Christ and the devil, in which Christ represented God. Holding the human race captive in his grasp, the devil fought to retain his slaves. But Christ incited the devil and death to attack Him and, in attacking Him, to destroy themselves. Now death had died, and the devil was destroyed. Christ the Victor arose from the dead to grant His life and His victory to all who believed in Him. With the aid of this picture Luther's exegesis could assign to Easter a more intrinsic importance in the work of Christ than could the Western exegesis that had interpreted Christ's death as only a sacrifice or as only vicarious satisfaction for human sin. For this Western exegesis Good Friday was the primary or even the sole event of redemption. But when Luther's exegesis described redemption as the victory of Christ, it made possible the inclusion of the resurrection of Christ in His redemptive work and thus also in the exegesis of passages about the Sacraments.

For these passages, too, needed to be related to the total redemptive work of Christ, instead of being confined

[30] See p. 170, note 42.

in their interpretation to the death of Christ. Baptism did indeed confer an intimate participation in the death of Christ. But Luther's exegesis of his favorite passage on Baptism, Rom. 6:4, described the full scope of this participation: "that as Christ was raised from the dead to the glory of the Father, so we, too, might walk in a newness of life." [31] For St. Paul the significance of Baptism was anchored both in the death and in the resurrection of Christ — in neither without the other. For Luther's exegesis too, even for his early exegesis, Baptism revolved around both death and resurrection. The same thing was true of the preached Word of God. It was a Word of the cross, and in his exegesis Luther was fond of quoting the saying of St. Paul at the beginning of 1 Corinthians about knowing nothing except Christ and Him crucified. On the other hand, his own exegesis of the fifteenth chapter of that epistle showed how important the resurrection of Christ was to his view of the atonement.[32]

Luther's exegesis taught that, like Baptism and like the preached Word, the Lord's Supper granted an intimate participation in the total redemptive work of the crucified and risen Lord, also in His resurrection. For as it was both His death and His resurrection that won the victory, so it was both His death and His resurrection that were shared in the Sacrament. In a remarkable passage in his treatise *This Is My Body* of 1527 Luther gave his exegesis of the words, "If anyone eats of this bread, he will live forever," though he did not quote them. The flesh of Christ, he wrote, "is an imperishable, immortal, indestructible flesh. . . . Once death tried to consume and devour it, but it could not. The flesh of Christ tore the stomach and throat of death into more than a hundred thousand pieces, so that death's teeth were

[31] Werner Jetter, *Die Taufe beim jungen Luther* (Tübingen, 1954).
[32] See p. 171, note 43.

pulled out and thrown away; but it [the flesh of Christ] remained alive. For the food was too strong for death, and the food consumed and devoured the eater. God is present in this flesh, it is a spirit-flesh. It is in God and God is in it; therefore it is alive itself, and it gives life to all who eat it, both to the body and to the soul." [33]

Since the Lord's Supper thus granted a share in the total redemptive work of Christ crucified and risen, it was a means by which that total redemptive work of Christ was applied to the total life of man. At times Luther's exegesis of the Gospels toyed with a departmentalization of Christ's redemptive work according to the various stages of human life: His holy birth atoned for man's sinful birth, His childhood obedience for man's disobedience, etc. [34] But this soon proved unmanageable, and most of Luther's exegesis interpreted the redemptive work of Christ as a whole. He did not distinguish as sharply as did later Lutheran exegetes between the "active" and the "passive" obedience of Christ. [35] It would seem more accurate to say that Luther's exegesis attributed a single obedience to Christ — His life, His suffering, and His death. [36] But there was one distinction to which it did return over and over, that between Christ's death and His resurrection. In this distinction the counterpart of the resurrection of Christ was, of course, the resurrection of the believer. And as a divinely appointed channel for conferring the power of Christ's resurrection, the Lord's Supper had a significance also for the hope of the resurrection.

At times Luther made the derivation of this from the sixth chapter of John direct and overt, as when he wrote that

[33] *This Is My Body* (1527), W, XXIII, 243—245.

[34] See the Torgau sermon of 1533, W, XXXVII, 53—59.

[35] Edmund Schlink, *Theologie der lutherischen Bekenntnisschriften* (3rd ed.; Munich, 1948), pp. 120—126.

[36] See also the Formula of Concord, S. D., Article III, 57, *Bekenntnisschriften*, p. 934.

Christ's flesh was "imperishable, as is everything that comes from the Spirit. It is a food completely different from perishable food. Perishable food is transformed into the body that eats it. This food, on the other hand, transforms him who eats it into itself and makes him like itself, as spiritual, alive, and eternal as it is itself, as He says (John 6:33): This is the bread from heaven, which gives life to the world." [37] A little later he put it even more dramatically: "In this eating [in the Lord's Supper] what happens is this, if I may use a crude illustration. It is as though a wolf were to eat a sheep and the sheep were such strong food that it would transform the wolf into a sheep. So it is with us. When we eat the flesh of Christ, physically and spiritually, this food is so strong that it transforms us into itself and changes carnal, sinful, mortal men into men who are holy and alive." [38]

Clearly Luther believed that according to the sixth chapter of John the Lord's Supper made the resurrection possible by transforming a person physically as well as spiritually. Luther generally refused to interpret this chapter sacramentally, as we have seen. His opponents opposed his exegesis of "This is My body," and their chief weapon came from this chapter: "The flesh is of no avail." [39] But from this same chapter came a eucharistic exegesis which Luther's opponents found even less acceptable than his exegesis of "This is My body." [40] The problem might be formulated a trifle extremely as follows: Only if the eating and drinking spoken of in this chapter were the eating and drinking in the Lord's Supper (an interpretation which Luther's exegesis denied) could the Lord's Supper prepare the body for the resurrection and make the resurrection possible (an interpretation which Luther's

[37] *This Is My Body* (1527), W, XXIII, 203.
[38] Ibid., p. 205.
[39] See pp. 122 ff.
[40] Helmut Gollwitzer, *Zur Auslegung von Joh. 6,* p. 166, note 84.

exegesis affirmed). This seems to have been the exegesis behind the formulations of church fathers like Irenaeus, whom Luther quoted on the physical effects of the Sacrament.[41]

At other times Luther proceeded more cautiously in his exegesis. Then he represented the Sacrament, not as the cause but only as the assurance of the resurrection. Christ "gives us His own body as food," Luther wrote in one place, "in order by such a guarantee to assure and comfort us that our body, too, is to live eternally, because here on earth it has had a share in an eternal and living food." [42] According to such an exegesis, the function of the Lord's Supper in relation to the resurrection would be subjective rather than objective: it assured men of that which was accomplished and made possible by other means. Luther did not iron out the inconsistencies between the idea that the Lord's Supper made the resurrection possible and the idea that it merely granted an assurance of it. His own position seems to have been that because the Lord's Supper made the resurrection possible, it also granted the assurance.[43]

Luther devoted as much attention to this question as he did because of the emphasis in his exegesis on the resurrection of the body. Where the Greek doctrine of the natural immortality of the soul had influenced Biblical exegesis, there Christian thought was concerned only with the "spiritual" effects of the Sacrament upon the soul. As has been pointed out, however, Luther's exegesis brought about a theological rediscovery of the body and of its role in both creation and redemption.[44] At times he expressed vigorous opposition to

[41] See p. 175, note 5, on patristic usage.
[42] *This Is My Body* (1527), W, XXIII, 155—157.
[43] See the work of Sommerlath referred to on p. 175, note 4.
[44] See p. 175, note 6.

the idea that the soul was naturally immortal.[45] But even when he was willing to countenance this idea, he nevertheless emphasized the resurrection of the body as the distinctive content of the Christian hope.[46] The difference between immortality and resurrection in Luther's exegesis was the difference between a hope based on man's natural abilities to live again and a hope based on God's power to make a man alive again. Luther's exegesis proceeded from the premise that special acts of divine intervention were necessary to make a man what he ought to be. Such special acts of divine intervention were the incarnation of Christ and the resurrection of the body.[47] Since in Luther's exegesis it was God "who alone has immortality and life," men could become immortal only if He communicated His immortality to them. When Luther's exegesis used the word "immortality," therefore, this did not refer to the shadowy life of the soul which had been its connotation in so much of the exegetical tradition; Luther used "immortality" as a synonym for "resurrection." [48]

Luther's clear-eyed realization that only God possessed immortality and that therefore only He could confer it gave a meaning to the traditional exegesis of "If anyone eats of this bread, he will live forever" that it could not have had without this realization. This realization was also a check upon the almost inescapable notion that according to this passage the Lord's Supper made men immortal through some inherent magical power. According to Luther's exegesis, the Lord's Supper united man to God, who thus communicated

[45] Carl Stange, *Luthers Gedanken über Tod, Gericht und ewiges Leben,* in *Zeitschrift für systematische Theologie,* X (1933), 490–513.

[46] Paul Althaus, *Die letzten Dinge* (3rd ed.; Gütersloh, 1926), pp. 271 to 288.

[47] Cf. *Commentary on Psalm 90* (1534–35), W, XL-III, 495; *Luther's Works,* 13, 82–83.

[48] But see my comment, *Luther's Works,* 1, xi.

His own immortality to them and made them alive through the resurrection of the body. Neither Luther's eucharistic exegesis of this passage nor his rejection of the eucharistic exegesis of the chapter as a whole would receive much support among the Biblical scholars of the twentieth century.[49] But even if one is obliged to question this exegesis, one does so in the name of Luther's own exegetical principles and practice! And that is more important than either acceptance or rejection of his exegesis as such.

[49] See pp. 259–260.

CHAPTER TEN

"Participation in the Body of Christ" (1 Cor. 10:16)

ONE of the most prominent exegetical motifs in Zwingli's view of the Lord's Supper was the motif of participation or fellowship.[1] And as its setting in 1 Corinthians indicates, the Lord's Supper had long been interpreted as a fellowship of Christians with one another.[2] The prominence of this idea in the New Testament suggests that the concept of the Lord's Supper as a fellowship among believers belongs in any doctrine of the Lord's Supper that lays claim to exegetical adequacy. In Luther's exegesis of passages on the Lord's Supper, as that exegesis was shaped in his controversy against Zwingli, the motif of fellowship was not very prominent.[3] If his doctrine of the Lord's Supper is interpreted only on the basis of this polemical exegesis, therefore, it is easy to conclude that he did not give attention to the notion of fellowship among Christians at the Lord's Table.[4] But when one turns from such polemics to his other exegesis, the motif of fellowship once more assumes an importance at least approximating that which it had in the New Testament. For as chapter two has sought to show, we must sometimes appeal from Luther the polemical theologian to Luther the Biblical theologian, just as we must sometimes appeal from

[1] See Hermann Sasse, *This Is My Body* (Minneapolis, 1959), pp. 389 to 398.

[2] Cf. the rich materials assembled in Werner Elert, *Abendmahl und Kirchengemeinschaft in der alten Kirche hauptsächlich des Ostens* (Berlin, 1954).

[3] See p. 43.

[4] See p. 182, note 23.

his exegetical practice to his exegetical principles — and vice versa!

The Lord's Supper, according to Luther's exegesis of Paul's words, was an intimate participation of Christian believers in one another. There was no other place in Christian experience where a participation so intimate existed.[5] From the church fathers Luther quoted the figure of speech that as the bread had been baked from many individual grains that had been ground up and as the wine was composed of many individual grapes that had been crushed, so Christians were gathered together from their isolation and separation into unity and intimacy at the common table.[6] The history of the exegesis of "participation" as fellowship shows how easily it has managed to become the determining element in the exegesis of Pauline teaching about the Lord's Supper.[7] When it has, the Lord's Supper has been said to be important in the Christian life because of the way the believers shared in it. What they brought to it and what they took away from it emphasized to their minds the closeness of "participation" that it represented. The curse of isolation and separation was part of the curse of sin, the proponents of this exegesis recognized. People thought primarily of themselves, and they used others for themselves. The Christian faith had as its purpose the elimination of that curse. It sought to break down the wall between individuals and to teach them "participation" in one another. And therefore in the night when He was betrayed the Lord had instituted a com-

---

[5] "The significance or purpose of this Sacrament is the fellowship of all saints, whence it derives its common name *synaxis* or *communio*, that is, fellowship; and *communicare* means to take part in this fellowship, or as we say, to go to the Sacrament." *Treatise on the Holy Sacrament* (1519), W, II, 743.

[6] Ibid., p. 748.

[7] For orientation on the problem of "participation" and of its meaning see Friedrich Hauck, s. v. κοινός in Gerhard Kittel (ed.), *Theologisches Wörterbuch zum Neuen Testament*, III (Stuttgart, 1938), 789—810.

mon meal in which sharing was central, so that by such a "participation in the body of Christ" men could be rescued from their isolation.[8]

Now all this was present in Luther's exegesis too; but here it was related to what he regarded as the basic "participation" in the Lord's Supper, namely, the participation of the church in Christ's body and blood. For the root of isolation from one's fellows was one's isolation from God; therefore the cure for it was not, first of all, a participation of men in one another but a restoration of their participation in God through the forgiveness of sins.[9] This was accomplished in the life, death, and resurrection of Christ. But the forgiveness did not come to a person automatically, simply by virtue of his participation in the human race. It had to be communicated by means or channels. The Lord's Supper was one such means. As chapter eight has tried to show, Luther's exegesis urged this availability of forgiveness through the means which God had appointed.[10]

The basic participation which Luther's exegesis found in the Lord's Supper, therefore, was the participation of the church and its members in Christ Himself through His body and blood.[11] In His last word to the church Christ had promised to be with the church to the consummation of this age.[12] The church was His body because He was continually present with His church. But in the Lord's Supper He was present in a unique way, by granting a "participation" in His body and blood to the recipients of the Sacrament. Through the Lord's Supper, according to this exegesis,

[8] Cf. Köhler, *Zwingli und Luther*, I, 286—287.

[9] Anders Nygren, *Agape and Eros*, tr. by Philip S. Watson (Philadelphia, 1953), pp. 733 ff.

[10] See pp. 157 ff.

[11] Cf. the remarks in the conclusion of Luther's *Confession on the Lord's Supper* (1528), W, XXVI, 495—496.

[12] See Luther's sermon of May 5, 1526, W, XX, 382—385 (Rörer).

Christian believers participated in one another, as members of any group eventually come to participate in one another; but primarily they participated in the body and blood of the Lord, and thus in one another. Luther's exegesis maintained that the Lord's Supper was indeed a participation of Christian believers in one another, and the most intimate fellowship they had. But this was due to their common participation in Christ. Such an exegesis of "participation" was of a piece with Luther's exegesis of "My body" as referring principally to Christ's own body and only derivatively to the church.[13]

Participation in the Lord's Supper was a participation in forgiveness. The community of the church was the community where men found forgiveness for their faults. At the Lord's Supper the members of the church did not represent merely their general sense of community, but they represented themselves as a community of forgiveness. From early times Christian exegesis had applied to the Lord's Supper the words of Jesus in the Sermon on the Mount: "If you are offering your gift at the altar, and there remember that your brother has something against you, leave your gift there before the altar and go: first be reconciled to your brother, and then come and offer your gift" (Matt. 5:23-24).[14] The Christian intuition behind such an exegesis of these words was a sound one, whatever their original intent may have been. For here at the table of the Lord forgiveness was called for, and the community that gathered here participated in forgiveness.

Luther's exegesis grasped the nature of that forgiveness profoundly.[15] His realistic understanding of man made it

[13] See pp. 154—156.

[14] Cf. Cyprian, Epistle 27, *ANF*, V, 306.

[15] So, for example, in his comments on the Lord's Prayer in the Large Catechism (1529), W, XXX-I, 206—208.

impossible for him to accept the naive idea that men could be brought to forgive one another genuinely and sincerely by the simple device of telling them that forgiveness was a good thing. He knew that only radical forgiveness would accomplish this, and that meant forgiveness by God in Christ. The only way a man could be brought to the point of overlooking the difference between himself and his brother was by the realization that in Christ God had overlooked the difference between Himself and sinful humanity.[16] Specifically, the Lord's Supper was a supper of forgiveness in the primary sense because it conferred upon men God's forgiveness of their sins. Those who gathered for the Lord's Supper were those who had an awareness of their own sins against God and who came to God for His forgiveness. That forgiveness by God communicated life and salvation, because it rescued men from the death of their sin and the sickness of their hostility to God. Salvation means restoration to health, because in much of Luther's exegesis God in Christ was the original Good Samaritan.[17] Through "participation in the body of Christ" in the Eucharist, men were restored to health and life and thus were made forgiven children of God once more.

By communicating life and salvation this forgiveness also enabled the believers to forgive one another's sins in the Christian community. Here Luther's exegesis of Matt. 5: 23-24 was explicit and strict. Either the forgiveness conferred by the Lord's Supper made this much of a difference, or the faith that pretended to accept that forgiveness was a counterfeit. With a vigor that has not always characterized Prot-

---

[16] "Through faith God gives you the Spirit, who transforms your heart, so that then you are very tender and gentle with your neighbor and you think: 'Ah, my God has acted this way toward me and forgiven me more than I can ever forgive! Why should I not also forgive my neighbor a little?'" Sermon of July 27, 1522, W, X-III, 251.

[17] See p. 183, note 27.

estant exegesis of this passage Luther's exposition stressed the importance of mutual forgiving as a condition of mutual participation in the forgiveness wrought by Christ.[18] Of course, Christians did not earn God's forgiveness by forgiving one another. God's forgiveness was a free gift, unearned and unmerited. But this gift was a power to change lives. The means which conveyed the gift also conveyed transforming power. In his exegesis of the sixth chapter of Romans, therefore, Luther emphasized that Baptism changed men's relation to God and therefore their relation to one another; if it did not do the second, it had not done the first.[19] And in his exegesis of 1 Corinthians he put similar stress upon the power in the Lord's Supper to change men and make them forgive one another's trespasses. The Christian fellowship was a twofold participation in forgiveness according to Luther's exegesis. It was a community in which, by Word and Sacrament, the communicant participated in the forgiveness of sins wrought by the body of Christ in its death. It was also a community in which, by the power of the life and salvation which this forgiveness granted, the communicants as the body of Christ were enabled to participate in the forgiveness of one another's sins. At the Lord's Table the church was given a "participation in the body of Christ" on both counts. Here Christians received the forgiveness of God, and here they also received and granted the forgiveness of Christian brethren to one another.

As the basic participation granted by the Lord's Supper was the participation of the church in Christ, and as the basic forgiveness in the Lord's Supper was the forgiveness of God, so the uniting bond in the Lord's Supper was the bond of

---

[18] *Commentary on the Sermon on the Mount* (1530–32), W, XXXII, 422–427; *Luther's Works*, 21, 148–155.

[19] *Lectures on Romans* (1515–16), W, LVI, 321–328; cf. also Ebeling, *Evangelienauslegung*, p. 441.

the Spirit. Luther's exegesis, like his entire theology, was rooted in the doctrine of the Trinity.[20] Because many of his interpreters have failed to recognize how basic the doctrine of the Trinity was to his exegesis, they have neglected to relate his doctrine of the Lord's Supper to the doctrine of the Holy Spirit rather than merely to the doctrine of Christ.[21] And yet the κοινωνία of the Lord's Supper was the peculiar province of the Holy Spirit in the church; for it was the grace which had come in the Lord Jesus Christ that assured men of the love of the Father and that expressed itself in the κοινωνία of the Holy Spirit.[22] In his exegesis Luther sought to follow the lead of the ancient church, which had put the phrases "the holy catholic church, the communion of saints (or perhaps the communion of the Sacraments)"[23] into the articles of the Creed after the Holy Spirit;[24] for the life of the church and the κοινωνία of the Sacraments were the special province of the Holy Spirit.

This view of the church's unity stood in opposition to any idea of unity based on something human. The bond among Christians could not be their common subjection to a church organization; for according to both exegesis and history, the forms of such an organization were human, and the bond in the church had to be divine.[25] The bond among Christians could not be their common liturgical forms; for Luther's exegesis recognized that even in the apostolic era these forms had been characterized by variety, and that they had not

[20] See pp. 52–53.

[21] Prenter, *Spiritus Creator*, pp. 130–172.

[22] On communion in the Lord's Supper cf. Paul Althaus, *Communio sanctorum* (Munich, 1929), pp. 75–79.

[23] Elert, *Abendmahl und Kirchengemeinschaft*, pp. 18 ff.

[24] On the backgrounds of this cf. *Bekenntnisschriften*, p. 61, note 3.

[25] Cf. Ernst Benz, *Bischofsamt und apostolische Sukzession im deutschen Protestantismus* (Stuttgart, 1953), pp. 11–16.

been able to bring about unity in the church.[26] The bond among Christians could not even be their theology; for as his negotiations with Martin Bucer and with the Bohemian Brethren amply showed, Luther was able to distinguish between what he called "the doctrine of the Gospel" and what he termed "the mode of speaking" theologically.[27] Organization, liturgy, and theology were all human ways of giving form to a divine imperative: the church had to be organized, it had to worship, and it had to think theologically. Their content was divine, for the content of all three was the Word and the Sacraments. But their form was not divine, and Luther's exegesis pointed out the flaw in any effort to achieve or guarantee the unity of the church by means of human forms.

The bond uniting the Christian community was rather the bond that was welded by the Holy Spirit Himself. The role of the Lord's Supper was to act as a means by which the grace of the Spirit was communicated. Organization, liturgy, and theology were all part of the church's response to that grace. As a response they contained that to which they responded, just as Luther's exegesis recognized that a prayer contained the Gospel when it pleaded the merits of Christ.[28] But it was not the church's response that made the church one; it merely testified to a unity already present. Both the unity and the response were created by God, not by man, as Luther's exegesis of John 17:21 insisted.[29] It was for the church only to accept God's created gift and to act in response to that gift. The Lord's Supper was a means of

[26] Jaroslav Pelikan, "Luther and the Liturgy," pp. 34—36.

[27] Jaroslav Pelikan, "Luther's Endorsement of the *Confessio Bohemica*," p. 840, note 63.

[28] *Commentary on the Sermon on the Mount* (1530—32), W, XXXII, 420; *Luther's Works*, 21, 146.

[29] See Luther's exegesis of this passage in his sermon of October 17, 1528, W, 28, 182—186.

grace to the church. Therefore it was also a means of unity. The peace of God passed all understanding; the bond among Christians was divine, not human. This was what Luther's exegesis recognized as the importance of the Lord's Supper for fostering the unity of the Spirit in the bond of peace.

Luther's exegesis of eucharistic texts often led to the admonition that the eating and drinking in the Lord's Supper were intended to make faith more personal and individual. In the Lord's Supper the Holy Spirit accentuated the "for me" of the Gospel, as Luther was wont to call it.[30] It is interesting that there was no explicit Biblical exegesis behind this idea of Luther's.[31] The primary emphasis in the admonitions of 1 Corinthians regarding the Lord's Supper was corporate rather than individual. And yet Luther's insight here was still exegetical, in the sense that it expounded a fundamental Biblical emphasis on individual responsibility and applied it to the Eucharist.

For Luther the idea that "participation in the body of Christ" could mean something individual and personal was part of this Biblical emphasis on the awesome responsibility of being a person before God. To put it into a formula, one had to do his own believing as he had to do his own dying.[32] Here, as Luther's exegesis often pointed out, parents would be willing to do anything to make their children believe.[33] They would be willing to risk their own salvation if they could guarantee their children's. But neither station nor position nor the affection of other people could take the

[30] *Commentary on Galatians* (1535), W, XL-I, 299.

[31] The closest thing to such exegesis is his use of "for you" in the passage cited in the previous note, but even here the word "you" is in the plural!

[32] Cf. Pauck, "Luther's Faith," op. cit., pp. 15—23.

[33] *Sermons on the Gospel of St. John: Chapters 1—4* (1537—40), W, XLVI, 745—746; *Luther's Works*, 22, 235—236.

place of what had to happen in "the shrine of the heart." [34] The believer had to be able to say, "*I* believe." [35] Similarly, he had to be able to find refuge in the grace of God that had been given to him personally. Luther's exegesis was filled with anecdotes that accentuated the importance of this personal appropriation of grace, especially in Baptism.[36] Of himself he said that when prayer, Scripture reading, and meditation all failed to drive away the devil, he would take comfort in his Baptism.[37] This emphasis on the fact that he, Martin Luther, had been baptized drove the devil away, because here he was relying on the grace of God that had been given to him personally.[38]

So it was in the Lord's Supper. When one heard the Word being preached — said Luther, the staunch proponent of the preached Word — one might suppose that this Word was not intended for him, that it meant everyone else in the church that day except him.[39] But when that Word was communicated to him in the Eucharist, when he was granted "a participation in the body of Christ" under the form of bread and wine, then he could have no further question about the person at whom this was aimed.[40] Because the communicant ate and drank personally and individually, he could know that this was meant for him. As the form of absolution was the declaration "I absolve thee" in the singular,[41] so the forgiveness conveyed by the Lord's Supper was for each communicant individually and personally.

[34] Ibid., W, XLVI, pp. 614—619; *Luther's Works,* pp. 91—96.

[35] Elert, *Morphologie,* I, 60—62.

[36] Cf. Luther's exegesis of Matt. 19:13-15 (1537—40), W, XLVII, 326—337.

[37] *Treatise on the Sacrament of Baptism* (1519), W, II, 732.

[38] Prenter, "Word and Sacrament," pp. 81—99.

[39] Cf. pp. 63—64.

[40] See p. 243, note 29.

[41] *Treatise on the Sacrament of Baptism* (1519), W, II, 733—734.

But that was only half of Luther's exegesis; for, as we have seen in chapter five, Luther's exegesis of a passage always included the doctrine of the church somewhere.[42] The Holy Spirit did indeed grant a personal "participation in the body of Christ" through the reception of the Lord's Supper, but such "participation" was possible only in the fellowship of believers with one another and with Christ. True individuality was to be found only through "participation" in the church. In the Lord's Supper one was strengthened in his membership within that community, and so it was that his individual relation to God was also strengthened.[43] Luther was therefore violently opposed to those who tried to take the Lord's Supper into their own individual hands and celebrate it privately, for the Sacrament belonged in the church.[44] Even the private communion of the sick, about which Luther had deep misgivings,[45] was an act of the church, by which the church shared the "participation in the body of Christ" with those who could not be present at its regular celebrations of the Sacrament. The excessive stress of Protestant exegesis on the individual rather than on the church has often caused this insight to disappear; and as the irony of the history of Pietism demonstrated, this has likewise meant the destruction of genuine individuality, especially in the Lord's Supper.[46]

In Luther's exegesis of "participation in the body of Christ" these two belonged together, the individual and the church. Whatever was significant for the one was significant

[42] See pp. 89 ff.

[43] Herman A. Preus, "The Christian and the Church," in *More About Luther*, pp. 125—214.

[44] Cf. his statement at table, W, Ti, V, No. 6361, pp. 621—622.

[45] Cf. Luther's letter to Anton Lauterbach, November 26, 1539, W, *Briefe*, VIII, 608—609.

[46] Cf. Hans Preuss, *Die Geschichte der Abendmahlsfrömmigkeit in Zeugnissen und Berichten* (Gütersloh, 1949), pp. 139—148.

for the other as well, for the only true individuality was in the church. Hence his exegesis included both meanings of "participation": that the Lord's Supper made individuals more personally aware of the meaning of Christ, and that it brought them together more closely in the church. Thus in the Lord's Supper the Holy Spirit strengthened and nourished the corporateness of Christian faith and life. Many Reformation scholars have failed to realize that the church was perhaps more prominent in Luther's exegesis than it had been in any exegete since Augustine.[47] Only in recent years has the study of the Reformation come to see the extent to which this was true, with consequences that have changed the whole interpretation of Luther's thought and exegesis.

Yet it is a mistake to treat Luther's doctrine of the church as merely part of a general awareness that life was corporate in character. He did indeed have such an awareness.[48] Throughout his writings he stressed the dependence of people on one another and the importance of the natural and historical groups in which people were organized to express that dependence. The basic element in Luther's theory of society was this realization that human life was corporate, and he did use the church as another illustration of this fact.[49] More fundamental than this theory in his thought, however, was his exegesis, which taught him that the church was a community, but a community of grace. The Lord's Supper was indeed a common meal; but so were the meals at Luther's house, especially when his students and colleagues came to dinner! [50] What made the Lord's Supper more than just a very solemn common meal was the fact that the cor-

---

[47] See p. 34, notes 9—10.

[48] See p. 153, note 54.

[49] See p. 152, note 53.

[50] Cf. Ernest G. Schwiebert, *Luther and his Times* (Saint Louis, 1950), pp. 597—598.

porateness nourished there was "a participation in the body of Christ," both an individual participation and a collective participation. The "body" in this text was the body of Christ in both of the senses described earlier: [51] the literal sense of "body" meant that the Sacrament granted the true body and blood of Christ, for Christians to eat and to drink; the spiritual sense of "body" meant that the group gathered here was the church, the body of Christ. A similar stratification characterized Luther's exegesis of "participation" in this text: basically it meant the communication of the true body and blood of Christ; derivatively it meant the fellowship of Christians with one another in Christ.

Individual and corporate, then, belonged together in Luther's exegesis. And that became most evident in his exegesis of "participation in the body of Christ." Nowhere was the relation of the Christian to God more completely vertical than in the Sacrament; nowhere was it more completely horizontal. Christ's community with the members of His church was both individual and collective. "Participation" meant a fellowship between Christ and each believer, and it meant a fellowship between Christ and the church as such. "Participation in the body of Christ" according to both these senses took place in the Sacrament, and neither was possible without the other. Luther's exegesis was based on the presupposition that a human being became an authentic person only when he was brought into participation in the life of God, and that this happened in and by the church.

Thus "participation in the body of Christ" in the Lord's Supper meant fellowship according to Luther's exegesis, just as it did according to the exegesis of other Protestants. But it meant fellowship because "participation in the body of Christ" truly present was constitutive of the "participation" by Christians in the worshiping community, and not vice

[51] See pp. 154—156.

versa. When Luther opposed what he regarded as a distorted exegesis of this "participation" in Zwingli's stress on fellowship in the Sacrament, he sometimes spoke as though this motif had no role at all in the exegesis of "participation in the body of Christ." But in the total picture of his exegesis this motif, too, had its place. It did not threaten the other motifs; it enriched them, as it was also enriched by them. Luther exhibited his exegetical skill by including "fellowship" in "participation," and he exhibited his exegetical precision by subordinating the first to the second.

CHAPTER ELEVEN

"Do This in Remembrance of Me" (1 Cor. 11:24)

LUTHER's exegetical method was obliged to consider, not only passages of the New Testament like "This is My body," which appeared to support his interpretation of the Eucharist, but also those passages which figured prominently in the interpretations of the Eucharist that were being set forth by his opponents. No passage was more prominent in the eucharistic exegesis of Luther's "Reformed" opponents than "Do this in remembrance of Me." [1] As a result, this exegesis was putting a heavier accent upon time and history than had much of medieval exegesis. For while the exegesis of "This is My body" had necessitated the use of spatial language, with all its possibilities for misunderstanding, the exegesis of "Do this in remembrance of Me" necessitated the use of temporal language, which had its own special possibilities for misunderstanding. [2] In the exegetical material summarized in chapter nine temporal language was important as well. [3] Yet the exegesis of "Do this in remembrance of Me," whether it was Luther's exegesis or that of his opponents, had to concentrate on the problem of "Christ and time." [4]

Among the many passages of Scripture that comprised the exegetical basis for Luther's interpretation of the Lord's

[1] Sasse, *This Is My Body,* pp. 375–382.

[2] See p. 140.

[3] See pp. 177–181.

[4] Oscar Cullmann's *Christ and Time,* tr. by Floyd Filson (Philadelphia, 1950), is an influential study of this issue in the New Testament.

Supper, "Do this in remembrance of Me" had its place. But most discussions of his exegesis have concentrated on his interpretation of passages which seemed to require the language of space rather than the language of time.[5] Now Luther's exegesis, like the Scriptures with which it operated, spoke about the Lord's Supper both in the language of space and in the language of time. Indeed, Luther's word for "present," like its English counterpart, could mean both "here" (a term drawn from the language of space) and "now" (a term drawn from the language of time).[6] Both ways of speaking would appear to be legitimate; both have also proved to be inadequate, but inadequate in different ways. For this reason a consideration of the view of time in Luther's exegesis may help to clarify many aspects of his exegetical works, including his exegesis of "remembrance."

Luther's exegesis interpreted Jesus Christ as the church's past, as the church's present, and as the church's future. He was the church's past, because Luther always maintained that the church was constituted by what Christ had been and said and done.[7] He was the church's present, because Luther interpreted the center of the church's life and worship as His presence with the church "even to the consummation of the age" (Matt. 28:20).[8] And He was the church's future, because Luther expounded the church's hope on the basis of the apostolic statement: "Beloved, we are God's children now; it does not yet appear what we shall be, but

[5] On the relation of spatial and temporal language cf. Paul Tillich, *Systematic Theology*, I (Chicago, 1951), 274–278; also his *Theology of Culture* (New York, 1959), pp. 30–39.

[6] Philipp Dietz, *Wörterbuch zu Dr. Martin Luthers deutschen Schriften* (Leipzig, 1870 ff.), II, 40.

[7] *Sermons on the Gospel of St. John: Chapters 1–4* (1537–40), W, XLVI, 649–657; *Luther's Works* 22, 130–138.

[8] *This Is My Body* (1527), W, XXIII, 149–153.

we know that when He appears we shall be like Him, for we shall see Him as He is" (1 John 3:2).[9]

Luther's exegesis of passages about the Word and the Sacraments likewise employed the themes of past, present, and future. The preached Word of the Gospel was a means of grace because it was the proclamation of past events, of the present Lord, and of the future which He secured.[10] Baptism was a means of grace because it was a Baptism into the death of Christ, an event in the past; because it made men dead to sin and alive to God in the present; and because, in the fundamental passage of Luther's baptismal exegesis, it promised that believers would "certainly be united with Him [Christ] in a resurrection like His" (Rom. 6:5).[11] And the Lord's Supper was a means of grace because it, too, united the church with its Lord as past, as present, and as future. In the words of St. Paul: "As often as you eat this bread and drink this cup [in the present], you proclaim the Lord's death [in the past] until He comes [in the future]" (1 Cor. 11:26).

According to Luther's exegesis of passages like this, the ground of Christian comfort in the Lord's Supper was the faith that the Sacrament was based on an event in the past. Luther was therefore able to emphasize "Do this in remembrance of Me" without making it fundamental to his exegesis. Because the exegesis of his Protestant opponents spoke so much about "Do this in remembrance of Me," Luther's own distinctive exegesis of this passage has not received its share of attention. Yet without his unique grasp of what was implied in the New Testament idea of memorial as summarized in this passage, Luther's exegesis of other passages

[9] See Luther's exposition of this passage, *Lectures on 1 John* (1527), W, XX, 697—698.

[10] See pp. 60—63.

[11] See p. 196, note 19.

is impoverished. In his exegesis of "remembrance" Luther stressed that the basis of the Sacrament was the suffering and death of Christ, an event in the past.

The blessings of the "remembrance" promised by this passage were the blessings achieved by the atonement; they were not achieved by the "remembrance" or even by the Sacrament. Against Carlstadt Luther wrote in 1525: "He [Carlstadt] gives . . . remembrance the power to justify, as faith does. The proof he gives is, he says, that it is written, That they have done this in remembrance of Me. What think you? It is written, They have done it in remembrance of Me. Therefore such remembrance justifies. . . . Such remembrance does not justify, but . . . they must first be justified who would preach, proclaim, and practice the outward remembrance of Christ." [12] In other words, as Luther's exegesis continually pointed out, the source of Christian faith and life was an unrepeatable happening.[13] Luther therefore related his exegesis of "Do this in remembrance of Me" to the suffering and death of Christ, just as the New Testament did. For not only did the New Testament date the institution of the Lord's Supper from the events of Holy Week, but it also made the suffering and death of Christ the content of the Lord's Supper. When Luther came to the exegesis of the words of institution, he put them into their setting in the history of the Passion; and his exegesis of the history of the Passion was, in turn, informed by his insistence that this was done once and for all.[14] Therefore the Lord's Supper had to be "in remembrance of Me"; for it communicated an event that lay in the past, the death of Christ. Only by insisting that this event was really past and truly incapable of

[12] *Against the Heavenly Prophets* (1525), W, XVIII, 197; *Luther's Works*, 40, 207—208.
[13] See pp. 242—243.
[14] See pp. 234—235.

repetition could Luther's exegesis include both "Do this in remembrance of Me" and "For the forgiveness of sins."

Another way of saying this would be that for Luther's exegesis the Eucharist could be "For the forgiveness of sins" because of God's act of remembrance.[15] Luther's own exegesis of "Do this in remembrance of Me" — for example, in his *Commentary on Psalm 111* of 1530 — was quite consistently on the side of the view that the "remembrance" was an act of the church.[16] The grammar of the sentence permitted another interpretation, namely, that the church did this in order that God might remember Christ.[17] Luther's exegesis of the term "remembrance" here did not make God the subject of the remembering. He maintained that the church did the remembering, just as Israel did the remembering of the Exodus in the Passover, whose celebration was the setting for the institution.[18] Nevertheless, Israel also pleaded with God to remember His deed.[19] And in the same *Commentary on Psalm 111* Luther could go on to say that God remembered the death of Christ and that the church was to remind God of it; and in support of this he could cite the passage "Do this in remembrance of Me." [20] When the church added "through Christ our Lord" to a prayer, it was reminding God of the death of Christ and pleading Him rather than its own worthiness as the basis of its petitions. Similarly, the grace expected from the Lord's Supper was

[15] Cf. Gregory Dix (ed.), *Treatise on the Apostolic Tradition of Hippolytus* (London, 1937), pp. 73–75, on the significance of "remembrance."

[16] *Commentary on Psalm 111* (1530), W, XXXI-I, 406–407; *Luther's Works*, 13, 364–365.

[17] On this whole problem cf. Hans Lietzmann, *Mass and Lord's Supper*, tr. by Dorothea Reeve (London, 1953 ff.).

[18] *Commentary on Isaiah* (1527–30), W, XXXI-II, 143.

[19] *Lectures on Genesis* (1535–45), W, XLII, 335–337.

[20] *Commentary on Psalm 111* (1530), W, XXXI-I, 417–418; *Luther's Works*, 13, 377.

the grace of Christ's death as God remembered it. Luther's exegesis made clear that Christians found their consolation in the declaration that God had been in Christ reconciling the world, and that this never had to be done again.[21]

It was this insistence on the unrepeatable in the relation between God and man that caused Luther's exegesis to stress continually the interrelations between Word and Sacrament.[22] From St. Augustine he often quoted the rule: "Let the Word come to the element, and a Sacrament comes to be." [23] Word and Sacrament belonged together; and the Word was central in the Sacrament, along with the eating and drinking.[24] From St. Augustine Luther likewise took the definition of a Sacrament as a "visible Word." [25] Thus Word and Sacrament belonged together both in the operation of God and in the obedience of the church. This principle had both exegetical and liturgical consequences for Luther. In the liturgy of the church this meant that Luther put a new focus upon exegetical preaching and that he urged a frequent reception of the Lord's Supper. His critique of Roman Catholicism accused it of neglecting the exegesis and preaching of the Scriptures, and of substituting the unbloody sacrifice for the reception of Christ's body and blood.[26] Word and Sacrament belonged together in the church; each needed the other.

One reason for Luther's stress on Word and Sacrament was the nature of the Word as a proclamation "in remembrance of Me," in remembrance of that past event whose blessings were the content of the Sacrament. For Luther

[21] *Commentary on the Psalms of Degrees* (1532–33), W, XL-III, 302.
[22] See p. 221.
[23] Reinhold Seeberg, *Lehrbuch der Dogmengeschichte*, II, 454–455.
[24] See p. 251, note 55.
[25] See p. 219, note 2.
[26] See p. 219, note 1.

exegetical preaching did not mean merely expounding Bible stories or Bible passages or Bible doctrines. As chapter three has shown, the Word of God was the action of God in redeeming His people, as this action found its climax and seal in the life, death, and resurrection of Jesus Christ. To preach the Word of God, therefore, meant to describe that redemptive action. When such preaching accompanied the celebration of the Lord's Supper, it was truly "in remembrance of Me." [27] On the one night of all nights when He was betrayed, Christ had instituted the Lord's Supper and had said: "Do this in remembrance of Me." The preaching of the living Word was a witness to the events surrounding that night, and as such it was the communication of that which was the content of this "remembrance." Both Word and Sacrament were meaningful as a "remembrance," because they conveyed the results of what had happened then. Without this point of reference in a past event neither would be valid. The ground of the "remembrance" was also the ground of both Word and Sacrament.

The same emphasis was present in Luther's exegesis of "Do this" in the passage "Do this in remembrance of Me." According to this exegesis, it was necessary to recite the words of institution because the command "Do this in remembrance of Me" included such recitation,[28] but also because this recitation connected the celebration of the Sacrament to the night when Christ was betrayed.[29] Thus the consecration had already been effected by Christ, and by repeating the word of His testament the church consecrated in union with His consecration. Luther directed

[27] Thus in the *Commentary on the Minor Prophets* (1524—26), W, XIII, 146, made even more explicit in the recension printed ibid., pp. 190 to 191.

[28] See p. 223, notes 15—16.

[29] Cf. Luther's introduction to his sermon for Maundy Thursday, March 25, 1529, W, XXIX, 219—220.

this against two conflicting exegeses of "Do this in remembrance of Me." In opposition to those exegetes who regarded the words of institution as not efficacious because the essence of the Sacrament consisted in subjective "remembrance" by the believers, Luther argued for the necessity of the words of the testament, because he wanted the Sacrament to be seen as an objective "remembrance." [30] Without the warrant provided by the words of the testament the "remembrance of Me" in the Sacrament would be a "remembrance" of what each individual believer thought about Christ, rather than the church's "remembrance" of the history of Christ, climaxing in the night when He was betrayed and when He instituted the Eucharist. On the other hand, Luther also directed his exegesis of "Do this in remembrance of Me" against an undue stress on "Do this" which had achieved wide circulation during the late Middle Ages, when it was thought that the celebrant effected a miracle by his recitation of the words.[31] In opposition to this exaggerated interpretation of "Do this" Luther's exegesis located the consecration in the act of Christ Himself on the night when He was betrayed. All that the celebrant did in obedience to "Do this" was to apply the power of that act to the elements before him.[32] Only in this dependent and derivative sense could the celebrant be said to consecrate.

It is interesting that Luther thus used his exegesis of "Do this in remembrance of Me" to rescue the doctrine of

[30] Cf. the careful study of Hans-Christoph Schmidt-Lauber, *Die Eucharistie als Entfaltung der Verba testamenti* (Kassel, 1957).

[31] See pp. 159—160.

[32] "If I were to speak, 'This is the body of Christ' over every piece of bread, certainly nothing would happen. But when, according to His institution and command, we say in the Lord's Supper, 'This is My body,' then it is His body — not on account of our speaking or our efficacious word [*thettel wort*], but on account of His command, because He has commanded us to speak and to act this way and has bound His command and action to our speaking." *Confession on the Lord's Supper* (1528), W, XXVI, 285.

the Lord's Supper from the implications in the Protestant exegesis of this same passage, but also from those in the Roman Catholic exegesis. When the "remembrance" of Christ in the hearts of the believers was made the efficient cause in the Sacrament, this was, in Luther's eyes, a false exegesis of "Do this in remembrance of Me"; for the power of that which was truly past, unrepeatable, and also unchangeable, had been replaced by the subjective feelings and "remembrance" of the communicants. Similarly, when the power of the sacramental miracle was put at the disposal of the consecrating priest, this represented a distortion of "Do this in remembrance of Me"; for the true miracle, as Luther was wont to remark in awe, was that the power of Christ's institution continued to be in force wherever and whenever the Sacrament was celebrated "in remembrance of Me." [33] It was the truly past character of that institution which guaranteed the Sacrament. By the miracle of faith that past had become the church's past; for faith identified the church with Christ, with His death and with His resurrection. And it was this Christ of the past whose body and blood were communicated to the church of the present under the forms of bread and wine.

The church was the company of those who had identified themselves by faith with this past event. When Luther said that the Word and the Sacraments were the constitutive elements in the church and the marks of its presence,[34] he meant that the church was a remembering community, which carried on its life by its acts of faithful "remembrance." Study of the church's history was, therefore, necessary.[35] Such study associated the church of the present with that

[33] See the discussions of this in Luther's *Sermons on Baptism* (1535), W, XXXVII, 636–639.

[34] Schlink, op. cit., pp. 269–276.

[35] See chapter four.

past which called the church into existence. It also assured the church of continuity with faithful believers in all centuries. Significantly, it was for his exegesis of passages like "Do this in remembrance of Me" that Luther sought proof of continuity with the church. In his earlier days, as chapter six has shown, he had felt able to defy the tradition of the church or even to ignore it altogether, almost as though there had been no church between Patmos and Wittenberg.[36] But in his mature thought, as chapter four has shown, he came to realize the importance of what had intervened between the New Testament and Luther.[37] What helped him to realize this importance was the construction other Protestants were putting on the right of private exegesis, the Anabaptists in their views of Baptism and various other Protestants in their various interpretations of the Lord's Supper. Liturgically, Luther held that the historic forms of the church's celebrations, while not necessary, served to support the "remembrance" of the community, in which it recalled both the original event that constituted the Sacrament and the company of the faithful departed who had participated in the Sacrament.[38] The "remembrance" was thus an integral element in the sacramental life of the church. The church, according to Luther, drew on its "remembrance" of the past to explain what it was doing in the Sacrament.

The church drew on that "remembrance" also as the standard of its faith and life. Especially was this true of its sacramental doctrine, which had to be exegetical to be correct. Luther insisted against his opponents on both sides that the proper basis for a doctrine of the Lord's Supper was a valid exegesis of the record of its institution. *This Is My Body: These Words Still Stand* was the title of one of

[36] See p. 114, note 19.
[37] See pp. 81–82.
[38] Jaroslav Pelikan, "Luther and the Liturgy," pp. 16–17.

his most important treatises on the Lord's Supper.[39] Its theme was that one should not judge a doctrine of the Lord's Supper by its conformity to reason. Luther charged that both the Roman exegesis of "This is My body" and the Zwinglian exegesis of "Do this in remembrance of Me" had trimmed the meaning of the Scriptures to meet the claims of reason.[40] Thus Luther's objection to transubstantiation was not that it was absurd — the objection most Protestants raised against it — but that it rationalized the mystery of the Sacrament.[41] The proper foundation for any doctrine of the Lord's Supper was in the exegesis of the deposit of the Christian memory, the words of Christ's testament. Only by the exegesis of that deposit from the past could the doctrine of the Lord's Supper in the present be evaluated. Where the relation between the present and the past in the life of the church was ignored or distorted, there the doctrine of the Lord's Supper was also distorted. There the exegesis of what was truly past was dismissed from its controlling position in the faith and life of the church.

Luther complained that this dismissal of the truly past was set forth as an exegesis of "Do this in remembrance of Me." Zwingli used his exegesis of this passage as the ground for the idea that the presence of Christ came about through the act of "remembrance."[42] When believers gathered for a celebration of the Lord's Supper, their collective "remembrance" of all that Christ had been and done was so strong that He became present in their midst. Although Zwingli tried various ways to make this exegesis sound less subjective than that, its leitmotif was this stress on the act of "remembrance" as the means by which the presence of

---

[39] W, XXIII, 64—283.

[40] Ibid., pp. 123—125; see also p. 121 above.

[41] *Confession on the Lord's Supper* (1528), W, XXVI, 439.

[42] Cf. Köhler, *Zwingli und Luther*, II, 137.

Christ (such as it was) was effected. At first this exegesis seemed to be the only way to emphasize "in remembrance of Me." By going through the actions through which He had gone and which He had prescribed, Christians were overwhelmed with their "remembrance" of Him. To their words of "remembrance" they added actions of "remembrance," and both were expressions of their thoughts of "remembrance." As one recalled a departed friend or relative when one visited the places he used to frequent and participated in actions he used to share, so Christians brought Christ to their consciousness and made Him present when, following both His example and His command, they gathered to "Do this in remembrance of Me." [43]

All this not only sounded very reasonable and plausible, but it also seemed to be a faithful exegesis of the command "Do this in remembrance of Me." When Luther rejected it, he was not, as some of his interpreters maintain, repudiating the Biblical idea of "remembrance." What he was repudiating was any exegesis of this passage that was anthropocentric or that made man and his "remembrance" the cause of Christ's presence in the Sacrament. When Christ said, "Do this in remembrance of Me," Luther maintained, He meant that the church was to perform this sacramental action in "remembrance" of, and reliance on, His Word and work. Such "remembrance" and reliance had as its foundation the conviction that the initiative in establishing any aspect of the relation between God and man was always God's. Therefore the Christ who was being remembered was the Christ who had become the Lord by His suffering, death, and resurrection. The "remembrance" enjoined by the passage meant the acceptance of His initiative in making Himself present through His body and blood in the Sacra-

---

[43] But see Köhler, *Zwingli und Luther*, I, 823—824, on the "objective" aspects of Zwingli's doctrine.

ment. To "Do this in remembrance of Me" meant to acknowledge His presence in the Sacrament in accordance with His
command and promise.[44]

The exegesis of "Do this in remembrance of Me," therefore, had to be Christocentric rather than anthropocentric.
It took as its point of departure, not the present in which
believers did the remembering but the past which they
remembered. And in that past were the life, death, and
resurrection of Christ, together with His promise: "This is
My body." The "remembrance of Me" in the Lord's Supper
consisted in reciting the history of His Passion and death,
and in receiving the blessings of that body and blood which
He gave into death. "Remembrance" was an act of faith,
of dependence on those deeds of redemption which Christ
had accomplished for men when they could do nothing for
themselves.[45] Thus Luther's exegesis of "Do this in remembrance of Me" found the deeper meaning in the Protestant
motif of memorial, because in Luther's exegesis the Lord's
Supper was a memento of the same Christ whose true body
and blood it simultaneously offered.[46]

This same emphasis also distinguished Luther's exegesis
from that of the late medieval doctors. For his exegesis of
"Do this in remembrance of Me" also enabled him to speak
as he did about the eucharistic sacrifice, as chapter 13 will
show.[47] He demanded that the sacrifice of Christ be left
in the past, where it properly belonged, and that there be
no talk about repeating it or extending or even re-present-

[44] Erich Seeberg, *Der Gegensatz zwischen Zwingli, Schwenckfeld und Luther*, in Wilhelm Koepp (ed.), *Reinhold Seeberg Festschrift*, I (Leipzig, 1929), 43—80.

[45] "You have not remembered the Lord when you merely mouth His name, but when you hang on Him and love Him with constant faith in your heart." *Notes on Deuteronomy* (1525), W, XIV, 613.

[46] See p. 132, note 105.

[47] See pp. 253—254.

ing it. Because the sacrifice was in the past, the church could have the memorial Sacrament in the present without having to be concerned about sacrifices of atonement any longer. Thus Luther's exegesis of "Do this in remembrance of Me" sought to rescue the Sacrament from the necessity of doing what it had never been intended to do. The sacrifice was past; the church had only to remember it, not to repeat it.

For this very reason Luther's exegesis was able to encompass all the various New Testament passages whose interpretation these chapters have been describing. And by his exegesis of the Gospel history as the focus for all of Christian faith and thought, Luther restored to theology the awareness of the past and of what it meant for the Lord's Supper. The fact that his controversies fastened upon the doctrine of the real presence of the body and blood of Christ in the Lord's Supper should not be permitted to obscure this fundamental insight. One of his great accomplishments as a theologian and exegete of the Sacred Scriptures was this realization that the exegesis of "Do this in remembrance of Me" and the exegesis of "This is My body," which were sometimes set in opposition to each other, actually required each other, just as they needed the exegesis of all the other passages that are being examined here. For, as chapter five of this book has shown, Luther constantly expounded the Scriptures as the history of the church. When he came to expound "Do this in remembrance of Me," therefore, he set this "remembrance" into the context of this history.

CHAPTER TWELVE

"You Proclaim the Lord's Death" (1 Cor. 11:26)

WHEN Luther's exegesis attacked the sacramental system of the medieval church, he was acting as a servant and a spokesman of the Word of God. This gave his attack a special form, for in the name of the Word of God he was able to accuse Roman Catholicism of subordinating the Word to the Sacraments and thus of distorting the meaning of both the Word and the Sacraments.[1] To undo the distortion and to restore the proper relation of Word and Sacrament, Luther and the other Reformers called upon a familiar formula from St. Augustine, according to which the Sacraments were the "visible Word of God."[2] This formula suited their purposes very well, because it summarized the statement of the apostle: "As often as you eat this bread and drink this cup, you proclaim the Lord's death until He comes." The motif of the visible Word thus became a primary mark of Protestant sacramental thought,[3] and it still is.[4] Recent

---

[1] "More importance attaches to the proclamation than to the Mass, since the prophet instructs us to proclaim the glory of the Lord but makes no mention of the Mass, except that he may allude to it with the word 'congregation.' For all the Masses stacked together are worthless without the Word of God. However, today this order has been reversed miserably." *Commentary on Psalm 68* (1521), W, VIII, 26–27; *Luther's Works*, 13, 27.

[2] Augustine, *Tractates on the Gospel According to St. John*, LXXX, 3, *NPNF-I*, VII, 344.

[3] Apology of the Augsburg Confession, XIII, 5, *Bekenntnisschriften*, pp. 292–293.

[4] See the brief but significant comments of Gustaf Aulen, *The Faith of the Christian Church*, tr. by Eric H. Wahlstrom and G. Everett Arden (Philadelphia, 1948), p. 376.

studies have shown its importance in the Reformed theological tradition,[5] but it also played a role in Luther's exegesis. Here its importance was enhanced by Luther's doctrine of the Word of God as such. Luther could designate the Lord's Supper as the visible Word because of what he taught about the Word of God. His exegesis of "You proclaim the Lord's death" was, therefore, parallel to his interpretation of the Word of God,[6] analyzed in chapter three above.

As chapter three has shown, what Luther taught about the Word of God was centered in his accent on the oral Word of preaching.[7] Far from minimizing the importance of the written Word in the Bible, this accent on the oral Word made possible a view of the Bible that assigned it a high place in the life and teaching of the church.[8] In the same way the stress on the Word as proclamation did not cause Luther to relegate the Sacrament to a secondary place in the church, for the Sacrament "proclaimed the Lord's death." It may be said, in fact, that Luther made the proclamation of the Word a Sacrament alongside the other Sacraments.[9] To put it another way, not only was the Lord's Supper the visible Word of God; but the proclamation of the Word of God was the audible Sacrament. Thus Luther discovered that Word and Sacrament, far from being antithetical, were actually co-ordinate. For if the Word of God was first the deed of God and then proclamation of that deed, it followed that the media which "proclaimed the

[5] Joseph C. McLelland's *The Visible Words of God* (Grand Rapids, 1957) is a careful exposition of this motif in Peter Martyr.

[6] See pp. 54—70.

[7] See pp. 63 ff.

[8] See p. 81, notes 41—42.

[9] As Regin Prenter says, "This connection between the preaching of the Gospel and the Sacrament does not mean a spiritualizing of the idea of the Sacrament but a sacramentalization of the message." *Spiritus Creator,* pp. 142—143.

Lord's death" — whether those media were audible, legible, or visible — belonged side by side.[10]

Such a co-ordination between Word and Sacrament would have been much more difficult if Luther had equated the Word of God exclusively with the Bible and not also with "proclamation." It is not a coincidence that those theologies which have equated the Word of God exclusively with the Bible have ended up by depressing the importance of the Sacraments into forms of instruction and reminder about what the Bible taught. As earlier chapters of this book have shown,[11] Luther's exegesis avoided both this tendency to depress the importance of the Sacraments and the opposite tendency to treat the Sacraments as a species of Christian magic. The first tendency has asserted itself when Scripture and Word of God were unequivocally identified, and the second when the doctrine of the Sacraments was dissociated from the oral and the written forms of the Word of God; both tendencies came from the neglect of Biblical exegesis.

Thus the several forms of the Word of God have needed one another to be rescued from the distortions to which each was subject. That fundamental insight, which came from Luther's exegesis, was especially productive for an understanding of the proper relationship between Word and Sacrament. If he had regarded the Word of God as only the Bible, then the dynamic connection between "proclaiming the Lord's death" in the Lord's Supper and "proclaiming" it through preaching would have been lost in his exegesis. Although Luther never did work out a satisfactory liturgical arrangement of a service with a focus on both the sermon and the Eucharist,[12] this is what he was interested in achieving; and exegetically his judgment about the relation of the

[10] See pp. 160–161.
[11] See pp. 164 ff.
[12] Jaroslav Pelikan, "Luther and the Liturgy," p. 29.

sacramental "proclamation" to the oral proclamation was sound. There have been very few theologians in the history of Christian exegesis who have managed to effect a proper co-ordination between Word and Sacrament. Though it is an oversimplification to put it this way, Roman Catholic thinkers have tended to stress the Sacrament at the expense of the oral Word, while Protestant thinkers have tended to stress the written Word at the expense of the Sacrament. It is a measure of Luther's stature as an exegete that he managed to bring them together as he did.

The co-ordination among the several forms of the Word of God in Luther's exegesis meant that whenever he discussed any one form, he took the others into consideration as well; for each had something to contribute to the understanding and interpretation of the others. Thus his exegesis of "You proclaim the Lord's death" had something to learn from, and something to contribute to, his exegesis of "proclamation" as such. What the oral and written "proclamation" supplied for the exegesis of "You proclaim the Lord's death" was the warrant and the meaning of the Sacrament.

Within the celebration of the Sacrament itself the warrant was provided by the recitation of the words of institution.[13] When the church repeated these through its minister, it declared its authorization for the act it was about to celebrate. This was part of the reasoning underlying Luther's suggestion that during the consecration of the elements it would be appropriate for the officiant in the celebration to stand facing the people rather than to stand before the altar facing God.[14] For the words of institution announced to the congregation the charter by which the congregation and its minister had obtained the right to consecrate and celebrate. Luther claimed in his exegesis of "This do in

[13] See the work of Schmidt-Lauber referred to p. 212, note 30.
[14] "Luther and the Liturgy," p. 28.

remembrance of Me" that the command "This do" included not only the actual eating and drinking but the blessing of the cup and the bread by means of this recitation.[15] In this exegesis he articulated a traditional intuition of the church that without the recitation of the words of institution the Sacrament was not a Sacrament, an intuition which the New Testament does not make explicit in so many words.[16] When the words of institution were recited orally in the service, this provided the celebration of the Sacrament with its warrant; thus "proclaiming the Lord's death" in the visible Word of God depended on the "proclamation" in the oral Word of God.

But the oral Word of God, in turn, depended on the written Word, as chapter three has shown.[17] Specifically, the warrant of the oral Word in the recitation of the words of institution itself had to be warranted by the written Word of God in the New Testament. Luther was not pedantic about this, and therefore his liturgies made use of a text of the words of institution which appeared at no one place in the New Testament.[18] But he did insist that the mere oral announcement of the priest did not suffice. This he directed against all the special devotions and services of the medieval church, which lacked an exegetical foundation in the written Word and depended only on someone's "supposition," his self-invented ideas.[19] On the other hand, it was not enough

[15] "Christ instituted the practice of eating [the Sacrament] when He said: 'Take and eat,' as the words show very clearly. . . . And He instituted the office of consecrating when He said: 'This do.' For 'to do' means to imitate everything that He did then." *Against King Henry of England* (1522), W, X-II, 216.

[16] Cf. *This Is My Body* (1528), W, XXVI, 290–292.

[17] See pp. 68 ff.

[18] "Luther and the Liturgy," pp. 10–13.

[19] "Into the ashcan with your suppositions, if I am supposed to base my salvation and blessedness on them! The command is: You must not imagine or suppose, but you must know and have a sure basis and testimony

to have a Bible lying on the altar to give a warrant for the Sacrament; but the written Word had to take oral form and thus authorize the church to "proclaim the Lord's death" through eating and drinking the Sacrament.

"Proclaiming the Lord's death" through the oral and written Word also provided the "proclaiming" through the visible Word with its meaning. Here, too, the oral Word was the usual means of "proclamation." One of the main preoccupations of Luther's liturgical writings and of his pastoral works on the Lord's Supper was his urging that the clergy deliver exegetical sermons to instruct people about the Biblical teaching on the Lord's Supper.[20] Worthy "proclaiming" through the visible Word depended on the kind of self-examination and self-understanding that was induced by the oral Word. To be rescued from the superstitious view and use of the Sacrament, the people needed to hear Biblical preaching about what the Sacrament meant. Then they would begin to realize that it was not there as a spectacle or as an atoning sacrifice but as a means of "proclaiming the Lord's death," the same death that was being "proclaimed" also by the oral Word.

As chapter three has pointed out, however, Luther also taught that the oral "proclamation" of the Word of God needed the written Word in the Scriptures if it was to be preserved from error.[21] He discovered that this was especially true of the oral proclamation about the Lord's Supper. When Zwingli tried to defend his doctrine of the Lord's

from the Word of God, telling you that this is pleasing to Him." *Commentary on the Sermon on the Mount* (1530–32), W, XXXII, 515; *Luther's Works*, 21, 261.

[20] "The principal purpose of any service of worship is the teaching and preaching of the Word of God." *German Mass* (1526), W, XIX, 78.

[21] See p. 85.

Supper by saying that God did not require one to affirm the impossible, Luther demanded that the exegesis of the Scriptures be the basis for any discussion about the Sacrament.[22] And when Zwingli made it known that his own exegesis of the Scriptures had come to him in a dream, Luther cried that neither dreams nor reason but only the Scriptures themselves could be trusted to provide the exegesis of the Scriptural statements about the Lord's Supper.[23] Thus he reiterated his principle, voiced at Leipzig, that the Scriptures were to interpret the Scriptures.[24]

In this exegesis of "You proclaim the Lord's death" Luther was fairly close to some of his opponents on the Protestant side, who also maintained that the Scriptures were to interpret the Scriptures, and who sought the meaning of the visible Word in the warrant provided by the written Word. But this exegesis is only half of the picture, for Luther also stressed far more than many other Protestants that in some sense the oral and written Word depended on the visible Word. It does seem that subsequent history has served to justify this stress. The Sacraments without exegesis degenerate into magic. On the other hand, an emphasis on the oral and the written Word without a correspondingly clear emphasis on the visible Word in the Sacrament has often debilitated both preaching and exegesis, making them impersonal, individualistic, and didactic.

Luther recognized that the oral and written form of the Word of God needed the visible Word of God to prevent it from becoming impersonal. He frequently commented on the intensely personal nature of the preached Word,

[22] Cf. *This Is My Body* (1527), W, XXIII, 123—125.
[23] Ibid., p. 161.
[24] See p. 113.

which was unmistakably addressed to the hearer.[25] And as a preacher Luther was himself the best demonstration of his own principle, for his preaching did involve and challenge his hearer personally.[26] So did his exegesis of the written Word, which always had a pronouncedly personal accent to it, as we have seen from his exegesis of the stories of Noah and Abraham.[27] But both preaching and exegesis could also be depersonalized to the point where the accent fell upon exegetical erudition or doctrinal correctness rather than upon a personal relation to the personal and living Lord. When this happened, one of the cures was the recovery of the personal element in Christian faith which was so prominent in the Lord's Supper.[28] For not only did "proclaiming the Lord's death" through preaching and exegesis prepare one for receiving the Sacrament, but "proclaiming the Lord's death" through the Sacrament enabled one to profit from preaching and exegesis by showing him that all this was spoken and written to him personally.[29]

[25] "Many proclaim Christ, but in such a way that they never understand or express His benefit and blessing. This is what the mob of preachers do, who proclaim at best nothing but the histories of Christ. But it is not Christian proclamation if you proclaim Christ historically; that is not proclaiming the glory of God. You must teach that the history of Christ is intended to grant us believers the blessings of righteousness and salvation, that He did everything according to the will of the Father, not for His own benefit but for ours. Thus we may know that everything that is in Christ belongs to us." *Works on the Psalms* (1519–21), W, V, 543.

[26] Cf. the introduction to *Luther's Works*, 51, xviii–xx.

[27] See pp. 98–99.

[28] See, in general, *Commentary on Psalm 51* (1532), W, XL-II, 315 to 316; *Luther's Works*, 12, 303–304.

[29] Thus the *Treatise on the Sacrament* (1526) said, according to its printed version (W, XIX, 504–505): "Therefore we also proclaim the death of Christ, according to the words: 'Do this in remembrance of Me.' But there is a difference. When I proclaim His death, that is a public proclamation in the congregation, which I am not giving to anyone individually. Anyone who accepts it, accepts it. But when I administer the Sacrament, I personalize it [*eigne . . . zu*] individually for the one who receives it. . . . This is something more than the public proclamation. For although

The personal intimacy between Christ and the church in the visible Word thus carried over into the church's reception of the oral and the written Word.

Yet for Luther this personal intimacy did not become something individualistic, to be stressed at the expense of the church. As chapter five has shown at length, the doctrine of the church was a major emphasis in Luther's exegesis, without which other emphases (like the priesthood of believers, for example) have come to mean something quite different from what Luther intended.[30] His view of preaching and of exegesis, especially the latter, has often been detached from his doctrine of the church, to the detriment of both. For then the right of the private interpretation of the Bible by anyone at all, competent or not, could become the excuse for the irresponsible rantings which Luther feared as much as he feared the papacy. Luther did indeed acknowledge the right of the private interpretation of the Bible, but in the same way that Paul acknowledged the right of speaking with tongues: with the proviso that such interpretation be carried on in the midst of, for the benefit of, and subject to examination by, the church.[31] But Luther's view of exegesis has sometimes come to mean that anyone who developed a private notion of interpreting the Scriptures which differed from someone else's private notion felt obliged to go off and found a new sect, which alone had the truth. It is no accident that this individualistic view of exegesis and preaching was accompanied by a neglect of the Sacrament. For, as we have seen, the Lord's Supper in Luther's exegesis was indeed intensely personal, as one ate and drank

that which is present in the Sacrament is present in the proclamation also and vice versa, the advantage is that here [in the Sacrament] it is directed to a specific person."

[30] See also p. 245, note 36.

[31] Cf., for example, Wilhelm Walther, *Für Luther wider Rom* (Halle, 1906), pp. 107—112.

for himself; but it was also intensely corporate, for it united the communicant with other believers in "one loaf." [32] This "one loaf" was also the proper locus for preaching and exegesis, and so the Lord's Supper helped to prevent both exegesis and preaching from becoming individualistic. [33]

A third danger in exegesis and preaching has been their tendency to become didactic and to stress doctrinal instruction at the expense of their other functions. This danger has become a reality whenever in Christian history preaching has acquired the style of a theological lecture and exegesis has assumed the function of ransacking the Scriptures for proof texts in support of the right doctrine. Protestant history has not been entirely free from this danger, as a study of its sermons and exegesis will show. [34] But if, as Luther taught and as his own preaching and exegesis demonstrated, the proclamation of the oral Word on the basis of the written Word had as one of its aims that the hearers should worthily receive the visible Word, then exegesis and preaching could not be a mere exposition of the right theological doctrine about the real presence or a mere recital of all the Biblical proof texts for that doctrine, vital though such doctrine and proof were. [35] Exegetical preaching had to call, summon, and invite the hearers. It had to instruct, but it was to do more. And this "more" was what it could easily forget without the depth which "proclaiming the Lord's death" through the Lord's Supper brought to both preaching and Biblical exegesis.

Thus there was a genuine co-ordination between Word and Sacrament in Luther's exegesis, and this co-ordination colored the interpretation of passages dealing with both

---

[32] On Luther's usage of this notion cf. Elert, *Morphologie*, I, 151—153.
[33] See pp. 200 ff.
[34] Jaroslav Pelikan, *From Luther to Kierkegaard*, pp. 49—75.
[35] Preuss, *Geschichte der Abendmahlsfrömmigkeit*, pp. 87—97.

Word and Sacrament. Co-ordination did not mean identity; for while the Word and the Sacrament both "proclaimed the Lord's death," they were also distinct from each other by virtue of their form and their function. This was important in Luther's exegesis of "You proclaim the Lord's death"; it was, if anything, even more important in his pastoral concern for applying this "proclamation of the Lord's death" to the needs of people.[36] The usefulness of the "proclamation" was enhanced and enriched by the generosity of God in providing several forms of the "proclamation," for these several forms served to make the "proclamation" relevant to the variety of human situations which needed it.

Martin Luther was an astute observer of human nature.[37] It would be a very interesting study to collect his statements about his friends or his colleagues at Wittenberg or the princes he knew or his opponents, to see the candor and the penetration of his judgments about people. He knew that Melanchthon was timid, that Zwingli was pedantic, that some of the princes were greedy — and that all these men covered this over with a show of zeal for the Word of God.[38] He also knew that Martin Luther had a nasty temper, which he liked to cover over with a show of zeal for the Word of God.[39] This canny insight into human nature made Luther acutely conscious of the need for dealing with a variety of human situations in the church. Much of what C. F. W. Walther collected from Luther in his book on *Law and Gospel* was pastoral rather than strictly doctrinal or exeget-

[36] Cf. Th. Heckel's introduction to his German translation of Luther's *Fourteen of Consolation* (1520), *Vierzehn Tröstungen* (Helsinki, 1941), pp. xv—xxviii.

[37] Willem J. Kooiman, "Luther as He Saw Himself," in *The Mature Luther*, pp. 76—93.

[38] Cf. *Confession on the Lord's Supper* (1528), W, XXVI, 405.

[39] See the passages cited in the unreliable but provocative book by Erik H. Erikson, *Young Man Luther* (New York, 1958).

ical; for in the passages quoted by Walther, Luther was often discussing the many fluctuations in human mood and consciousness and the way the "proclamation" was to be addressed to men amid these fluctuations.[40]

Luther's awareness of these fluctuations caused him to reflect in his exegesis on the way the various forms of the "proclamation" were peculiarly adapted to the various situations of men. The most obvious instance of his reflection on this variety was, of course, his doctrine of infant Baptism. In his exegesis of passages on Baptism he took the position that the unique need of the infant was uniquely met by the distinctive quality of Baptism and by no other form of the Word of God.[41] Thus God addressed His Word of redemption to the infant through Baptism. But the Lord's Supper, too, spoke to unique needs. From his own intense personal crises Luther knew that there were times in the life of a Christian when neither prayer nor preaching nor exegesis could provide him with the assurance he needed.[42] At such times the Lord's Supper was often — not always, but often[43] — the way for the redemptive Word of God to be addressed to a specific human situation. Luther's exegesis played continual variations on the theme that God had not been stingy with His Word of redemption but had put it into various forms, so that regardless of the human situation or need there would be a "proclamation" especially appropriate to it.[44] Thus it was that "proclaiming the Lord's death" in the Lord's Supper supplemented the other forms of the "proclamation."

[40] C. F. W. Walther, *The Proper Distinction Between Law and Gospel*, tr. by W. H. T. Dau (Saint Louis, 1929), pp. 5—6.

[41] Cf. the *Lenten Postil* (1525), W, XVII-II, 86—87. Luther had occasion to refer to this sermon later in his polemical treatise *On Anabaptism* (1528), W, XXVI, 144—145.

[42] Boehmer, *Road to Reformation*, pp. 87—117.

[43] Karl Holl, *Luther*, pp. 149—153.

[44] Smalcald Articles (1537), W, L, 240—241.

But in his polemics against certain strains in medieval exegesis Luther stressed that it was nevertheless the same "proclamation of the Lord's death" that was being administered in the various forms.[45] There was continuity from one form of this "proclamation" to another, because the fundamental content of the proclamation was always "the Lord's death," God's redemptive deed in Jesus Christ. The continuity of the "proclamation," despite the variety of its forms, was also the guarantee for Luther that the variety of human needs and situations did not destroy the unity of the church.[46] For the church was not built on human situations or ideas but on the "proclaimed" Word of God, which was always the same amid the variety of its own forms and amid the variety of human situations. In this way Luther's exegesis could recognize that men's needs did differ; he could take the variety seriously and yet keep the unity.

Luther's exegesis of "You proclaim the Lord's death" concentrated on the connections between the visible Word, on the one hand, and the Word as oral and as written, on the other hand. But in Luther's exegesis the Lord's Supper as visible Word of God was connected also to two other senses of the term "Word of God" — what we have called in chapter three the "cosmic sense" and the "historical sense." [47]

The Word of God in the cosmic sense was the Logos, through whom the speaking of God existed before creation

[45] Wilhelm Pauck has summarized this half of Luther's teaching as follows: "It is my conviction that there is no characteristically Protestant sacramentalism that can be regarded as the *'pendant'* of the Roman Catholic teaching and practice. The signs of the sacraments celebrated in Protestant churches, Baptism and the Lord's Supper, are effective only because of the Word and it is the Word that constitutes the true nature of the sacrament." *Heritage of the Reformation*, pp. 305–306.

[46] See, for example, Luther's comments in *Against King Henry of England* (1522), W, X-II, 219–220.

[47] See pp. 52 ff.

and in creation.[48] The Lord's Supper united the church with
this Word of God in the cosmic sense. For that reason
Luther's exegesis of the Sanctus in the liturgy, as it was
taken from Isaiah, took the occasion to speak of the God
whose glory filled heaven and earth. In Luther's German
setting of the Sanctus — "Isaiah, mighty seer, in days of old" —
this sense of reverence before the God of the universe was,
if anything, even more profound.[49] Although Luther's exegesis of the words of institution did not often indulge in
reflection about the cosmic meaning of the bread and the
wine, he did occasionally speak about the symbolism of the
elements as images of the natural world. The crushed grape
and the ground grain symbolized man's affinity with the
world of plants and animals and showed him his place in
the entire cosmos of God — with angels and archangels and
with all the company of heaven.[50] Redemption rather than
creation was the primary theme of Luther's exegesis, here
as elsewhere. Yet creation did receive more attention in
Luther's exegesis than most interpreters have recognized.

Part of Luther's provocation for considering the implications of the Lord's Supper for creation as well as for
redemption in his exegesis was his conflict with the Protestant
opponents of his exegesis of "This is My body." They objected that this exegesis was impossible because of the limitations of space and time: the body of Christ was at the
right hand of God in heaven and therefore could not be
concealed within the host on the altar. To this objection
Luther replied with a variety of exegetical and speculative
arguments, including the contention reviewed in chapter

[48] *Sermons on the Gospel of St. John: Chapters 1—4* (1537—40),
W, XLVI, 541—561; *Luther's Works,* 22, 5—29.

[49] The hymn appears in W, XXXV, 455; cf. the valuable introductory
materials, ibid., pp. 230—231, placing it into the context of the *German
Mass* of 1526.

[50] See *Treatise on the Sacrament* (1526), W, XIX, 511.

seven,[51] that the body of Christ was not limited by space to some one place but was present everywhere. In developing this contention Luther spoke occasionally of the consolation that came from the realization that the body of Christ received in the Lord's Supper was the body of the same Christ by whom the entire cosmos was upheld and held together.[52] As we have seen, he often referred to the statement in Leviticus about a man being terrified by the rustling of a leaf, apparently because the falling of the leaves used to terrify him in the hours of his early struggles.[53] But then he added that "proclaiming the Lord's death" granted deliverance from this terror too, and the assurance that the universe was friendly. And this Lord, this Word of God in the cosmic sense, was the one who gave the benefits of His death to the church through His true body and blood in the Lord's Supper.[54]

Principally, then, Luther used this relation between the visible Word and the cosmic Word as a devotional and pastoral device for consolation and encouragement. He sometimes acknowledged that its implications went beyond the personal and pastoral to the exegetical, the theological, and even to the philosophical. Sometimes he connected his exegesis of "This is My body" to his definition of how God was in the world — truly present, yet not empirically available.[55] Sometimes he said that as the bread and wine were changed by the Word of God into bearers of the body and

[51] See pp. 139 ff.

[52] "The body that you receive and the Word that you hear belong to Him who holds the whole world in His hand and is present everywhere." *On the Adoration of the Sacrament* (1523), W, XI, 450.

[53] So, for example, in the *Lectures on Genesis* (1535–45), W, XLII, 127–128; *Luther's Works*, 1, 170–171.

[54] See the discussion of Karl Jäger, *Luthers religiöses Interesse an seiner Lehre von der Realpräsenz* (Giessen, 1900), pp. 62–80.

[55] On this presence of God in the world cf. *Lectures on Genesis* (1535 to 1545), W, XLII, 9–10; *Luther's Works*, 1, 11.

blood of Christ, so the universe had been changed by the Word of God into a bearer of the body of Christ.[56] It was on the basis of statements like these that some of Luther's opponents charged him with pantheism.[57] Even though this charge was obviously false, Luther did speculate about the implications of his eucharistic exegesis for his view of the cosmos. When someone challenged his speculation, he insisted that one should not speculate but should stick to exegesis.[58] And then, when the controversy was over, he went right back to speculating about it! For it was almost unavoidable for Luther's exegesis of "This is My body" to have considerable implications, not only for devotional and pastoral thought but also for philosophical and metaphysical thought. Lutheranism has repeatedly found itself drawn back to these implications of Luther's exegesis; and under the impact of modern physics and metaphysics, as well as of recent exegesis, Lutheran theology is having to face them again today.[59]

Through the idea of the Logos, Luther's exegesis of "This is My body" contributed to his doctrine of the Word. Yet the Word in the Eucharist meant principally, not the Word of God as Logos in the cosmic sense but the Word of God in the historical sense as Jesus Christ. For the very foundation of the church was the Word of God in the historical sense, the "Lord's death," through which God had chosen to act redemptively and to reveal Himself as Lord and Savior. In communion with this special deed of God the church lived to "proclaim the Lord's death" and to celebrate it: The

[56] This problem is discussed in *The Babylonian Captivity of the Church* (1520), W, VI, 510—512.

[57] Franz Hildebrandt, *Est*, p. 103.

[58] W. Link, *Das Ringen Luthers um die Freiheit der Theologie von der Philosophie* (Munich, 1940).

[59] Erwin Metzke's *Sakrament und Metaphysik* (Stuttgart, 1948) is a penetrating discussion.

Lord's Supper as a "proclamation of the Lord's death" was a divinely instituted means for binding the church of the present to that event in the past.[60] Through the Lord's Supper, as through the other forms of the "proclamation," the Holy Spirit made the grace of God in the death of Jesus Christ contemporary.

In this way the Lord's Supper as "proclamation" imparted to the church the benefits of God's redemptive deed in "the Lord's death." For the historical Word of God, the death of Christ, could not be repeated. Thus the deed as deed could not be contemporary to anyone who did not live at the time of Pontius Pilate. But when the church "proclaimed the Lord's death" in the Sacraments, the blessings won by that deed in the past did become contemporary.[61] The crucifixion remained in the past, but the cross could become a present-day reality; and it did when the "proclamation" spoke to faith and faith responded. The benefits and blessings of "the Lord's death" according to Luther's exegesis were forgiveness of sins, life, and salvation:[62] the destruction of the power of sin, the creation of a new man in Christ, and the restoration of a man's wholeness and soundness as a child of God and a member of the healthy body of Christ.

What was the importance of the exegesis of "This is My body" for this exegesis of "You proclaim the Lord's death"? After all, both Baptism and preaching also "proclaimed the Lord's death," and they did so without any special presence of the body and blood of Christ in them. What, according to Luther, did "This is My body" add to "proclamation"? This is an interesting question, because Luther's exegesis

[60] See p. 210.
[61] See pp. 242 ff.
[62] See pp. 181 ff.

of the two passages did not give a consistent answer to it.[63] Sometimes Luther expounded "You proclaim the Lord's death" to mean that the Lord's Supper conferred nothing except what the "proclamation" conferred, and took the view that he accepted the literal sense of "This is My body" simply because the Bible taught it, without inquiring into any benefits that might accrue from the presence.[64] At other times, however, Luther's exegesis spoke very warmly, almost mystically, about how Christ's very body dwelt in the communicant through the Lord's Supper, granting an intimacy with Him that was not available anywhere else.[65]

The very least that the Eucharist granted were the benefits of Christ's death and resurrection. Whether or not this necessitated Luther's exegesis of "This is My body," it certainly did make necessary a more than cognitive definition of what was implied by "You proclaim the Lord's death"; for this "proclaiming" not only showed but also granted what it showed. Sometimes Luther went on to say that in the Bible a deed not only granted what it showed but also contained what it represented;[66] this would mean that Luther's exegesis of "This is My body" was a necessary complement to the Protestant exegesis of "You proclaim the Lord's death." If this was indeed so, it is noteworthy that Luther was one of the few to discover this connection between the exegesis of the two passages. And that illustrates once more the complexity of Luther's exegetical work. He interpreted one text at a time; yet his exegesis of any one text usually involved the exegesis of many other texts, as well as all the principles we have discussed in Part One.

[63] Schlink, op. cit., pp. 253–256.

[64] So in the remarkable words of *On the Councils and the Church* (1539), W, L, 648.

[65] See p. 226, note 29.

[66] See p. 132.

CHAPTER THIRTEEN

"Once for All the Sacrifice of Himself" (Heb. 9:26)

ONE of the most prominent motifs in medieval eucharistic exegesis was its idea that the Mass was a sacrifice.[1] More than any other aspect of this exegesis, the notion that the Mass was a sacrifice which somehow repeated the sacrifice of Christ on Calvary provoked Luther's vigorous dissent.[2] For this represented a denial of the New Testament teaching that Christ "has appeared once for all at the end of the age to put away sin by the sacrifice of Himself." At the same time Luther's repudiation of the sacrificial exegesis of "This do" in the Lord's Supper must not be permitted to obscure the sense in which the Lord's Supper still had sacrificial meaning according to Luther's exegesis. Here, as elsewhere, Luther brought care and precision to the task of Biblical exegesis, and this chapter seeks to trace some of the care and precision with which his exegesis interpreted the Biblical view of "sacrifice."

As we have pointed out earlier, Luther's main work as a professor and theologian was the exegesis of the Old Testament.[3] In this work he was aided not alone by his prodigious memory[4] but especially by his capacity for ferreting out the basic meaning of Biblical words and phrases. He discerned the different terms which the Scriptures used

---

[1] Gustaf Aulén, *Eucharist and Sacrifice,* tr. by Eric H. Wahlstrom (Philadelphia, 1958).

[2] Hence his violent denunciation of the Mass as a "dragon's tail." Smalcald Articles (1537), W, L, 204.

[3] See pp. 45—46.

[4] Meissinger, *Der katholische Luther,* p. 84.

to describe the same thing, as, for example, "justification" and "forgiveness." [5] He was also sensitive to the tendency of the Bible to describe different things by the use of the same term; here he sought to distinguish the several meanings and to relate them to one another. Such distinguishing and relating was, according to Luther, one of the principal assignments of the expositor of the Scriptures.

As an expositor of the Scriptures, especially of the Old Testament, Luther had to give detailed attention to the sacrifices described and prescribed in the Scriptures. We have described some of this in chapter five.[6] This exegesis brought him to the observation that the word "sacrifice" had been used in the Scriptures to designate two distinct types of action. Luther sometimes distinguished these two types of action as "sacrifices of atonement" and "sacrifices of thanksgiving."[7] A "sacrifice of atonement" was an action by which the favor of God was secured; its relation to the favor of God was that of cause to effect. A "sacrifice of thanksgiving," on the other hand, came from a person who already stood in a reconciled relation to God; its relation to the favor of God was that of effect to cause. The Scriptures used the word "sacrifice" for both types of action, and so did the early fathers of the church. It was, therefore, important that exegesis distinguish between the two meanings.

Failure to distinguish between the two meanings was, according to Luther, one of the sources of paganism in the ancient world. In his exegesis of the Old Testament,[8] especially in his monumental exposition of Genesis,[9] Luther pon-

[5] Thus already in the Lectures on Romans (1515–16), W, LVI, 42.
[6] See pp. 106 ff.
[7] Sermon on the Visitation of Mary, July 2, 1539, W, XLVII, 835.
[8] So, for example, in his Commentary on Psalm 117 (1530), W, XXXI-I, 230; Luther's Works, 14, 10.
[9] Lectures on Genesis (1535–45), W, XLII, 183–185; Luther's Works, 1, 247–250.

dered the question: How could the primitive revelation and promise given to Adam and again to Noah perish in the memory of so many nations and be replaced by pagan religion? The blurring of the distinction between "sacrifices of atonement" and "sacrifices of thanksgiving" was one of the basic reasons for this change. Since the basis of patriarchal religion was a covenant of grace with God, the patriarchs recognized that their sacrifices were not a means of appeasing God's wrath or of winning His favor but only a means of expressing gratitude to God and of bearing witness to God's grace given in the covenant. But when others saw the patriarchs offering up their sacrifices and then also discerned that the patriarchs stood in a special covenant with God, they concluded that the sacrifices were the basis of the covenant, and that God was gracious to the patriarchs because of sacrifices. Imitating the actions of the patriarchs rather than their faith, the Gentiles thus became pagans.[10]

Here Luther's exegesis discerned a persistent tendency of man to turn his signs of gratitude toward God into devices for getting into God's good graces. So persistent was this tendency to confuse "sacrifices of thanksgiving" with "sacrifices of atonement" that Luther used it not only in his exegesis, as a way to explain the history of primitive religion in relation to the Old Testament, but also in his polemics, as a way to account for the fall of the church and the rise of notions like merit and satisfaction in the sacramental system of the church.[11] His reading of the history of the early church, which was more discerning than it was extensive,[12]

---

[10] Cf. *Sermons on Deuteronomy* (1529), W, XXVIII, 671–677.

[11] "They cite the example of the holy fathers who used this canon [of the Mass] and regarded the Mass as a sacrifice, for example, Gregory, Bernard, Bonaventure, and others. To this I reply that nothing is more dangerous than the works and lives of the saints if they are not based on the Scriptures." *The Abuse of the Mass* (1521), W, VIII, 527.

[12] See p. 83.

produced the conclusion that in the history of the Christian Church men had very early begun to use their prayers, services, and Sacraments as a way of making atonement to God. When they did this, the church moved from its early apostolic purity into the corruption that Luther believed he was called to purge out of it. The dating of this fall of the church varied considerably in Luther. Only rarely did he date it, as the radical Protestants tended to do, at the end of the first century.[13] Oftener the seventh century or even a later century was the dividing line.[14] But wherever and whenever it happened, the failure of Biblical exegesis to distinguish "sacrifices of thanksgiving" from "sacrifices of atonement" had been fateful, indeed fatal, for true Christian faith.

One of the metaphors which Luther's exegesis used to describe reconciliation through the death of Christ was the image of the "sacrifice of Himself."[15] It was not the only metaphor, not even the most distinctive metaphor in his exegesis. Unlike some later exegetes, Luther recognized that the Scriptures employed a variety of images to depict what had taken place in the atonement. But both Scripture and tradition did have recourse to the idea of "the sacrifice of Himself" as a figure of speech for the atonement,[16] and there-

[13] Karl Ecke, *Schwenckfeld, Luther und der Gedanke einer apostolischen Reformation* (Berlin, 1911).

[14] "St. Gregory [Gregory I, who was pope 590–604] was the last bishop of Rome. Since him the church in Rome has had no more bishops to the present day . . . but only popes, that is, masked devils." *Against the Papacy at Rome, Founded by the Devil* (1545), W, LIV, 229.

[15] Christ "is the Son of God who, in pure mercy and love, surrendered Himself . . . and offered Himself as a sacrifice to God for us miserable sinners. . . . Therefore Christ is the Lover of those who are in anguish, sin, and death — and the sort of Lover who gives Himself for us and becomes our Priest, that is, who interposes Himself as the Mediator between God and us miserable sinners." *Commentary on Galatians* (1535), W, XL-I, 299.

[16] See the very discerning comments of Eugene R. Fairweather, "Introduction" to *A Scholastic Miscellany: Anselm to Ockham*, LCC, X, 54–58.

fore the idea appeared in Luther's exegesis too. Only seldom did he take up the cultic sacrifices of the Old Testament without referring them to the "sacrifice" of Christ.[17] The picture of Christ as the sacrificial Lamb that takes away the sin of the world was one of the most familiar liturgical and artistic symbols of this connection between the sacrifice of Christ and the sacrificial worship of Israel.[18] At times Luther took the idea of Christ's "sacrifice of Himself" to mean simply that the human race brought Christ as its sacrifice to God.[19] But in his more profound discussions of the idea of "sacrifice" Luther pointed out — partly as an exegesis of the story of the sacrifice of Isaac — that God not only demanded the sacrifice but also provided it.[20] Thus the sacrifice itself was Gospel rather than Law. And this was pre-eminently true of Christ's "sacrifice of Himself" on the cross, a sacrifice which God not only demanded but provided.

Christ's "sacrifice of Himself" was the only "sacrifice of atonement" in the proper sense of the word. Luther was disturbed in his exegesis when the Old Testament seemed to say that the sacrifices prescribed in the Pentateuch were a way to win God's mercy or to make up for sin.[21] Clearly this was the way many people in the Old Testament had understood them, and the text sometimes seemed to support this understanding. Some Christian exegetes had suggested that this had been true of the Old Testament, but that the coming of Christ had changed this; at times Luther seems to

[17] An interesting exception is the *Commentary on Psalm 111* (1530), W, XXXI-I, 393–426; *Luther's Works*, 13, 351–387.

[18] See Luther's exposition of this picture, *Sermons on the Gospel of St. John: Chapters 1–4* (1537–40), W, XLVI, 676–684; *Luther's Works*, 22, 161–170.

[19] For one of Luther's fullest explanations of sacrifice and priesthood see his *Commentary on Psalm 110* (1535), W, XLI, 174–215; *Luther's Works*, 13, 309–334.

[20] See p. 36, note 18.

[21] Cf. Bornkamm, *Luther und das Alte Testament*, pp. 69–74.

have accepted this exegesis.[22] But his most mature reflection on the problem led him to conclude that the way of salvation had always been the same.[23] He therefore said in 1532: "It was not the purpose of sacrifices or of services under the Law to justify or to placate God. Since the sin of Adam this purpose has been reserved for the one sacrifice of Christ, of which the sacrifices of the Law were a kind of shadow." [24] When the power of atoning to God for sin was ascribed to the sacrifices of the Old Testament cultus, Luther's exegesis added that this was done in anticipation of Christ's "sacrifice of Himself." For this alone was the "sacrifice" with which God was truly pleased and for which God was willing to forgive men their sins.

And Christ had done this "once for all at the end of the age to put away sin by the sacrifice of Himself." Early in his exegetical career, while he was expounding this passage in the Epistle to the Hebrews, Luther had already come to the realization of what this meant.[25] "Once for all" meant that Christ's "sacrifice of Himself" had happened at a specific time and place in history, when He suffered under Pontius Pilate. Some theologians have been inclined to speculate about the timeless character of the death of Christ, on the basis of an exegesis of the words in Rev. 13:8, "the Lamb

[22] In a sermon on Heb. 8:3, delivered in 1537, there is an interesting statement (W, XLV, 397): "This passage . . . proves mightily that since the death of Christ and until the end of the world no sacrifice can avail any longer except the sacrifice of praise. . . . In the Old Testament there were many priests who were to sacrifice, but they accomplished nothing. No one ever received the forgiveness of sins through their sacrifice. Therefore the entire priesthood of the Old Testament had to cease, and God had to send His Son. . . . Therefore the blood of goats does not avail before God any longer."

[23] See Bornkamm's interesting discussion of "Moses the Christian" in *Luther und das Alte Testament,* pp. 126—139.

[24] *Commentary on Psalm 51* (1538), W, XL-II, 455; *Luther's Works,* 12, 399.

[25] *Lectures on Hebrews* (1517—18), W, LVII, 217—218.

slain from the foundation of the world." [26] If this exegesis were correct, these words would describe the death of Christ as parallel to all of human history and thus applicable to each moment in history. But Luther was one of the few exegetes since St. Augustine to give basic thought to the meaning of time and of history in the plan of God, and therefore to the "once for all" in the history of God's dealings with the human race. [27]

Such exegesis led Luther to the realization that as an event which happened "once for all," Christ's "sacrifice of Himself" was unrepeatable. It could not be repeated, because the historical event of Christ was unique (as indeed every historical event was). [28] What is more, it did not need to be repeated; for God in His grace and freedom had declared this to be the one "sacrifice" with which He chose to be pleased. [29] Because of its intrinsic worth and because of God's choosing, Christ's "sacrifice of Himself" was the only genuine atonement ever offered to God. And by the resurrection God had made it known that the atonement was satisfactory. [30] He would never have to be propitiated again,

[26] Cf. Francis Turretinus, *Institutio theologiae elencticae,* II (Geneva, 1689), 215.

[27] See p. 54, note 21.

[28] See Luther's remarks on this in his *Commentary on Romans* (1515 to 1516), W, LVI, 327.

[29] Christ was "the sacrifice which God Himself has appointed and with which God is pleased. . . . Because God Himself has appointed this sacrifice, we should have no doubt that this sacrifice completely accomplished everything it was intended to accomplish. . . . Christ suffered this on account of you and your sins. God laid them upon Him, and in all obedience He bore them . . . so that when you confess that you are a sinner and have angered God, you might . . . comfort yourself with the suffering and atonement of our Lord Christ." *House Postil* (1544), W, LII, 229.

[30] "Thus His death not only signifies but also accomplishes the forgiveness of sin as a most sufficient satisfaction. And His resurrection is not only the guarantee [*sacramentum*] of our righteousness, but it also accomplishes it in us if we believe it." *Commentary on Romans* (1515–16), W, LVI, 296.

and no further "sacrifice of atonement" was either necessary or possible.

Thus "sacrifice" in the sense of "sacrifice of atonement" was a term that could be applied properly only to Christ's "sacrifice of Himself." But Luther's exegesis of the Scriptures showed him that in spite of this qualification the other sacrifice could not be made a peripheral element in the Bible. All his life he lectured on the Old Testament, where the concept of sacrifice was very prominent. Because of his controversy with Rome, Luther was especially interested in the denunciations of sacrifice that figured so noticeably in the books of the prophets. If the prophets had the right to denounce forms of worship which had divine sanction and command, then certainly Luther had the right to denounce purely human ordinances and traditions.[31] But in his exegesis he also paid attention to the positive value of sacrifices in the Old Testament. He pointed to their didactic value.[32] But he also recognized that they were a form of worship in themselves.[33] Sometimes he spoke very perceptively about the meaning of sacrifice in worship, as he expounded passages dealing with the Levitical priesthood of the Old Testament. The worship of God in the Old Testament had been inseparable from the element of sacrifice.

[31] "I have often admired this boldness of the prophets, that they spoke so contemptuously about sacrifices, contrary to the Law of Moses and the rites of their people. If the pope were able from the Word of God to prove his sacrifices and ceremonies, the way the Jews could their sacrifices, I should surely never have dared to raise any objection. But since he has instituted and commanded them without the Word, indeed against the Word, we condemn him with full right." *Commentary on Psalm 51* (1538), W, XL-II, 450—451; *Luther's Works*, 12, 396.

[32] "The ceremonies were intended to be understood as pictures or symbols, to remind those people of the promise of Christ until He came to establish the right service of worship of God which the Law typified." *Commentary on Psalm 110* (1535), W, XLI, 152; *Luther's Works*, 13, 293.

[33] *Commentary on Psalm 51* (1538), W, XL-II, 454; *Luther's Works*, 12, 398.

But worship was inseparable from "sacrifice" in the New Testament too. Christ's "sacrifice of Himself" did not eliminate the need for "sacrifice" in Christian worship. If anything, "sacrifice" could become more prominent in Christian worship than it had been in Jewish worship, for the very reason that the need for an atoning "sacrifice" had been met by the death of Christ.[34] Now for the first time it was possible to understand the true meaning of "sacrifice" in worship without injecting the notion of atonement. Luther's exegesis of the prophets pointed out that the believers in Old Testament times had been in constant danger of obscuring the meaning of their "sacrifices." Now the church had been delivered from its dependence on "sacrifices," and therefore it could begin to bring true "sacrifices," just as its deliverance from dependence on good works was the only way it could become capable of true good works.[35]

As he tried to state this paradox in a form that was meaningful to the church of his time, Luther fastened upon an idea that had never quite disappeared from the teaching and exegesis of the church but had certainly been quiescent for a time: the universal priesthood of believers.[36] But this idea was based on exegesis, and therefore it must be extricated from the interpretations put upon it by its later exponents if its significance for the interpretation of the Sacrament is to become clear.[37] The universal priesthood of believers did not mean in Luther's exegesis that every Christian was his own priest, needing no mediator between God and himself. What it did mean for Luther's exegesis was that every Christian was a priest to every other Christian and a mediator

[34] See p. 242, note 22.
[35] Jaroslav Pelikan, *Fools for Christ*, pp. 85—117.
[36] A classic statement of this was in the *Sermons on 1 Peter* (1523), W, XII, 316—320.
[37] *Christian Liberty* (1520), W, VII, 35.

between God and his brother, a "little Christ." The doctrine of the universal priesthood of believers was not individualism, rugged or otherwise, but part of Luther's exegesis of the Scriptures as "the history of the people of God." [38]

In that "people of God" Christians exercised their priesthood. From his exegesis of the Old Testament, Luther saw that a priest had the function of mediating between God and man in both directions.[39] He sometimes called these two directions the sacramental and the sacrificial: the sacramental mediated God to man, the sacrificial mediated man to God.[40] Because of his stress on the universal priesthood Luther was able to see how prominent and central the element of "sacrifice" still was in Christian worship, that is, in the worship of the church. For by "sacrifice" Luther did not mean the individualistic "personal sacrifice" which was so prominent in medieval monasticism and in later Protestant Pietism. He meant the action of the church by which the church offered itself up to God in its corporate worship, uniting itself to Christ's "sacrifice of Himself once for all." In the New Testament no less than in the Old, worshiping God meant bringing Him a sacrifice. Christ was the only Priest, Luther's exegesis of Hebrews said, and yet believers were priests; [41] Christ was the only Sacrifice, and yet they were to bring their sacrifices to God in the worship of the church.

Luther's exegesis of the Bible found one of its continuing themes in grace, and therefore it had to emphasize thanksgiving. In both Greek and Latin the words for "grace" and for "thanksgiving" are the same. Chapter eight has already discussed Luther's exegesis of "grace" as "forgiveness." [42]

[38] See pp. 89 ff.

[39] *Commentary on Psalm 110* (1535), W, XLI, 183; *Luther's Works*, 13, 315.

[40] *The Babylonian Captivity of the Church* (1520), W, VI, 526.

[41] *Lectures on Hebrews* (1517–18), W, LVII, 165 ff.

[42] See pp. 157 ff.

But it is interesting that many interpreters of Luther's theology and exegesis are unable to interpret his ideas about thanksgiving. For Luther thanksgiving was so basic in the Christian life precisely because the life of grace was a gift. Thanksgiving was always in response to a gift, as Luther pointed out in his exegesis of "O give thanks to the Lord" in the Psalms.[43] The giving of thanks thus included an acknowledgement of it as a gift rather than a reward. One did not need to give thanks for that which he had earned, Luther pointed out in his exegesis. But when one had been the recipient of an unearned gift, then thanksgiving was the least (and the most) he could do.

Thanksgiving was also the outgrowth of a new relation between God and man. God's gift of grace in Christ was distinguished from human gifts by the basic change it brought about in the recipient. It was the grace of a new creation.[44] Luther's favorite way of talking about this in his exegesis was to speak about the gift of the Holy Spirit.[45] This was not a static gift to be clutched or saved. It was a dynamic gift, which effected a radical transformation in the recipient and made him a new being. Thanksgiving for the gift of grace was, therefore, not simply gratitude for favors received but the expression of that transformation which has been wrought by the Holy Spirit. Failure to recognize this meant the substitution of the Law for the Gospel. Despite its emphasis on thanksgiving, therefore, Luther's exegesis did not make gratitude the basis of Christian morality.[46] The basis of Christian morality was the change which the Holy Spirit worked through the means of grace, and the dedication to

[43] See Luther's *Commentary on Psalm 118* (1530), W, XXXI-I, 68–77; *Luther's Works*, 14, 47–51.

[44] Cf. Johann Haar, *Initium creaturae Dei* (Gütersloh, 1939).

[45] Prenter, *Spiritus Creator*, pp. 224–238.

[46] Cf. Renatus Hupfeld, *Die Ethik Johann Gerhards* (Berlin, 1908).

God which that change made possible. Thanksgiving was the expression of such dedication.

The fundamental significance of the Lord's Supper in Luther's exegesis was, therefore, its function as an instrument of the grace to which thanksgiving responded. Through the grace communicated in the Sacrament the Holy Spirit accomplished the dedication out of which thanksgiving proceeded. The element of thanksgiving pervaded the entire Christian life, just as the grace given in the Word and the Sacraments affected the entire Christian life. Thanksgiving, therefore, was thanksgiving for the grace granted through the Word and the Sacraments, and it was the grace thus granted that made the thanksgiving possible. In this dynamic way Luther's exegesis joined thanksgiving and the Lord's Supper, because they were connected by the emphasis on grace. When thanksgiving was spoken of as duty in the legalistic sense of the word, its connection with the Lord's Supper was either destroyed or distorted. But when, on the other hand, the grace of the Lord's Supper was not related also to thanksgiving, its meaning shriveled up.[47] This is why it is so important to realize that in Luther's exegesis both forgiveness of sins and thanksgiving had a role to play.

As Luther's exegesis joined the forgiveness of sins and thanksgiving in the Lord's Supper, so he also connected "sacrifice" and thanksgiving. A "sacrifice" was always related to God's demands, for "sacrifice" was an act of obedience. This applied both to "sacrifices of atonement" and to "sacrifices of thanksgiving"; they were valid only if they were based on an explicit commandment of God. In his exegesis Luther fiercely attacked the monks, accusing them of substituting their self-invented deeds of piety for the acts of

[47] See Brilioth's *Eucharistic Faith and Practice* for a statement of this proposition.

worship which God had prescribed.[48] They supposed that their mortification and fasting were a true "sacrifice" merely because they were uncomfortable when they did such things. But for a true "sacrifice" the command of God was necessary. Luther said in his exegesis of Deuteronomy that without the command of God a man was like the priests of Baal; flagellation did not guarantee the validity of a "sacrifice." [49]

While a "sacrifice" was always related to God's demands, thanksgiving was always related to God's gifts. But since the grace of God in the Holy Spirit was not just one gift among other gifts but a unique gift of God, a unique thanksgiving was also in order. The church thus needed to have a way of thanksgiving that truly expressed the free and unique character of the gift for which it was offering its thanks. At the same time it needed to have a form of "sacrifice" through which the universal priesthood could be sure to meet the demands of God. If it were not for Christ's "sacrifice of Himself once for all," no other "sacrifice" would be possible or beneficial. If it were not for this "sacrifice of atonement," the thanksgiving of the church would be no different from the thanksgiving of the entire creation. But by virtue of Christ's "sacrifice of Himself once for all" the members of the church had been transformed, and they offered up the willing "sacrifice" of New Testament priests. They gave thanks to God for His marvelous gift.

[48] "Though they boast that they are the servants of God and the brides of Christ, none of the monks, nuns, or priests either do or understand this. . . . If you want to know it and find it, you must not seek for it on the basis of your own ideas." *Commentary on the Sermon on the Mount* (1530 to 1532), W, XXXII, 468; *Luther's Works*, 21, 204—205.

[49] "The rule of St. Francis attracts so much attention that the monks deny Christ on its account and follow St. Francis. The spectacular life of the priests of Baal — when they stabbed themselves with lances and ripped themselves with knives — gave more of an impression of holiness than the teaching of the prophet Elijah." *Sermons on Deuteronomy* (1529), W, XXVIII, 600.

In this way the Christian "sacrifice of thanksgiving" was a fulfillment of God's demands, for it offered God the kind of "sacrifice" He desired. At the same time it was an expression of God's gifts, for in its thanksgiving the church acknowledged its continuing dependence on His giving grace. And the two — God's gifts and God's demands — were congruent.[50] When in the cross of Christ God demanded and then proceeded to give what He had demanded, this demonstrated clearly what Luther's exegesis saw already foreshadowed in the sacrifice of Isaac: that it was God's way to demand a "sacrifice" and then, in His gift, to provide the "sacrifice," so that His gifts and His demands were indeed congruent.[51] Here Luther's exegesis recognized a basic feature of the will and way of God — adumbrated in the Old Testament, revealed in Christ, and manifested in God's dealings with the church. This feature was well summarized in the epigrammatic prayer of St. Augustine: "Give what Thou commandest, and command what Thou wilt." [52] The Gospel was the disclosure of that congruence between gift and demand in Jesus Christ.

Luther's exegesis recognized that the Lord's Supper uniquely manifested this evangelical congruence. On the one hand, it was based on a command of God: "Do this in remembrance of Me." Luther's exegesis made much of the imperative mood in that verb.[53] The celebration of the Lord's Supper was not optional in the church, although the forms for its celebration were; Luther held to both of these prin-

[50] "We say that all the commandments of God are fulfilled, not by our perfect deeds but in the abundantly forgiving grace of God." *Against Latomus* (1521), W, VIII, 56; *Luther's Works*, 32, 157.

[51] See p. 36, note 18.

[52] See p. 10, note 13.

[53] For example, in his *German Answer to the Book of King Henry* (1522), W, X-II, 256.

ciples.[54] In the Lord's Supper, therefore, the church confronted God's demand that something be done and that something be brought (bread and wine) for the accomplishment of God's demands. On the other hand, the Lord's Supper was fundamentally a gift. The "main thing" in the Sacrament was something about which Luther spoke often, though not consistently.[55] One of the things which he called the main thing in the Sacrament were the words "given and shed"; [56] for they stressed the gift-character of the Supper, in contrast to the notion that the Sacrament was "a sacrifice [of atonement] and a good work." [57] The power of the Sacrament consisted in the congruence between demand and gift, between the imperative and the indicative mood. In the Lord's Supper, consequently, "sacrifice" and thanksgiving came together.

Luther's exegesis, therefore, began by asserting the dependence of the Lord's Supper on Christ's "sacrifice of Himself once for all," just as the starting point for Luther's doctrine of Baptism was the Baptism of Christ.[58] Already in his early writings Luther expressly ruled out any interpretation of the Lord's Supper as "sacrifice" that overlooked this dependence on the original sacrifice of Christ.[59] Sacrifice

[54] Jaroslav Pelikan, "Luther and the Liturgy," pp. 23—25.

[55] The German word was *heubtstück*; on Luther's varying use of it cf. *Bekenntnisschriften*, p. 691, note 3.

[56] Thus in the Small Catechism (1529), W, XXX-I, 319.

[57] Jaroslav Pelikan, "Luther's Endorsement of the *Confessio Bohemica*," in *Concordia Theological Monthly*, XX (1949), 840.

[58] In one of his last sermons, preached on January 6, 1546, Luther said (W, LI, 111): "You must not separate your Baptism from the Baptism of Christ; but you must enter the Baptism of Christ with your Baptism, so that Christ's Baptism becomes your Baptism and your Baptism becomes Christ's Baptism and there is only one Baptism. . . . We should know and believe that Christ was baptized on our account, and thus say that His Baptism is mine and my Baptism is His Baptism."

[59] Thus, for example, in *The Babylonian Captivity of the Church* (1520), W, VI, 523.

or not, the Sacrament derived its meaning from the suffering, death, and resurrection of Christ; each aspect of Luther's exegesis must, therefore, be related to his doctrine of atonement through the cross of Christ. And when the aspect under consideration is as integral a part of his exegesis as the idea of "sacrifice" was, this requirement becomes even more stringent. The Lord's Supper united the church with its Lord in His death, a death which was a "sacrifice of Himself once for all." The roots of the Sacrament were in the event on the cross; and, as earlier chapters have pointed out at greater length, Luther's exegesis thus made the death of Christ and its benefits the content of the Lord's Supper.[60]

On this basis Luther branded it as blasphemous for Christian theologians to speak of the Lord's Supper as a repetition or even as a continuation of Christ's "sacrifice of Himself once for all." [61] Certain medieval exegetes had spoken of it that way, and some of their statements so exaggerated this idea of the repeated "sacrifice" that the significance of the original "sacrifice" became merely that of the first in a long series: Christ's "sacrifice of Himself" had inaugurated the daily "sacrifices" of the Mass. At the Council of Trent (1545 to 1563) these statements were modified; [62] and since Trent, Roman Catholic theologians have been rather more careful in the way they speak of the sacrificial effect of the Mass.[63] Even now, however, they speak of the Mass as a "sacrifice" that avails — but only in union with the "sacrifice" of Christ on the cross. Luther's opponents in his own day were not so circumspect in their language about the sacrifice. He ac-

[60] See p. 171.

[61] "Therefore the pope's sacrifice is an unheard-of abomination [grewel wunder]." *The Abuse of the Mass* (1521), W, VIII, 516.

[62] Erwin Iserloh's *Die Eucharistie in der Darstellung des Johannes Eck* (Münster, 1950), pp. 130—190, is a careful presentation.

[63] Council of Trent, Session XXII, *Canons and Decrees of the Council of Trent,* ed. by H. J. Schroeder (Saint Louis, 1955), pp. 144—150.

cused them of minimizing the importance of Christ's "sacrifice of Himself" in favor of the "sacrifice" of the Mass, of ignoring the "once for all," and thus of confusing "sacrifices of atonement" with "sacrifices of thanksgiving."

If the Lord's Supper was to be a "sacrifice," then, it had to be a "sacrifice of thanksgiving." Or perhaps the term "sacrifice" could be used for the offerings of bread and wine which the church brought to the altar: God accepted this "sacrifice" and set it aside for His purposes by the consecration. These were the two senses in which Luther's exegesis would permit the word "sacrifice" to be applied to the Lord's Supper, and he interpreted the applications of the word to the Sacrament in the church fathers as instances of such usage. When used that way, the word "sacrifice" was appropriate, and it expressed something about the Sacrament that was difficult to express any other way. What Luther managed to do by his careful exegesis was to eliminate from the motif of "sacrifice" all the connotations that contradicted the Biblical image of Christ's "sacrifice of Himself once for all." In the treatise *This Is My Body: These Words Still Stand* of 1527 Luther summarized his exegesis of "sacrifice" this way:

"It is certain that Christ cannot be sacrificed over and above the one single time when He sacrificed Himself. Thank God, even the papists now recognize that the daily sacrifice and the sale of this sacrifice to make up for our sins, as we have carried it on and maintained it heretofore, is the greatest blasphemy and abomination there has ever been on earth. None of the old theologians maintained, taught, or wrote this. For Irenaeus calls it a sacrifice in the sense that one sacrifices the bread and wine, out of which the Sacrament is made through the Word of God, only as an expression of thanksgiving, so that thereby one confesses that God nourishes us, as used to happen in the Old Testament. . . . Others call it a sacrifice because in it we remember the single sacrifice which Christ offered up on our behalf once and for all. Thus every year we call Easter 'Resurrection' or the 'Day of Resurrection' and say, 'Christ is risen today!' This does not mean that Christ arises every year, but that every year we recall the day of His resurrection. It is in this sense that St. Augustine calls the Sacrament a sacrifice." [64]

[64] *This Is My Body* (1527), W, XXIII, 273.

Conclusion

LUTHER the expositor was a virtuoso. No modern exegete can fail to be moved by the depth of the Reformer's insights into the meaning of the Biblical text. Next to his exegesis most present-day commentaries seem either pedantic or shallow or both. When one turns from such commentaries to Luther's exegetical works, as presented in the subsequent volumes, one immediately recognizes the master's touch. Where conservative commentators are often timid, Luther is bold and creative. Where critical commentators are often irresponsible, Luther knows himself to be the servant of the Word of God, not its master. Where scholarly commentators sometimes seem interested in every detail of the text except its theological meaning, Luther manages to find theological meaning in the most unpromising parts of the Bible. Where Roman Catholic allegorical commentators often practice an exegetical alchemy that sets out to turn lead into gold but ends up turning gold into lead, Luther labors to discover the literal and historical sense of the text. Where Protestant commentators often become so preoccupied with the literal sense that they cannot tell prose from poetry, Luther's eye is always sensitive to the spectrum of meanings in both the Old and the New Testament. Surely the judgment of men like Ebeling and Bornkamm is correct: that Luther was one of the most important figures in the history of Biblical exegesis. He was, in a sense he could not have known when he took his degree in 1512, a true *Doctor in Biblia*.[1]

---

[1] See pp. 46—47 above.

Yet a virtuoso is often a failure as a composer — and worse than a failure as a member of an orchestra. Many of the features which we find most attractive and powerful in Luther's exegesis are also the ones which we find most difficult to follow. It would be an oversimplification to say that we are in a position to imitate some of Luther's exegesis, while we are obliged to depart from his pattern in other ways. Rather, what is impossible about Luther's exegesis is often his most telling and persuasive interpretation of the Scriptures. To put the problem in a somewhat exaggerated form: A virtuoso certainly finds nuances in the score which a less talented performer often misses. But does this mean that the less talented performer should seek to emulate the virtuoso? Now it is clear that the analogy between exegetical skill and musical virtuosity has decided limitations. No one is asked to stake his life and his hope on a performer's reading of the score! The central message of the Scriptures must be clear and unmistakable, whether the church has a Luther to interpret that message or not. And it must be possible for the church to discover the meaning of the Word of God for problems and situations with which Luther never dealt. What is at stake here is no merely aesthetic contrast, but the very life of the church in the Gospel.

That is what makes the contemporary relevance of Luther's exegesis so important, but also so problematical. As we have said in the Introduction to this volume, it is not an editor's prerogative to decide the question of this relevance for his readers.[2] Inevitably one's own theological assessment of an exegete from the past will affect his historical interpretation of that exegete. Completely objective history is no more possible in the history of exegesis than it is in the history of theology or of painting. Some of the problems

[2] See Introduction, p. x.

in determining the relevance of Luther's exegesis come from a consideration of his exegetical principles, outlined in Part One of this volume. Others arise from a study of Luther's exegetical practice, sketched in Part Two of this volume. Still others emerge from the contrast between Luther's situation and our own, with the inescapable realization that some of the techniques and theories available to Luther have been closed off to us. This Conclusion, therefore, can do little more than review for the present situation the principles analyzed in Part One, as these principles take embodiment in the exegetical practice summarized in Part Two. Perhaps the most useful form for any such review, following an effort at a reasonably objective account, is a series of brief questions.[3]

1. *The Bible and the Word of God.* As a polemical theologian in his conflict with both Roman Catholicism and Protestantism, Luther identified the Bible with the Word of God.[4] This identification made itself felt in his exegesis of "This is My body."[5] By means of this identification he tended to make the doctrine of the Word of God a matter of knowledge. But as an exegetical theologian in his exposition of the Biblical text, Luther noted the rarity of such an identification in the Scriptures themselves.[6] This insight asserted itself in his exegesis of "You proclaim the Lord's death,"[7] in which he made the Eucharist the visible Word of God, as well as in his exegesis of "For the forgiveness of sins."[8] By means of this insight he made the doctrine of

[3] In Chapter XVI of *The Riddle of Roman Catholicism* I have employed a similar method.

[4] See pp. 67—70 above.

[5] See pp. 142 ff.

[6] See p. 67 above.

[7] See pp. 219—236 above.

[8] See pp. 166 ff.

the Word of God a matter of grace and the means of grace rather than a matter of mere knowledge. The question that emerges from this contrast is: Is it possible to formulate the doctrine of the Word of God today in such a way that the distinction between revelation and Scripture, but also the connection between them, may be safeguarded?

2. *Scripture and Tradition.* As the spokesman for a Biblically oriented Protestantism, Luther stressed the sovereignty of the Scriptures over all tradition and dogma, however ancient.[9] This stress enabled him to repudiate the sacrificial interpretation of the Eucharist, despite its noble antiquity, on the basis of the Scriptural declaration that Christ had "appeared once for all at the end of the age to put away sin by the sacrifice of Himself," [10] and even to repudiate the eucharistic exegesis of the sixth chapter of John.[11] But as a Biblical interpreter, Luther made use of tradition and dogma to find a meaning in the text that many other spokesmen for a Biblically oriented Protestantism were unable or unwilling to recognize as valid exegesis.[12] This difference appeared in his insistence on what he called "the old meaning" of passages like "This is My body," [13] also in his traditional exegesis of "participation in the body of Christ" to mean the real presence in the elements.[14] The question raised by both his principle and his practice is: Is it possible for exegesis today to assert the sovereignty of Scripture over tradition (including the tradition of Luther's exegesis of Scripture) and simultaneously to affirm a continuity and affinity with the tradition and dogma of the Christian centuries?

[9] See pp. 71—88 above.
[10] See pp. 237—254 above.
[11] See pp. 145—146 above.
[12] See p. 187 above.
[13] See pp. 143—144 above.
[14] See pp. 191—204 above.

3. *The history of the people of God.* As a man of scholarship, Luther employed the best historical-critical scholarship available to him and demanded that the historical sense of the Scriptures receive the normative place in exegesis.[15] Therefore he took the phrase "body of Christ" in "participation in the body of Christ" in its "historical" rather than in any "spiritual" sense.[16] But as a man of faith, Luther continually extracted something more than the simple and single historical sense from the Scriptures, and even found the ministry of the Word in the narratives of Genesis.[17] Thus he was even willing, at least in his earlier exegesis, to give the "spiritual" sense of "body of Christ" a certain pre-eminence over the "historical" or "natural" sense.[18] This forces one to ask the question: Is it possible to practice a spiritual or Christocentric exegesis of the Old Testament today without accepting Luther's Christological exegesis or losing the "historical" sense in the vagaries of unbridled allegorism?

4. *Commentary and controversy.* As an obedient expositor of the whole Bible, Luther endeavored to incorporate the full range of Biblical language into his theology.[19] He therefore had room in his system for a pronounced emphasis on the memorial aspects of the Eucharist, summarized in the phrase "in remembrance of Me," despite his primary insistence on the real presence.[20] But as a theological controversialist, Luther often gave the impression that he was concentrating on one strain of Biblical language to the exclusion, or at least the overshadowing, of others. This im-

---

[15] See pp. 89–90 above.
[16] See p. 194.
[17] See pp. 103–105 above.
[18] See pp. 155–156 above.
[19] See pp. 32–47 above.
[20] See pp. 205–218 above.

pression is conveyed by his almost exclusive emphasis on "the forgiveness of sins" as the benefit of the Eucharist.[21] This circumstance compels the question: Is it possible to involve oneself in theological controversy (whether for Luther or against Luther or without Luther!) without being forced into an overemphasis that belies the work of the expositor?

These questions are obviously little more than examples, and they could be multiplied with ease. But they do serve to illustrate both the fascination and the embarrassment one feels in the study of Luther the expositor. As contemporary Protestant theology is re-examining the task of exegesis afresh, it is beginning to sense this fascination and to confess this embarrassment. Even some very dedicated defenders of Luther's eucharistic doctrine confess that they cannot follow Luther's eucharistic exegesis in all its aspects.[22] Conversely, even some very vigorous critics of Luther's doctrine of justification must pay tribute to his method of exegesis.[23] Here as elsewhere it is a distortion of the work of Luther to regard it as some sort of new revelation. For in his exegesis — as in his doctrine, piety, and ethic — the Reformer represented himself as a son of the church and as a witness to the Word of God revealed in Jesus Christ and documented in the Sacred Scriptures. To that church, to that Word, to that Christ, to those Scriptures Luther the expositor pointed.

He still does.

[21] See pp. 157—173 above.

[22] Cf. Hermann Sasse, *This Is My Body* (Minneapolis, 1959), pp. 351 to 356.

[23] See the statement of the Roman Catholic historian Joseph Lortz, *Die Reformation in Deutschland,* 3rd ed. (Freiburg, 1949), I, 190.

INDEXES

Index

By WALTER A. HANSEN

89, 91, 102, 107, 133, 134, 246, 259
of Pietism 201
of primitive religion 239
of religion 160
of sacramental piety 165
of theology 5, 7, 19, 23, 31, 32, 33, 109, 256
post-Biblical 93, 118
Protestant 228
sacred 132
social 36
theological and ecclesiastical 6
History of the Peloponnesian War, by Thucydides 36
Hofmann, Fritz 96 fn., 112 fn.
Holl, Karl 35, 41 fn., 42 fn., 230 fn.
Holy Infant 148
Holy Spirit 62, 84, 104, 116, 130, 151, 181, 197, 198, 199, 201, 202, 235, 247, 248, 249
Luther's doctrine of 67
Holy Trinity 52
Holy Week 208
Holy Writ or Holy Church, by George Tavard 74 fn.
Homiletical works, Luther's 44
Homoousios 79 fn.
House Postil, by Luther 243 fn.
Hübner, Friedrich 13 fn.
Humanity, Christ's 21, 22
Hupfeld, Renatus 247 fn.
Hussite poison 114
Hussites 117
Hypocrites 92

Idealism
false 149
non-Christian 148
Idolatry 66, 88, 165
In Memoriam Ernst Loh-

meyer, Werner Schmauch (ed.) 146 fn.
Incantation, formula of 172
Incarnation 107, 148, 189
paradox of 149
reality of 149
Infallibility, papal 73
Initiative, divine 11
Initium creaturae Dei, by Johann Haar 53 fn., 247 fn.
Institutio theologiae elencticae, by Francis Turretinus 243 fn.
Instruction to the Clergy to Preach Against Usury, by Luther 102 fn.
Interpretation(s) 5, 6, 10, 14, 23, 42, 44, 57, 81, 82, 93, 105, 122, 131, 133, 138, 139, 147, 148, 153, 157, 164, 184, 185, 187, 206, 209, 212, 220, 222, 227, 245, 256, 258
allegorical 89
ancient and hallowed 119
Biblical x, xii, 8, 20, 22, 31, 72, 113, 166
distorted 120
early Christian, of Old Testament 15
eucharistic, of John 6:55 ff. 145 fn., 174
fetishistic 145
literal 103
Luther's, of Eucharist 205
Luther's, of First Commandment 66
of atonement 170
of Luther and his theology 39
of Luther's eucharistic doctrine 45
of Luther's thought and exegesis 202

of Reformation 71, 74
of "rock" 115
of Scriptures 18, 19, 41, 77, 114, 129
of space, mass, volume, motion, and the like 141
spiritual 107
suppressed, of Christianity 8 fn.
symbolic, of "body" 144
Interpreters x, 48, 65, 197, 232, 247, 258
Intervention, divine 189
Irenaeus 74, 188, 253
Isaac 36, 96, 97, 101, 104, 105, 241, 250
Isaaks Opferung christlich gedeutet, by David Lerch 23 fn., 36 fn.
Isaiah x, 183, 232
Iserloh, Erwin 252 fn.
Ishmael 96, 97, 100
Islam 117
Israel 50 fn., 55, 57 fn., 58, 59, 92, 165, 209
apostasy of 94
new 94
true 93, 94
worship of 241
Israelites 57 fn.

Jacob 91, 92, 93, 96, 97, 101, 104, 105
Jäger, Karl 233 fn.
James 87
Jedin, Hubert 73 fn.
Jensen, John M. 52 fn.
Jerome, St. 28, 76, 81, 114, 115
Jesus Christ 12, 18, 29, 53, 59, 60, 61, 62, 114, 145, 181, 197, 211, 231, 234, 235, 250, 260
as church's past, present, future 206
true humanity of 21
Jesus of Nazareth 16 fn., 53, 133
Jetter, Werner 185 fn.

INDEX TO SCRIPTURE PASSAGES